"An amazing book. An instant classic. Staff Sergeant Brown is a true guardian who saved countless lives with supernatural marksmanship skill in a moment of great need, but he has also proven himself to be a true warrior-wordsmith who will save even more lives, as the lessons from this book are learned and applied in our current violent times. Absolutely "required reading" for law enforcement and mental health professionals, but also profoundly valuable for anyone who wants to understand violence and mental illness in our society today."

—Lt. Col. Dave Grossman (USA, ret.), author of
On Combat, On Killing, and *Assassination Generation*

"In vivid and thoroughly researched detail, Andy Brown masterfully weaves two tragic stories that display how interventions were thwarted and clear warning signs of danger were overlooked due to politics and military pressures. In parallel accounts he craftily weds the stories of the vivid dysfunction of a troubled young airman and the reckless arrogance of a senior officer and aviator. As Andy Brown clearly displays, if warnings had been heeded, the behavior of both men would not have led to disastrous ends. Disturbing as these stories are, this is an important and well-written read."

—Gregory K. Moffatt, Ph.D., author of
Blind-Sided: Homicide Where it is Least Expected and *A Violent Heart*

"The compelling true story of a law enforcement officer who kills a mass murderer and then meticulously digs out the twisted circumstances that brought them together that fateful day. Rich in fascinating detail and page-turning narration, *Warnings Unheeded* delivers memorable insights into the kind of slaughter that so often fills news cycles these days, and the resilience heroes need to fight back from the emotional toll of protecting other lives."

—Charles Remsberg, author of the
Street Survival book series for police

WARNINGS UNHEEDED

WARNINGS UNHEEDED

Twin Tragedies at Fairchild Air Force Base

SSgt Andrew P. Brown
US Air Force, Retired

Published by WU Press
Spokane, Washington
www.FairchildHospitalShooting.com

Warnings Unheeded: Twin Tragedies at Fairchild Air Force Base

ISBN: 978-0-9978634-0-6

Interior Design: Gray Dog Press

Printed in the United States of America.

This book is dedicated to the men and women of Fairchild Air Force Base, June 1994.

Maj Thomas E. Brigham M.D.
Anita L. Lindner
Taylor McKenzie Sigman

Capt Alan W. London Ph.D.
Christin Francis McCarron

Col Robert E. Wolff
Lt Col Kenneth S. Huston

Lt Col Arthur "Bud" Holland
Lt Col Mark C. McGeehan

Lt Col Delwyn Baker
TSgt Patrick Deaton
Mark Hess
Deena Kelley
MSgt Dennis Moe
Marlene Moe
Lorraine Murray
Hazel "Joy" Roberts
Michelle Sigman
John Urick
Anthony Zucchetto

Pauline Brown
Ruth Gerken
Omer Karns
Orson Lee
Kelly Moe
Melissa Moe
SSgt Joseph Noone
SSgt Laura Rogers
Sam Spencer
Eva Walch
Janessa Zucchetto

Military to Standard Time Conversion

0100	1:00 AM
0200	2:00 AM
0300	3:00 AM
0400	4:00 AM
0500	5:00 AM
0600	6:00 AM
0700	7:00 AM
0800	8:00 AM
0900	9:00 AM
1000	10:00 AM
1100	11:00 AM
1200	Noon
1300	1:00 PM
1400	2:00 PM
1500	3:00 PM
1600	4:00 PM
1700	5:00 PM
1800	6:00 PM
1900	7:00 PM
2000	8:00 PM
2100	9:00 PM
2200	10:00 PM
2300	11:00 PM
0000 or 2400	Midnight

Air Force Rank and Abbreviations

General	Gen
Lieutenant General	Lt Gen
Major General	Maj Gen
Brigadier General	Brig Gen
Colonel	Col
Lieutenant Colonel	Lt Col
Major	Maj
Captain	Capt
First Lieutenant	1st Lt
Second Lieutenant	2nd Lt
Chief Master Sergeant	CMSgt
Senior Master Sergeant	SMSgt
Master Sergeant	MSgt
Technical Sergeant	TSgt
Staff Sergeant	SSgt
Sergeant	Sgt
Senior Airman	SrA
Airman First Class	A1C
Airman	Amn
Airman Basic	AB

Andy Brown 2016

Andy Brown is an Air Force law enforcement veteran from Port Orchard, Washington. After serving in Idaho, Greece, Washington, Hawaii and New Mexico, he returned to the Spokane, Washington area where he works for the Department of Homeland Security. He spent seven years researching and writing *Warnings Unheeded*. This book is part of his ongoing effort to share the lessons learned from the tragedies and his experience with the effects of trauma.

Author's Note

This narrative nonfiction book was written using reports of investigation, witness statements, medical records, personal interviews, newspaper articles, recorded law enforcement and fire department radio transmissions and the letters and journals of the people involved.

I read hundreds of statements written by witnesses to the events depicted in this book. As in many high-stress incidents, the perceptions and observations of eye witnesses can differ. On the rare occasion where I encountered differing witness accounts, I went with the majority consensus.

These stories are told using the words of those who lived and died during the events. Some quotes have been corrected for minor errors in spelling and grammar, but the spirit of the text remains unchanged.

The letters and journal entries of Dean Mellberg contain multiple spelling and grammatical errors. Mellberg's writing was intentionally left uncorrected and appears as it was originally written.

Actual names are used with few exceptions. Many of the witness statements were name redacted. In many cases I was able to identify and validate the source of the statement through context and research. When the source of a statement could not be definitively identified, the quote or information is attributed to "an airman" or "a sergeant." In one instance, the unattributable information was substantial and a fictitious name was used to improve the reader's experience. In other instances, fictitious names were used at the request of the source or when the use of a real name created an invasion of privacy concern. When a fictitious name is used an asterisk (*) appears next to the name when it is first introduced.

"The Provost must have a horse allowed him and some soldiers to attend him, and all the rest commanded to obey and assist, or else the Service will suffer; for he is but one man and must correct many and therefore he cannot be beloved. And he must be riding from one garrison to another to see that the soldiers do not outrage nor scathe the country."

Articles of War, Charles I of England, 1629

Contents

Foreword xiii

Shots Fired 1
Port Orchard 5
Lansing 9
92nd Bomb Wing 15
Basic Training 21
Lowry AFB 29
Airman Brown 33
Mountain Home AFB 37
Iraklion AS 41
1991–1992 Air Shows 45
Fairchild PMEL 55
Fairchild Mental Health 63
1993 Air Show 79
Stateside 83
Wilford Hall 87
Patient Squadron 105
Reassignment 111
Black Rock Desert 115
Yakima Valley 119
Cannon AFB 125
Discharged 135
Deployed 143
Mister Mellberg 147
Return to San Antonio 151
Lt Col Mark McGeehan 153
Preparation 165
20 June 1994 171

Police Response 207
Base Housing 225
Hospital Aid..229
Survivors 251
Victim Twenty-Three..255
Czar 52 257
Sheriff's Investigation..279
Politics and Media..281
Memorial 285
Lawsuit 291
Accountability and Change 295
Trauma to Recovery 299
Afterword..319

Reference Material..325
Bibliography..339
Acknowledgments 343
Index..345

Foreword

By Massad Ayoob

Have you ever read a book written by someone who stopped a mass murder? I can think of only four, and you are holding the most recent in your hand.

Andy Brown is, to my mind, a genuine American hero. "Those who ride to the sound of the guns" is not a testosterone-fueled cliché. Rather, it is the very definition of not only our armed services, but also our domestic emergency services—police, fire, paramedic. Andy had one foot in each of those worlds on the day when destiny called to him, and both those feet raced toward the deadly danger from which he had sworn an oath to protect others.

Every crisis is managed in three stages. The ideal is *prevention:* you are alert to the warning signals that tell you danger is coming, you act upon those signals, and you keep the crisis from happening at all. Next comes *intervention:* it's happening now, and you get in there and stop it, freezing the damage where it is, and as physicians say in the Hippocratic Oath, prevent *further* harm. Finally, there is *postvention,* a term so often neglected most people don't even recognize the word: It's over, and all you can do is pick up the pieces. You do what you can to heal the wounded, you grieve for the dead, you console their loved ones…and, if you are wise, you learn the lessons from the terrible life-ending crisis with a view toward preventing it from happening again. Thus, the postvention in the best of all worlds feeds into the next cycle of prevention, and if you had to diagram it, it would look like a circle or perhaps, a yin-yang symbol.

This book starkly and powerfully illustrates all three. Prevention? As the crisis built over a long and increasingly ominous period, the warning signals were never transmitted to Andy Brown. He worked in a large organization, and the larger bureaucracy is like a gigantic dinosaur: the farther its brain is from the feet on the ground, the longer it takes the signal from the one to get to the other. Denial, wishful thinking, and the momentum of "it's policy to do it *this* way" combine to slow reaction until prevention is no longer possible.

Intervention? Andy Brown handled it brilliantly, with a combination of courage and skill that had allowed him to perform what most combat instructors would call "a feat of arms." We will never know how many lives Brown saved with his swift and decisive action on that terrible day.

Postvention? Our nation does not treat its heroes as well as it should. Andy was not handled well by his superior officers in the aftermath of this crisis, in my opinion. It tells you something about Brown that he treads rather lightly on this in the book. You'll see no tinge of self-pity. Instead, with the same selfless courage that drove him to put his life on the line on the day you'll read about, he focuses on the "learn from this to keep it from happening again" element of postvention. From that awful day to today, his focus has been on others, not upon himself.

He is a good man. You will see it also in the way he treats the perpetrator of that atrocity. I and others tend to focus on the end product—a monster who acted out true evil. Andy Brown is compassionate enough to focus instead on how the man he had to fight to the death became what he was at the end.

That benevolent focus begins with the title, and carries through the last chapter. Andy reminds us all that uncorrected recklessness can be every bit as deadly as unchecked madness and malice. The parallel story he weaves into this excellent book shows us why experienced aviators say, "There are old pilots and there are bold pilots, but there are no old, bold pilots."

There are specific lessons in this book which can prevent lethal tragedy. Lessons for bosses, subordinates, and co-workers. Lessons for law enforcement, and for psychologists, and for human resources personnel. But there are also general lessons for us all that can save lives, though perhaps not so dramatically nor so heroically as Andy Brown saved uncounted lives when he "rode to the sound of the guns."

—Massad Ayoob, May 2016

Massad Ayoob is an internationally recognized lethal-force expert with more than forty years' experience as a police officer, author, and firearms and self-defense instructor to law enforcement officers and private citizens.

WARNINGS UNHEEDED

Shots Fired

"Fairchild Police to all posts and patrols, we have an alarm at the ER. Informational, we have an individual in the hospital running around with a shotgun."

I had been a patrolman for five years, but today was only my second day working bike patrol. After spending the first hour of my shift patrolling the housing areas of Fairchild Air Force Base, I stopped by the Offutt gate to escape the summer sun. My visit with the guard was cut short by the radio call, and before the transmission ended, I had strapped on my helmet and stepped out of the air-conditioned gate shack to my bicycle. The severity of the situation set in as I rode away from the gate.

As I approached the intersection of Offutt and Graham I was suddenly aware that, unlike my patrol car, my bicycle wasn't equipped with lights and a siren. I slipped the key ring from my duty belt. The keys to my dorm room, car, and handcuffs dangled from my mouth as I blew a chrome whistle and turned onto Graham, pedaling hard down the two-lane asphalt road. As I rode toward the scene, the world around me slowed and went silent. I felt calm, almost numb.

Several vehicles rolled past me on their way out of the area. The occupants shouted frantically, their voices muted. I kept pedaling toward the hospital. Although I couldn't hear them, their urgency told me there was trouble ahead.

"Fairchild Police to all responding patrols, the individual just ran out of building 9010 across from the hospital, firing off rounds out of his shotgun."

I passed a housing area on my right and could see building 9010 ahead. A crowd of men and women dressed in civilian clothes, Air Force uniforms, and hospital whites streamed down the road, fleeing the hospital campus. I coasted through the crowd, scanning them and the surrounding area for a threat. I was intently focused on finding the man with the gun and didn't hear the radio.

"Fairchild Police, Fairchild Security, just received a notification from the hospital, you have individuals down. Repeat. You have individuals down."

I shouted to the crowd, "Where is he?" They collectively pointed behind them as they fled, yelling. "There's a man with a gun!" "He's shooting people!" "He's over there!"

As I emerged from the crowd, I heard the deep boom of gunfire. The sound reverberated off the hospital buildings to my right and the military houses behind the perimeter fence to my left. I coasted and searched for the source of the gunfire. In the distance, a man dressed in black, with a long gun at his hip, appeared in the middle of the road. As he walked toward me, he swung the weapon to his right and fired toward the housing area. He then swung the weapon to his left and fired toward the hospital.

Still coasting, I leaned right and glided up a sidewalk ramp in front of the hospital annex building. I leapt from the bike and drew my Beretta as I knelt on the sidewalk. My hands gripped the pistol and brought it in line with my target as I yelled, "Police! Drop your weapon! Put it down!" The man continued toward me and fired again to his side. I yelled again, "Police! Drop it! Put it down now!" His pace quickened and he aimed the rifle in my direction. My finger moved to the trigger of my Beretta and slowly applied pressure. The hammer came back smooth and dropped sharp, propelling my first shot toward the man with the gun.

* * *

When the shooting ceased, a trail of shell casings, bullet holes, and blood led through the hallways and parking lots of the Fairchild Air Force Base hospital campus. Medical teams worked to locate and triage the wounded, while law enforcement officers searched for a rumored second gunman and investigators attempted to identify the shooter.

As word of the shooting spread, at least one Fairchild airman correctly predicted the shooter would be identified as his former co-worker, Dean Mellberg. Mellberg had previously been assigned to Fairchild's calibration laboratory before being sent to the psychiatric ward of a military hospital in Texas. TSgt Payton Kendall*, a lab supervisor, said, "Dean scared all of us. ... I was always real careful not to piss him off, because I was afraid this would happen. ... I was scared even after he left ... All along I felt sure that he'd come back. ... I didn't know who he'd target: the lab, the commander, the doctors, the wing commander. I didn't know, and that's what scared me."

Sgt Sam Prescott* previously worked with Mellberg at Cannon Air Force Base in New Mexico and had a similar experience. Prescott said, "During the period I knew Dean, my feelings that he was dangerous progressed daily." Prescott frequently warned his co-workers to be careful when alone with Mellberg, and he warned them to be even more cautious when gathered in a group. Prescott recalls how he learned of the shooting. "About 0200 the morning after, I was asleep on my sofa with the TV on. I thought I dreamed about Mellberg going on a shooting spree at some Air Force base." In the dream, Prescott chastised his co-workers, "I told you so. Damn it, why didn't you listen? I told you he'd get you."

When Prescott went to work the next day one of his co-workers asked, "How did you know?"

"How did I know what?"

"You know, about Mellberg."

Prescott's knees went weak when he realized his dream had been prompted by news reports that aired while he slept.

Jeff Cook had worked as a medical technician at Fairchild's mental health center and had transferred to another base. He learned of the shooting when his mother-in-law called him after seeing reports on the local news. She asked him, "Who could do something like that?"

Without hesitation, Cook said, "It was Dean Mellberg."

According to an article in *The Spokesman-Review*, Susan Brigham, the wife of Fairchild's psychiatrist Thomas Brigham, had a similar reaction. "When I first heard [about the shooting] that afternoon on the television, I knew Tom was dead, and I knew who did it."

Four days after the hospital tragedy, a B-52 bomber with four airmen on board crashed near Fairchild's flight line. The crew had been practicing maneuvers for an upcoming air show.

The tragedy of these events is compounded by the fact that they were predictable and therefore preventable. The pilot of the B-52, Lt Col Arthur "Bud" Holland, was unquestionably a skilled aviator, but he had become reckless. One aviator said, "He was one of the most senior active pilots we had. … He was considered one of the best. … However, I did reach a point where … I didn't want him flying on my airplane anymore." Several Fairchild airmen had refused to fly with Holland. His maneuvers became so dangerous some aviators would have sacrificed their careers to save their lives. One pilot said, "I did not ever want to fly with Colonel Holland again, even if it meant that I couldn't fly anymore as an Air Force pilot." Several airmen voiced their concerns to their superiors, to no effect. It was no surprise when the air show practice flight ended in tragedy. As one pilot said, "A lot of us ... would sit around ... and talk about Lieutenant Colonel Holland, and we predicted the worst air show disaster in history when we found out that he was gonna fly."

Port Orchard

As a kid I lived in a 1920s farmhouse in the waterfront town of Port Orchard, Washington. The big white house sat on a hill overlooking a large grass field next to a wooded piece of state land. Through the years, parts of that field raised vegetable gardens, goats, pigs, and chickens; but more importantly, it raised children. Born in 1970, I grew up in an era without video game systems, when you could only get four television channels and cartoons only aired on Saturday mornings. Our field was the neighborhood rally point, where we played hide-and-seek, tag, kickball, football, and baseball. We dug holes and climbed trees; we built forts and strong friendships.

I taught myself to ride my garage sale bicycle by coasting down our long steep driveway. My friends and I rode around catching bad guys like the motorcycle cops I saw on the television shows *CHiPs*. We played cops-and-robbers like the patrolmen in the show *Adam 12*. I also emulated the firefighters and paramedics on the TV show *Emergency*. Firefighters and policemen, who used their wits and the tools of their trade to save lives, were my heroes. But the cops carried guns, and I had an early fascination with firearms. I routinely carried a toy die cast replica of a Colt Model 1911 .45 Automatic in the pocket of my holey jeans. My dad didn't own many firearms, but when I was seven he bought me a Daisy lever-action BB gun. I regularly practiced shooting pop cans and pinecones and eventually graduated to a .22 rifle. It never occurred to me to shoot at living things, and I was troubled to see the man next door shooting birds with his pellet gun just for the fun of it. I didn't object to hunting—we ate the animals we raised on our property—but I couldn't tolerate killing without cause. When I was younger, if my mom found a spider in the house, I'd come running, pleading, "Don't kill it!" I'd catch it in a cup and set it free outside.

I didn't like to kill, but I loved playing war. Starting at age seven, my friends and I practically lived in the woods of the state land. Dressed in our Army surplus uniforms, with web belts and canteens, we patrolled the trails along Olney Creek, among the ferns and moss-covered cedars and firs. We battled imaginary armies and filled the tranquil woods with the plastic rattle of replica M16 rifles. Our parents' only stipulation was to be home before dark—which came quickly in the thick woods of the Pacific Northwest. By the time we emerged from the tree line into the light of the setting sun, our uniforms were wet and heavy with bog mud. My mom would stop me at the front door, defending her clean floors. I'd stand on the lawn, shivering in my underwear, while the garden hose, cold as creek water, washed away the day's adventure. Then I'd head inside for a warm bath and a hot meal. Mom was a great homemaker and raised five kids on the income my dad made as a Bremerton firefighter. She was a talented cook and made excellent meals on a tight budget, though I do remember days when the only thing we had for dinner was buttered macaroni and bread.

When I was ten years old, Mt. Saint Helens erupted one hundred miles south of our home. It was Sunday morning, 18 May 1980. We watched news footage showing the entire side of the mountain exploding and falling away. A dark plume billowed 80,000 feet high, eventually spreading 520 million tons of ash over eleven states, reducing visibility to ten feet in some areas. The accumulation of fine ash closed roads and caused power outages. The intense heat converted snow and glaciers into thick rivers of ash and debris that charged through valleys, destroying homes and bridges.

Practicing the Boy Scout motto, "Be prepared," I filled our bathtub with drinking water, gathered paper face masks, and inventoried the food in our pantry.

Eastern Washington received the brunt of the fallout. In Spokane, 250 miles east of the mountain, a black mass with gray billowing edges spanned the horizon. The threat of falling ash caused Fairchild Air Force Base to cancel their open house and air show, turning away sixty thousand visitors. Some visiting aircraft fled to their home bases, racing ahead of the ominous cloud that turned the midday sky midnight black and blanketed the ground with up to five inches of ash. Thankfully, our town was upwind of the mountain and out of the reach of the mudflows. Port Orchard only received a light dusting; but closer to the volcano, rescue crews would discover, fifty-seven people lost their lives.

By the time I started high school, I was a slim six-foot-two teenager with shoulder length blond hair. I listened to Ozzy Osbourne, AC/DC, and Iron Maiden. I rode a motorcycle and wore the heavy metal uniform: blue jeans, T-shirts, and a black leather biker jacket.

South Kitsap High School had the same social cliques as other schools, but I wasn't overly concerned with fitting in with any particular crowd. I got along with most people, but I was more comfortable with the blue collar kids and spent much of my time in auto shop.

I dated a couple of girls in high school—nothing serious until my senior year, when I met a girl who was two years behind me in school. Before long we were talking about a future together. She picked out names for our future children and practiced her signature using her married name, Brown. I teased her that if we had sons, I wanted to name them Hash and Dark.

I went through several jobs in my teens, earning just enough to take my girl to the movies, put gas in my motorcycle, and go camping at the lake with my buddies. I bused tables and washed dishes at a Denny's in nearby Bremerton. I flipped burgers at the A&W in Port Orchard and mounted tires and pumped gas at the 76 gas station on Bethel Road near Highway 16.

The owner of the gas station encouraged us to sell overpriced oil, wiper blades, and windshield washer fluid while we checked under the hoods of our customers' vehicles. I was always relieved when they brushed off my sales pitch, even though it meant I wouldn't get the fifteen-cent commission.

One afternoon, I was working alone when a man walked up from the highway. He was unshaven, and his face and mechanic's overalls were black with engine grease. He told me he was having trouble with his truck and needed a fuse but had left home without his wallet. I bought him a box of fuses; he thanked me and walked back down to the highway. The following day after school, I showed up for work and my co-worker told me the State Patrol had been looking for me. He smiled and pointed to a business card and a dollar bill pinned to a bulletin board. The man I had helped was Trooper Gail Otto with the Washington State Patrol, and he had come back to repay me.

As a teen driver I had met quite a few law enforcement officers and had always respected them as they issued me tickets for various minor traffic offenses. I admired police officers and saw them as flawless superheroes. Seeing Trooper Otto on his day off made me realize that although they have an extraordinary job, law enforcement officers are ordinary people. I started to think that maybe someday I could be like them.

At age eighteen, I was too young to be a police officer, but I did the next best thing. I became a volunteer firefighter at South Kitsap County

Station 8, in Port Orchard. I was issued a big Motorola pager and a set of turnout gear: a heavy coat, pants, boots, and helmet that I strapped to the back of my motorcycle. We lived far away from the fire station, so when we got a call, more often than not I'd arrive after the trucks had already left. One of the first calls I made it to occurred late at night, around Christmas. The pager announced a residential chimney fire. I raced to the station, put on my gear, and climbed into the jumper seat of the pumper truck. My adrenaline surged as the big diesel ran with emergency lights and sirens. We pulled up to the house, the air brakes hissed, and I leapt from the truck, waiting for the command to pull the hoses and charge the lines. I was surprised at the apparent lack of urgency as I followed a seasoned firefighter through the front door of the home. We stood in the living room and he spoke briefly with the homeowner before kneeling down in front of the woodstove. He opened the stove door and squirted the orange embers inside with an ordinary household spray bottle. Steam billowed up the stove pipe, extinguishing any flames that may have been in the chimney. The firefighter closed the stove door and suggested the homeowner have his chimney cleaned and inspected. We left. My first structure fire had been snuffed out with the equivalent of a child's squirt gun.

In June of 1988, I graduated and moved into a tiny basement apartment in Bremerton while I figured out what I wanted to do in life. I took a job at the Silverdale Cinema, which was fun but didn't pay well. After paying rent, I had little money left for food and gas. When a local food bank didn't pick up the canned goods we collected for them at the theater, my boss started sending the food home with me. I could barely support myself, let alone a future family. I needed to find a career. My father and grandfather had both served in the Navy. I had a brother in the Army and a sister in the Air Force. I had gotten a taste of public safety and hoped to become a military police officer or firefighter. I joined the Air Force after hearing they took the best care of their people. I signed up in August and spent a cold winter in the damp confines of my basement apartment, waiting for my enlistment date. In February 1989, I flew to Texas to begin basic training at Lackland Air Force Base. I didn't know where I would be stationed after training, but my girlfriend planned to join me after she got out of school.

Lansing

Gary and Lois Mellberg lived down a dusty road in a modest home on a ten-acre parcel in Lansing, Michigan. Gary serviced vending machines, and Lois taught school in the Waverly Community School District, where both of her sons attended.

The younger son, Dean, had trouble fitting in at school. He was moderately overweight and his round, acne-scarred face was surrounded by unkempt, reddish-brown hair. His clothes were mismatched and ill-fitting. A classmate recalls the first time he saw Dean, he was wearing a green-and-yellow striped, short-sleeve turtleneck shirt. Most of his classmates remember Dean as very quiet; he shuffled down the hallways staring at the floor with an odd grin on his face. Those who tried to talk to him found the conversation to be one-sided. When he did speak, it was in a rigid, halting style, and he avoided eye contact. He looked like he was searching the room for the appropriate words. His responses usually didn't fit in the conversation, as he often parroted common phrases and clichés, usually in a whisper.

From 1989 to 1992 Dean attended Waverly High School, a single-story brick building with a student body of about one thousand. Many students found Waverly to be full of opportunity and a place with incredible teachers. Those who didn't fit into one of the popular cliques saw it otherwise.

The hallways of Waverly High were filled with conversation and laughter as students swapped books in and out of their lockers between classes. For Dean the halls were a gauntlet of humiliation. Several of his classmates said he was picked on relentlessly. His tormentors knocked books out of his hands or tripped him, sending his books and papers scattering among the feet of passing students. One student liked to sit behind Dean in class and flick his ears. Others put tacks on his chair or gum in his hair. With no apparent coping mechanisms, Dean seemed to withdraw into himself, making him an even easier target. As one self-proclaimed jock put it, "he was treated like the average nerd who didn't defend himself." Although he was five foot ten and one hundred ninety pounds, he never fought back; he just grinned and acted as if it were normal.

9

Students also teased Dean about his mother, whom they knew as a substitute teacher. The students said Lois Mellberg had long red hair, which she kept up as much as she could. One student said, "Sometimes it looked like she just rolled out of bed." Another said she regularly wore a pair of seventies-style knee-high maroon leather boots that she paired with a plaid skirt, slacks, or jeans. One former student said if Dean was in Lois's classroom, she talked him up in front of the other students. Another classmate said, "I recall an instance when after classes were over for the day, Dean and his mother were in the hall and she appeared to be scolding him … shaking her finger in his face, poking him in the chest and seemingly belittling him for whatever reason."

While most kids knew Dean Mellberg as the quiet kid who was constantly picked on, others saw a different side of him. His media production class divided into groups to work on video projects. Dean's group cast him as the hero of their video, *Super Dean*. While performing, Dean took on a stage persona: he appeared focused and spoke clearly. When the class watched the *Super Dean* video, everybody laughed. Dean sat at his desk with a proud look on his face and seemed to enjoy the attention.

When the students in Mrs. Politowski's biology class partnered up to dissect frogs, Dean was left without a partner. Mrs. Politowski had to repeatedly remind Dean to stop playing with the dead frog as he mumbled, giggled, and laughed to himself. After class, Dean snuck the frog into his pocket and carried it around school, occasionally pulling it out and using it as a hand puppet to entertain his classmates.

In his junior year, Dean's classmates recall, he was a disruption in Ms. Thorp's creative writing class. During writing time, he frequently laughed aloud and giggled to himself. When the students were told to write a paper describing their twentieth reunion, one student wrote, "Dean would be there on parole from the insane asylum."

Dean signed up for Waverly's award-winning choir program. When Mrs. Sauter noticed some of her students making fun of him, she sent Dean down to the office while she made it clear to her class that she would not tolerate the mistreatment of another student. Dean found choir to be a sanctuary. Though he never progressed out of beginning choir, he continued with the program for the four years he was at Waverly.

Dean Mellberg accepted direction very well. Mrs. Sauter described him as very nice and eager to please. She taught the class choral posture, feet flat on the floor, sitting upright on the edge of their chair to best project their singing voice. When they weren't singing, students were allowed to relax in their chairs. Mrs. Sauter said Dean rarely relaxed; he maintained a perfectly rigid military posture at all times, even more so when in her class. When Mrs. Sauter used Dean as an example of how to sit, he smiled proudly, sitting rigidly in his chair with his palms flat on his thighs. Some students took advantage of Dean's eagerness to please. Someone once convinced him to sing off key at the top of his lungs during rehearsal. Another student convinced him to make paper airplanes out of concert brochures, and when Mrs. Sauter was in front of the class, her students quietly awaiting instruction, Dean sent the airplanes flying around the room.

During homecoming week on "opposite day," some kids wore their clothes inside out or backward; others dressed as the opposite sex. No one took it to the extreme that Dean did. He came to school wearing a dress, a curly wig, and makeup, mascara, and lipstick. He painted his fingernails and shaved his legs. When Mrs. Sauter attempted to start class, she couldn't get Dean to break character or stop touching up his makeup. Mrs. Sauter had seen several "different" kids in her career but never anyone like Dean. She questioned what was going on at his home, and found his behavior so upsetting that she spoke to a school counselor, who quickly dismissed her concerns.

Although Dean appeared harmless to most students, Sharon O'Meara* saw his creepy side. Sharon had a locker next to Dean's and saw how some of the other students treated him. "He had old clothes and would often be dirty. If he got a haircut and came to school clean, it was even worse for him." Sharon described herself as a chubby tomboy during her freshman and sophomore year and said she "had a propensity to protect kids who were 'different,'" as she always felt that way too. Sharon said the teachers "turned a blind eye" to Dean's mistreatment, but she helped him pick up his books and tried to uplift him by talking to him and sitting with him in the hallway during lunch.

In her junior year, Sharon grew into a beautiful young woman, and Dean's interest in her became increasingly sexual, to the point that she avoided her locker. She couldn't avoid Dean in the classroom. During one class, she noticed Dean staring at her while masturbating at his desk. She says she told him to "put that away," and when he refused to stop, she walked out of class. According to Sharon and other female students, Dean had a history of masturbating in class. Sharon said the teachers were dismissive. "Once or twice they may have said something; but other than that, nobody said or did anything. ... He clearly had something wrong mentally. I finally confronted him, per my father's advice, at our locker and reminded him how I was always friendly to him and I would kick his ass if he ever masturbated in front of me again. He laughed but never did it again, and we never spoke again."

Ben, another of Dean's classmates, recalls he had a temper. In Mr. Lockhart's English class, Dean was being picked on by a bully. "It was getting out of control, and I remember Dean breaking his pen and getting ink all over himself ... and just rushing around the room making animal growling noises and trying to scare people. ... I don't think the teachers even knew what to do. ... Usually the teachers would kick an offender out of class or something like that, but then nobody knew what to do with the aftermath. Dean would just sit there, having absorbed it, his face all reddened with embarrassment and anger."

Dean spent his free time in the school library reading military history books, and he was involved with the Civil Air Patrol. His father had been in the Army and was a Vietnam veteran, so when an Air Force recruiter came to the high school, Dean approached her. Sometime later he walked into the recruiter's office and took the vocational aptitude test. His test scores were average but indicated a strength in electronics. He signed up for a career as a precision measurement electronics laboratory (PMEL) technician with plans to enlist upon graduating from high school. He went to the Military Entrance Processing Station in Lansing, to complete the delayed enlistment process. While there he provided contradictory information on two medical forms. On 15 May 1992, he indicated he had never broken any bones and had never been treated for a mental condition. On 22 May 1992, he indicated he *had* been hospitalized, *had* suffered broken bones, and *had* been treated for a mental condition which he referred to as "family counseling" sessions when he was twelve years old. Neither the examining physician nor other staff followed up on the admission of prior mental health counseling; if they had, he might never have been accepted into the Air Force.

Dean got his hair cut military style and looked forward to a fresh start in the Air Force; but according to his peers and teachers, joining the military was the last thing they thought he should do. Basic military training is designed to break a person of their individuality, in order to rebuild them into a military professional. Students who associated with Dean predicted the military would simply break him. If those same students had been asked to vote for who was most likely to go on a shooting spree, Dean Mellberg would have been the last person to come to their mind. As one former student put it, "To say he was harmless was an understatement." It would appear that everyone knew who Dean Mellberg was, but no one really *knew* him.

In June of 1992, Dean accepted his high school diploma as his class-mates chanted his name. Two weeks later he headed to Lackland Air Force Base for basic training.

92nd Bomb Wing

A Fairchild B-52 and KC-135 performing mid-air refueling.
Credit: Capt Derek B. Riggan, Courtesy of FAFB Historian

The Cascade Mountains run through Washington State, dividing it in two: Western Washington, with its wet climate and moss-covered forests; and Eastern Washington, whose farms, orchards, and ranches receive only a fraction of the coastal rainfall. The mountains offered a natural barrier against enemy attack during World War II, prompting the US Army Air Corps to build an aircraft repair depot in far eastern Washington. The repair depot was built on the flatlands above the city of Spokane—a ponderosa-pine-treed oasis in the valley of the Spokane River. Over the years, Spokane Air Depot was renamed Fairchild Air Force Base and became the home of the 92nd Bombardment Wing. Among other squadrons, the wing was the home of the 325th Bomb Squadron and the 92nd Air Refueling

15

Squadron, with the B-52 Stratofortress and the KC-135 Stratotanker. The KC-135 was a militarized version of the Boeing 707 airliner, modified to perform high-altitude refueling. The B-52 was an even larger long-range bomber. Fairchild was also the home of the Air Force's Survival, Evasion, Resistance, and Escape (SERE) School, commonly known as Survival School. Spokane's extreme climate and diverse geography of mountain wilderness to the north and desert plains to the west provided an ideal location for survival training.

For about as long as anyone can remember, Fairchild Air Force Base has been hosting open houses, allowing the public a chance to see the aircraft up close. In the early years, military pilots performed aerial demonstrations, which eventually grew into large air shows featuring parachute stunt teams and military and civilian aerobatic planes. The air shows eventually became part of Spokane's week-long Lilac Festival, and drew crowds of more than 100,000 people, especially when the Air Force's Thunderbirds or the Navy's Blue Angels were slated to perform grand finales in their small, maneuverable jets.

Fairchild had been a SAC base since 1947, one of several Air Force bases that fell under the Strategic Air Command. During the Cold War, SAC controlled the country's land-based nuclear missiles and nuclear-capable bombers. Since 1957, Fairchild's B-52s and KC-135s worked as a team in that mission. The bomber could deliver conventional or nuclear munitions anywhere in the world, and the tanker ensured it had enough fuel to reach its target. The planes performed their missions well but they weren't designed to perform aerobatics.

At Fairchild's air shows, the B-52 and KC-135 had always been relegated to static display. Air Force regulations prohibited the two planes from performing in air shows. Even straight and level fly-bys were discouraged. The large, multi-engine aircraft were known as *heavies* and did not have the quick handling characteristics of the crowd-pleasing single-engine fighters.

In June 1986, Gen John Chain Jr. became the commander-in-chief of SAC. Weeks after he took over, General Chain waived the regulations restricting the large planes from conducting aerobatics and directed Fairchild to put together an aerial demonstration team to show off the capabilities of SAC's heavies. The team, known as the Thunderhawks, would be SAC's version of the Blue Angels and Thunderbirds. The Thunderhawks developed a routine and demonstrated it for Chain and other SAC officials.

Chain rejected the maneuvers, directing the team to "keep the aircraft closer to the field."

After the Thunderhawks developed and performed a revised routine for Chain, he approved the new maneuvers. An anonymous Fairchild pilot told *The Spokesman-Review* reporter, Jim Camden, the flight profile appeared more dangerous after it was revised. The newly approved flight profile included maximum-performance climbs, a mock low-level bomb run, and simulated aerial refueling. The first maneuver in the Thunderhawk routine was the most spectacular. It consisted of a series of two S-shaped, steeply banked turns at low altitude. The stunt was designed to show the top and bottom of the two planes as the Thunderhawks passed in front of the spectator area. They called the maneuver "the snake."

On Friday, 13 March 1987, the Thunderhawks were scheduled to practice the maneuvers in preparation for their debut flight at Fairchild's upcoming air show. On that cool, damp afternoon, a KC-135A and a B-52H took off in tandem. At the end of Fairchild's runway, the B-52 executed a tight right teardrop turn and flew back toward the flight line. The KC-135 mirrored the B-52 with a left teardrop turn. The B-52 descended to 200 feet and initiated the snake as it passed the proposed spectator area. The bomber banked hard to one side, revealing the top of the large aircraft before immediately banking in the opposite direction to reveal its underbelly before it flew away from the airfield.

Seconds later, the KC-135 approached from the opposite side of the airfield and descended. Witnesses said the plane looked to be flying lower and slower than planned, possibly putting it in line with the turbulent air left in the wake of the B-52. As the tanker approached the spectator area it banked left forty-five degrees. Abruptly, the wing dropped to nearly ninety degrees vertical, the left engines stalled and the plane lost altitude. The crew struggled to regain control and managed to level the wings, but it was too late to gain speed or halt the descent. The plane went down in an area surrounded by aircraft hangers, squadron buildings, and the Base Exchange—an Air Force department store. The crash site was adjacent to the flight line, in an area that would have been occupied by air show spectators.

The KC-135 broke up and burst into flames as it plowed a path three hundred yards long, killing all six crewmembers onboard. A seventh Thunderhawk team member, boom operator, SMSgt Paul Hamilton, was watching the performance from his car parked near the flight line. The plane skidded along the ground, tore through a fence, and smashed into Hamilton's car, killing him.

Four days later, a memorial service for the seven airmen was held at Fairchild's chapel. The service concluded with the playing of taps, a twenty-one-gun salute, and a KC-135 executing a flyover of the base chapel.

General Chain insisted the Thunderhawk maneuvers were not aerobatics—he called them "low-level flying maneuvers that look neat from the ground." But pilots and aircraft engineers said the maneuvers approached or exceeded the aircraft's capabilities, especially at low altitude. An anonymous pilot said, "What they did was leave themselves absolutely no margin for error." Chain and other SAC officials expressed an interest in continuing the air show program. But after a congressional inquiry, Air Force officials promised concerned members of Congress that its heavies would no longer perform in air shows. The Thunderhawks team was disbanded.

Two months after the 1987 crash, Fairchild's air show continued as scheduled without the Thunderhawks. A Fairchild B-52 and KC-135 did get some time in the spotlight, flying low passes over the airfield.

From the beginning, Fairchild has lost its share of aircraft and airmen in plane crashes. Every mishap is followed by an investigation to determine the cause. Be it weather, mechanical malfunction, or pilot error, every tragedy is a learning opportunity—a chance to improve crew training, maintenance standards, or flight safety regulations. The crews will never be forgotten by their friends and loved ones. The mishaps are forever burned into the minds of the unfortunate airmen who witness the tragedy. But after a span of accident-free flying, the hard-learned lessons of the past are sometimes forgotten. Following the 1987 Thunderhawk air show practice crash, Fairchild's planes continued to perform aerial demonstrations, most notably the B-52. The maneuvers were impressive, but nothing appeared overtly dangerous until 1991.

Fairchild AFB, March 1987, KC-135 crash site showing remains of SMSgt Paul Hamilton's vehicle and a B-52 in background. Press photo

Fairchild AFB, March 1987, KC-135 debris with B-52 in background. Press photo

Thunderhawk crewmembers killed on 13 March 1987

Lt Col Michael W. Cornett
Capt Christopher L. Chapman
Capt Frank B. Johnson
Capt James W. Litzinger
1st Lt Mark L. Myers
SSgt Rodney S. Erks
SMSgt Paul W. Hamilton

Basic Training

Joining the Air Force doesn't automatically make someone a confident military professional who works well in a team, pays attention to detail, and performs under stress. Those traits are ingrained in new recruits by military training instructors (TIs) like Sgt Phil Kemph. Sergeant Kemph joined the Air Force at age eighteen and worked as a cryptographic systems technician for several years before applying for the special duty assignment. At twenty-five, he was well into his second year as a TI at Lackland Air Force Base, Texas. Kemph had spent the last six weeks training a group of young men, and recently watched them graduate as a flight of new airmen. On the evening of 29 June 1992, Kemph stood in front of the 3702nd Training Squadron waiting to receive a fresh batch of recruits.

The 3702nd was one of several training squadrons on Lackland, each one located in its own three-story recruit housing and training (RH&T) facility. The first floor of the RH&T facility was the administrative heart of the squadron. It held the orderly room and the offices of the training superintendent and squadron commander as well as the dining hall, laundry room, and trainee classrooms. The trainees were housed in the second- and third-story dormitories that radiated out from four sides of the RH&T facility. Concrete drill pads sat underneath the dorms, shaded from the San Antonio sun.

Sergeant Kemph paced back and forth on the drill pad as he waited for the new recruits. Each step sent a sharp metallic click echoing across the brightly lit drill pad. TIs walked hundreds of miles a month teaching airmen "drill and ceremony" and marching them to appointments. To extend the service life of their footwear, they wore taps—small horseshoe-shaped steel plates on their heels and soles. The click of an approaching TI's footfalls sent shivers through young trainees.

Kemph wore a dark blue broad-brimmed campaign hat and a woodland camouflage uniform that he'd had tailored at his own expense to fit his six foot four, 225-pound frame. His shirt pocket flaps were sewn flat; starched creases ran the length of his sleeves as well as his pant legs, which were neatly bloused at the top of combat boots that shone like black leather mirrors. Kemph taught his airmen the proper wear of their uniforms, and even in the damp Texas heat, he was a flawless example of military dress and appearance.

A blue Air Force bus carrying a group of new recruits, including Dean Mellberg, pulled up to the 3702nd. As they looked out the windows at what would be their home for the next six weeks, a TI leapt up the steps, shouting commands from the front of the bus. The recruits, still wearing civilian clothes, grabbed their bags and streamed off the bus. They were directed to stand in a formation of columns and rows under the dorm. TIs instructed them to stand tall in the position of attention—head and eyes forward, heels together, feet at a forty-five-degree angle, arms at their sides, hands closed, thumbs pointing down the seam of their pants. They stood at attention as TIs moved through the ranks, stopping to shout in the face of anyone who drew their attention. It was intentionally stressful, designed to strip them of their individuality, and motivate them to forget everything they knew about civilian life and the freedom to do as they chose. Basic training had begun. From the moment the group—now known as Flight 407—arrived, they would be told what to do and how and when to do it. To avoid their TI's scrutiny, they would strive to do as they were told, do it fast, and do it right the first time.

In the Air Force, single airmen's living quarters are called dormitories. Unlike what you may find at a college, the dorms at basic training were large open bays with precise rows of small, gray, metal-framed beds, the mattress wrapped tight in white linen, and wool blankets that reeked of mothballs.

The trainees filed up the stairs and into their dorm, where they were assigned a bed and a wall locker. They surrendered their civilian belongings and were issued several sets of uniforms, boots, shoes, and underwear. Their heads were shaved, their individuality was gone, and their previous social status was now irrelevant. They were addressed as airmen, usually followed by their last name. They were all on the same level, with a shared mission of graduating from basic training; if they wanted to succeed, they would need to work as a team.

Sergeant Kemph had six weeks to teach the recruits the fundamentals of Air Force life: discipline, drill and ceremonies, core values, physical fitness, and uniform standards. It was a great responsibility, and along with it came the duty of identifying anyone who wasn't fit for military service.

From the beginning Kemph had concerns about Airman Mellberg. He was slightly overweight, sweated profusely, and was extremely nervous. It was common for trainees to take a few days to adjust to the training environment, but Kemph sensed something wasn't right about Airman Mellberg.

Kemph regularly gathered the airmen around him and instructed them on how to prepare and maintain his dorm for inspection. Every issued item had a specific place in their wall locker. A proper display took hours to set up, uniforms hung precisely and evenly spaced, T-shirts folded a meticulous six inches wide, and footwear aligned uniformly under a perfectly made bed. On a Saturday morning early in the flight's training, Kemph conducted bed drills. He had the airmen lie in their beds with the lights out, wearing their physical conditioning (PC) gear: shorts, T-shirt, and running shoes. When he turned on the lights, the flight went to work, making and aligning all sixty beds. After five minutes, Kemph stopped them and made corrections on their performance. Then they got back into bed and did it again. By the end of the day, the beds were perfect.

Kemph inspected the dorm regularly, his footsteps clicking on the white tile floor, his command voice echoing down the bay when he found a discrepancy. An airman could fail inspection for a stray thread extending from the seam of a shirt or failing to remove the tiny garment inspection tags from the pockets of newly issued uniforms. The threads and tags seemed to grow overnight on previously inspected uniforms. TIs sometimes communicated failure by flipping an improperly made bed or dumping the contents of a failing wall locker on the floor. If one airman failed, they all felt the punishment. They developed a sense of urgency, alertness, and attention to detail. The airmen offered help shining boots or making beds and received help ironing uniforms or folding T-shirts. Before long, their confidence grew. They were no longer motivated solely by fear but by their developing pride in themselves, their flight and their squadron.

As a flight progressed through training and showed they knew what was expected of them, the TIs eased up a little. But if the flight slacked off, the TIs came down hard. Kemph used a technique he called the duffle bag drag to remind the flight of his standards. He ordered the airmen to empty their wall lockers and stuff all of their property in their duffle bags. He marched them around the squadron with their duffle bags on their backs before giving them an hour to put everything back in inspection order. If it wasn't perfect, they did it again until it was.

The TIs were a constant intimidating presence. To the airmen, they didn't appear to have a soul, let alone a personal life or a family. Kemph was at the squadron several hours after the airmen had gone to bed and was back again well before they woke up. He spent at least part of every Saturday and Sunday at work, leaving little time for his family. TIs received few accolades for the sacrifices they made. But as Kemph said, "The rewards of seeing sixty undisciplined civilians grow into one flight of airmen that worked as a well-oiled team" was all the recognition he needed.

As the rest of Flight 407 settled into the training environment, Mellberg still hadn't adapted. Kemph said, "He just never fit in with the rest of the flight … he never fit into the team." He was "wound pretty tight." His hands were always clenched to the point that his knuckles were white.

Every airman in basic training had a turn working as a dorm guard. The guard stood at the dormitory entrance, opening the door only for authorized individuals. Dorm guard duty was performed in two-hour shifts, day and night, which could cut into precious sleep time. Like all senior flights, Flight 407 also performed dorm guard duty for new flights until they were capable of doing it themselves. The female flights didn't perform as much additional dorm guard duty since there were fewer female flights in the squadron. Some of the airmen of Flight 407 quietly grumbled about the disparity. Mellberg obsessed over it. When he complained, Kemph told him to let it go. When Mellberg continued to complain, Kemph told him he must have "huge balls," which prompted Mellberg to file a sexual harassment complaint against his TI.

The airmen spent every day of their training together as a flight. From the time reveille sounded at 0500, their day was filled with PC, drill practice, attending classes, and various group appointments. Prior to lights out at 2100, they usually had some spare time to iron their uniforms, shine their boots, set up their wall lockers, and prepare the dorm for inspection. Most of their time was spent in the squadron. Lackland had a mini-mall and recreation centers with snack bars that offered the trainees a small taste of freedom, but they were off-limits until their later days of training and even then only accessible if they earned permission from their TI. On the rare instance where a trainee was allowed out of the squadron, they were still expected to maintain their military bearing.

Every trainee was required to keep at least two copies of Air Training Command Form 341 in their pocket at all times, filled out with the airman's name, squadron, and flight number. The 341 was an excellence/

discrepancy report and was part of an accountability system. A trainee couldn't go anywhere on Lackland without being scrutinized by a sharp-eyed TI. The sound of a TI barking, "Airman! Give me a 341!" was a common occurrence. It was followed by the airman standing at attention getting "pointed instruction" while fumbling to surrender the 341. If a TI from another squadron pulled a 341, it eventually made its way back to the airman's TI with a note describing the infraction.

On his eighteenth day of training, Mellberg was allowed out of the squadron to walk to a medical appointment. Afterward, instead of returning to the squadron, he stopped at the mini-mall. A TI saw him attempting to purchase a soft drink and confronted him, demanding a 341. The TI then drove to the 3702nd to brief Sergeant Kemph. When Mellberg returned to the dorm, Kemph yelled for him to report to his office. Mellberg knocked once on Kemph's door and entered, speaking softly: "Sir, Airman Mellberg reports as ordered." Mellberg stood at attention in front of Kemph's gray metal desk, his red hands clenched. He denied going to the mini-mall even after Kemph showed him his 341. When Mellberg continued to lie, Kemph jumped from his chair, his thighs catching the underside of his desk, flipping it toward Mellberg who jumped backward, knocking into a shelf, spilling books onto the floor. Kemph, no longer playing the part of an angry TI, left the dorm yelling for the airman to clean up the mess. When he returned, both he and his office had returned to normal. He verbally counseled Mellberg for dishonesty and going to an off-limits area. Kemph also decided it was time for Mellberg to be evaluated by Behavior Analysis Services (BAS), a mental health clinic for basic trainees.

Kemph filled out an evaluation request form and noted his observations of Airman Mellberg: nervousness, excitability, low self-esteem, excessive sweating, being "constantly uptight," and an inability to interact effectively with fellow trainees. Kemph brought the request downstairs to the 3702nd's orderly room, where it was reviewed by the section supervisor and the training superintendent, SMSgt Joe Rodriguez III, who, after meeting with Mellberg, concurred with the TI.

On 23 and 24 July 1992, Mellberg was seen by a BAS psychologist who said that Mellberg appeared frightened and nervous; he was overly rigid, prefacing every sentence and virtually every other word with *sir*. After interviewing Mellberg, the psychologist sent a report to the 3702nd indicating that he had a generalized anxiety disorder with strong obsessive traits. In his report, the psychologist strongly recommended Mellberg for immediate administrative discharge and referral to civilian mental health-care. The report said that if Mellberg were allowed to stay in the Air Force, he should be excluded from duties involving nuclear weapons, security duties, and weapons handling.

Senior Master Sergeant Rodriguez reviewed the BAS report and concurred with the psychologist's recommendations, as did the squadron deputy commander, who forwarded the report to the squadron commander. It was the squadron commander who would make the final determination to retain or discharge Airman Mellberg. Rodriguez's decision to concur with the report came naturally. He had three years' experience as a TI and five years' experience as the 3702nd training superintendent. He was well respected by his TIs, who described him as "all business." He managed the training of around 8,000 trainees a year and had the duty to ensure only qualified airmen graduated from basic training. In addition to his experience, he received annual mental health training to guide him in that effort. After reading the report and meeting with Airman Mellberg, Rodriguez could tell he wasn't fit for military service. He said, "The way an airman sits, fidgets, stares, the inflection or lack of it when responding to certain questions tells a lot about an airman. … This kid did not talk much and had a look and stare that showed he was not playing with the system. I believe he had serious mental problems."

Maj Margaret Arnold* had only been in command of the 3702nd for two weeks, having come from the public affairs career field. Rodriguez recalled being introduced to her in the office of the Basic Military Training School (BMTS) Commander, Col Ronald Jackson. Colonel Jackson told Major Arnold she was fortunate to have a training superintendent with so much experience, and if she relied on Rodriguez's counsel, she would not have any problems. Rodriguez said that after the two of them left the colonel's office, Major Arnold stopped him and made it clear that, as an officer, she did not need advice from her enlisted personnel.

Senior Master Sergeant Rodriguez said that when Airman Mellberg returned to the squadron orderly room from his BAS appointment, the charge of quarters was advised to watch him for potential harm to himself or others. Mellberg was put in a holding area near the squadron orderly room while he waited for Major Arnold's decision. The next morning Arnold called Mellberg into her office and spoke with him. She then summoned Rodriguez and asked him why Mellberg had no belt or bootlaces. Rodriguez said he tried to explain the precautions but the major refused to hear it. According to Rodriguez, Arnold was more concerned that Mellberg was not properly dressed to see the commander than she was about his mental health. He said the major told him, "I don't see anything wrong with the airman. I want him returned to training ASAP." Rodriguez said he asked to speak with the major in private but she replied, "No, get him back in training."

Air Force BMTS was run by non-commissioned officers (NCOs), the enlisted men and women of the Air Force. The officers in BMTS held administrative desk jobs and, with few exceptions, rarely interacted with the trainees. Some TIs felt that certain BMTS squadron commanders took their positions for the sole purpose of having the experience on their résumés. One senior NCO who spent fifteen years at BMTS was of the opinion that many BMTS squadron commanders "were there to punch their ticket and really didn't give a flip about training." Arnold may not have earned the respect of those in her command, but she did earn a nickname. The TIs privately referred to her as Major Maybelline, because she "seemed more interested in her makeup … than in instilling discipline."

Mellberg had evaded discharge from the Air Force but he was apparently oblivious as to why he had been referred to BAS in the first place and why he was allowed to continue basic training. He believed the referral was punitive and would later complain, "I was sent for this appointment as reprisal for making … [a sexual harassment] complaint." He told his mother that Arnold intervened because he was "diligent and patriotic."

Sergeant Kemph was surprised to see Mellberg return to Flight 407, but he had fulfilled his duty, and trusted that his superiors had fulfilled theirs. Other than a group therapy session at the BAS four days later, Mellberg received no further mental health treatment. Despite the BAS psychologist's recommendations that he be excluded from weapon handling, he received basic firearms training and qualified with the M16 rifle. Kemph said other than still being "wound tight," Mellberg kept a low profile. After graduation, he and the other airmen of Flight 407 dispersed to Air Force bases around the country to attend technical school and learn the basic skills of their Air Force career fields. Airman Mellberg flew to Lowry Air Force Base in Colorado, and Sgt Phil Kemph set about preparing his dorm for the next sixty civilians he would transform into airmen.

Lackland Air Force Base, Recruit Housing & Training (RH&T) facilities.
Credit: Andy Brown

Lowry AFB

Lowry Air Force Base, near Denver, Colorado, was the home of the Precision Measurement Equipment Laboratory Technical School. PMEL (pronounced p-mell) was a section within the Air Force maintenance component responsible for testing and calibrating electrical and mechanical instruments in a laboratory setting. Mellberg would spend the next eight months learning the skills needed for his career as a lab technician.

The PMEL students lived in three-story dormitories, with two airmen to a room. On the day Mellberg arrived, 12 Aug 1992, he was pranked by two students who were further along in the program. The students donned officer's uniforms and walked through the dorm halls, where they conducted a mock inspection of Mellberg's room and verbally reprimanded him for a messy room and an improperly made bed. It was typical military hijinks, and Mellberg seemed to take it in stride.

Tech school is a structured military environment. To prevent discipline problems, new PMEL students, known as *pingers*, were subject to many restrictions, which were gradually lifted, in three phases, over a thirty-six-day period. Initially the airmen had curfews, were restricted to base, and had to be in uniform if they left the dormitory. Eventually they earned the right to wear civilian clothes while off duty, could venture off base, and had later curfews. The three-phase program was designed to ease the transition from the strict control of basic training to a more relaxed professional atmosphere. Most students welcomed the newfound freedoms, but Mellberg's classmates noticed he wasn't adapting. Every weekday, the students formed up outside their dormitory to march to the school. One airman recalls, "Everyone else marched with a relaxed posture except him. He was very stiff ... his steps were even, and his boots smacked the ground very hard, as if he were trying to impress someone ... I once asked him why he marched that way. He just smiled and shrugged."

Mellberg's classmates observed that he "appeared to be a loner, always sitting by himself." He sat in the back of the classroom; and although he didn't participate in class discussions, he did pose questions to the instructors, the nature of which usually resulted in laughter from his classmates. His classmates teased him but they also invited him to socialize with them off duty. A few airmen attempted to interact with him during school as well. One classmate remembers, "I tried to talk to him during break sometimes at school, but I felt the conversation was a little one-sided, with me doing most of the talking." While most airmen socialized during break, an instructor observed, "Mellberg would go outside during break periods and march around in a square, doing facing movements."

An airman recalls a time when Mellberg accepted an invitation to join his classmates for an evening of watching videos. "We went to a video store near the base to rent some movies. … We found some movies but lost track of Mellberg and found him again, in the X-rated section. Some of the guys egged him on and pointed out some more nude women. He acted really goofy and made remarks about their breasts and begged to get one." The airmen declined and returned to the dorm with the movies they had selected. One airman said Mellberg acted hyper for the rest of the evening to the point where they eventually kicked him out of the room. He said, "It seemed he was a totally different person that night."

Mellberg scored above average on written tests. His academic average earned him a Distinguished Performer award in Electronic Principals. On paper he was an apt pupil, but he struggled to apply the course material in the laboratory. His medical records show that late in his training he was admitted into the hospital "for observation as a result of post electric shock." It was rumored that "he wanted to listen to the electrons that were flowing in a piece of equipment" and was shocked from ear to finger. As a result, he was the butt of further jokes and insults.

Mellberg spent most of his free time in his dorm room studying or playing video games on his computer. He neglected his personal hygiene to the extent that his instructors had to tell him to take showers. His video game habit may have interfered with his sleep. Students noticed his "eyes always appeared to be red, like he was constantly rubbing them." On one occasion, Mellberg went missing during class and was found standing in an unlit janitor's closet holding an open bottle of ammonia.

Mellberg had trouble getting along with his roommates throughout tech school. They complained about his "frequent masturbation" and "unusual acts." After an argument with one roommate, Mellberg stood in the room holding a can of lighter fluid. When the roommate asked what he was doing, Mellberg told him he "should not go to sleep, because he was going to douse him with lighter fluid and set him on fire." When the threat was reported to the training staff, Mellberg was command directed to undergo a mental health evaluation and was driven to the appointment by a school staff member.

A second instructor recommended Mellberg for a mental health referral because "he wasn't grasping course material and had a tendency to stare at the walls for prolonged periods." The instructor said he was told that Mellberg had already been referred to mental health. In a separate instance, another instructor identified Mellberg as "a person I thought clearly needed mental health help." When he brought his concerns to his supervisor, he recalls, "I was told to let him go because he had a ninety-eight grade point average and would be out of school soon enough."

In spite of the statements from these instructors, no mental health records pertaining to Mellberg were ever located at Lowry AFB or the nearby Fitzsimmons Army Medical Center.

Mellberg continued to struggle with the practical lab exercises. The students worked in pairs and, according to one report, "it is likely Mellberg was intentionally paired with a strong partner." Because of this emphasis on teamwork, virtually no one failed the lab portion of the course. In April of 1993, after eight months of tech school, Mellberg graduated and received orders to Fairchild Air Force Base. A classmate observed he still hadn't adjusted to the norms of military life: "He never changed his marching style. Even when I left tech school to go to my first duty station, he was still marching like he was in basic training or the British Royal Guard." An instructor was similarly concerned. He called Fairchild's PMEL shop and warned them to keep an eye on Mellberg's performance. He expressed concern about Mellberg's difficulty "applying concepts to real-world events."

Airman Brown

I started basic training at Lackland Air Force Base in February of 1989. At age 19, it was the most difficult experience I had yet encountered. I wrote letters home and received several in return, which helped ease my homesickness, especially the perfume-scented letters from my girlfriend. The stress of basic training faded as I learned what my TI expected of me. The experience taught me discipline and the importance of teamwork; it boosted my confidence and instilled in me a military bearing that is with me to this day. As impactful as it was, the weeks I spent in Flight 268 of the 3711th Training Squadron are now just a fragmented blur of memories occasionally triggered by the scent of mothballs or Kiwi boot polish.

All basic trainees were required to memorize Air Force regulations, history, and organizational structure. Among other things, we learned that a group of airmen numbering from a few to one hundred can make up a flight, the smallest unit in the Air Force. A flight was usually given a letter designation such as alpha flight, bravo flight, and so forth, and is led by a flight chief, usually a senior NCO.

Several flights make up a squadron, which is usually led by an officer with a rank from captain to lieutenant colonel. It is the lowest level of command and is identified by a number and its function, for example, the 377th Security Police Squadron or the 92nd Services Squadron.

A group, such as the 92nd Medical Group or 92nd Mission Support Group, is made up of several squadrons and is usually commanded by a colonel.

A wing, such as the 92nd Bombardment Wing, is composed of several groups and is usually commanded by a colonel or higher. The wing commander is typically responsible for all operations of the base and is usually referred to as the base commander.

As I neared the end of basic training, I learned that I had been selected to train as a law enforcement specialist in the security police career field. I was not only excited at the prospect of becoming a cop but also looked forward to leaving Lackland AFB. I would soon discover the Law

Enforcement Tech School was a mere five-minute bus ride from the basic training squadrons, and I was to spend six more weeks at Lackland.

Our Tech School was similar to a civilian police academy. We studied law and learned how to take written statements and write reports and traffic tickets. We practiced traffic stops and responding to domestic disputes and other scenarios we would likely encounter.

We were introduced to the Beretta model 92FS semiautomatic handgun, which was given the military designation M9. The M9 was our primary arm, and we would carry it holstered with a round chambered and the safety in the fire position. I hadn't fired many handguns up to that point; and although the large grip of the M9 didn't fit my hand well, I was enamored of its mechanical craftsmanship.

The M9 is a hammer-fired double action/single action handgun. The initial trigger pull is long and heavy, as it performs two actions: drawing the hammer to the rear and releasing it to drop on the firing pin. When the gun fires, the slide moves rearward, simultaneously ejecting the spent shell casing and cocking the hammer. As the slide returns to battery, it strips a fresh cartridge from the magazine and loads it into the chamber. With the hammer now cocked, subsequent pulls of the trigger require significantly less pressure and perform the single action of releasing the hammer.

We shot our first qualification course with the M9 in tech school, something we would repeat every six months at our duty stations. We fired thirty-six rounds at a cardboard silhouette target with a nine-inch circle penciled onto it. We shot from distances of seven, fifteen, and twenty-five yards, and if you managed to get at least thirty rounds in the circle and all thirty-six on the target, you earned expert status.

The ammunition we used to qualify was 9mm NATO ball. The cartridge was made with a round-nosed projectile composed of 124 grains of lead covered by a thin jacket of copper. Ball ammo is inexpensive and well suited for target practice, but in a defensive shooting the round projectile tends to pass through an offender without disrupting their behavior. Ammunition with a hollow-point projectile is more suited for defensive use. Hollow-points are designed to better transfer their ballistic energy by expanding when they strike their target. As I became more knowledgeable about firearms and ballistics, I was dismayed to learn that the NATO-approved ball ammo was our only authorized defensive round, even while serving in the continental United States.

I spent most of my spare time at tech school studying the course material, which helped me earn the distinction of honor graduate. My classmates and I left tech school proudly wearing our blue berets, headed to Fort Dix, New Jersey, for Air Base Ground Defense School where we traded the berets for Kevlar helmets and flak jackets. We spent time in the field learning the skills of our wartime mission.

We built and manned bunkers, foxholes, and hasty fighting positions. We practiced combat tactics, squad movement, and patrolling outside the perimeter. We learned how to deploy Claymore mines and hand grenades. Armed with blank-firing M16s and M60 machine guns, we defended our mock base and resources from opposing force role players. It reminded me of playing war in the woods of Port Orchard.

Upon graduation, I received orders to my first duty station, Mountain Home Air Force Base, Idaho, where I would be assigned to the 366th Security Police Squadron. Mountain Home: it sounded beautiful.

Airman Basic Andy Brown, Basic Military Training photo, 1989

Mountain Home AFB

I am a security policeman.
I hold allegiance to my country, devotion to duty, and
personal integrity above all.
I wear my badge of authority with dignity and restraint, and
promote by example high standards of conduct, appearance,
courtesy, and performance.
I seek no favor because of my position.
I perform my duties in a firm, courteous, and impartial
manner, irrespective of a person's color, race, religion, national
origin, or sex.
I strive to merit the respect of my fellow airmen and all with
whom I come in contact.

I memorized the Security Police Creed and, to the chagrin of my co-workers, quoted it often.

I flew home for a week and was met at the airport by my family and girlfriend. I was happy to see her, but being in uniform and fresh from training, I was conditioned to not violate the regulation banning the public display of affection. Understandably, she misinterpreted the familial hug I gave her. She said the military had changed me. I spent the week catching up with family and friends and trying to maintain our relationship before heading to Idaho.

Mountain Home was a misnomer. On a June afternoon in 1989, I was the sole passenger on a blue Air Force bus leaving the Boise airport. The bus rolled down the highway through forty miles of Idaho's high desert flatlands to the small town of Mountain Home. The whining engine and road noise made conversation impossible. The driver turned down a lonely road and headed out into the desert. As we bounced along the two-lane road, the driver gestured out the window and yelled, "That's Idaho's state forest!" I searched the expanse of dirt and tumbleweeds stretching to the distant mountains on the horizon. When I realized he was referring to the clumps of sagebrush dotting the landscape, I leaned my head against the window and nodded off. I woke up twelve miles later at the end of the road—the gate to Mountain Home Air Force Base.

I checked in with the 366th Security Police Squadron orderly room and spent the next few days in-processing. I was assigned a dorm room, issued equipment, attended newcomer orientation briefings and delivered my personnel and medical records. I was assigned to a flight, and rode with experienced patrolmen until I could be certified to work the road on my own. I memorized the base regulations and state laws. I emulated the professionalism of my mentors and absorbed all the job knowledge they shared with me. When I made my first solo traffic stop, I was filled with the same nervous anxiety that surged through me as a newly licensed driver whenever I saw blue lights flashing in my rear view mirror. I felt that same anxiety the first time I apprehended a DUI suspect or responded to a domestic dispute or a vehicle accident. But as I gained experience, my confidence grew. Whether I was issuing a speeding ticket in a housing area or assisting a driver who had locked their keys in their car, I took pride in knowing I was serving my community.

We worked three swing shifts and three midnight shifts, followed by three days off; our sleep cycle was in constant flux. Many of our days off were spent in training or working traffic and crowd control at base-wide celebrations and events. We worked holidays and weekends in temperatures ranging from below zero to above one hundred.

We often pulled twelve-hour shifts when manning got low, but even our eight-hour shifts typically took ten hours to complete. We arrived at the squadron an hour early to line up at the armory window to be issued our weapons, ammo and radios. Then we attended guard mount—standing in formation as our flight chief inspected our crisp uniforms and polished boots before assigning us our duties for the day. We inevitably stayed late writing reports on incidents that always seemed to occur right before shift change. Commiserating over the sacrifices that came with the job strengthened the bond we shared as security policemen.

The security police career field was separated into two specialties, security and law enforcement. Security specialists carried the M16 rifle and usually rode in trucks, guarding base resources such as aircraft and the flight line. Law enforcement specialists staffed the base gates or patrolled the base. Our job was similar to that of a small-town cop, only our town had a uniform of the day and a chain link and barbed wire perimeter fence. I knew that fences and gates were only a deterrent to criminals; nevertheless, I was perturbed to discover that Mountain Home's perimeter fence consisted of three strands of barbed wire stretched between wooden fence posts. At least we were secure from marauding cows.

The primary mission of the security police was air base defense, which meant the majority of our training focused on security and resource protection. The law enforcement mission was secondary, and despite the efforts of our training section, which worked with limited resources, our law enforcement training was minimal.

I knew that the job could require me to step into harm's way to defend myself or others, and I didn't feel the training we received or the tools we carried prepared me for the job. We didn't carry batons, pepper spray, or TASERs. But aside from that, I felt underequipped tactically and mentally. I subscribed to *Police* magazine and read through all of the informative articles, but I still felt I was missing something. I wasn't sure what I was looking for. I wished there were a sacred book of secrets that seasoned law enforcement officers passed down to their rookies. In the meantime, I went to the gym as often as possible and religiously practiced the officer safety techniques I had learned from *Police* magazine and my mentor patrolmen.

Whenever I was on duty, I wore bullet-resistant body armor and patrolled the base with my windows down so I could be aware of my surroundings. When I was on a call, I never turned my back on the subjects. During traffic stops I walked backward while returning to my patrol car so I would be ready to respond to an emerging threat.

When some of my co-workers jokingly called me paranoid, I told them, "I'm not paranoid. I'm prepared." They weren't in the majority, but there were some who had been lulled into a false sense of security, believing that major crime doesn't happen on military bases.

Our policies, both written and unofficial, were of the same mindset. Security police were verbally reprimanded for appearing too aggressive if they approached a traffic stop with their hand resting on their duty belt near their holstered handgun. Our use of force policy authorized us to use deadly force if a subject demonstrated the intent, opportunity, and capability to cause serious bodily injury to us or someone else. But that same policy handicapped us by stating if we were responding to an incident where we "could reasonably expect to meet an armed adversary," we could have our shooting hand on the pistol grip but could not draw the pistol from the holster until we had reasonably determined deadly force was necessary. If I was working with a partner I could trust and we were out of public view, we disregarded that policy. When we responded to late-night building intrusion alarms, we frequently searched the building with our handguns drawn and at the ready. One of those partners I trusted was Erik Turner.

Erik was a patrolman on my flight. Like me, he was nineteen years old, from Washington State, and away from home for the first time. We shared a common dedication to the job and seemed to know what the other was thinking when we backed each other up on calls. We had a passion for the job, but we also had compassion for our fellow airmen. If we thought someone genuinely made a mistake in committing a minor offense, we cut them a break. When we responded to noise complaints in the dormitories, we'd warn everyone at the party to keep it down and that if we had to come back we would be checking ID cards. We knew that would likely result in finding underage drinkers, and we took no pleasure in apprehending someone for an offense we were guilty of on a regular basis.

Although I drove the 580 miles to Port Orchard, Washington, as often as I could to spend a day with my family and my girlfriend, the long-distance relationship didn't last. I was heartbroken, but I found a new devotion in law enforcement and my security police family.

I spent most of my off-duty time at the home of Erik and his wife, Tracy, who lived in a mobile home park in the town of Mountain Home. It was a sanctuary from dorm life and a favorite hangout of the cops we worked with. There was a lot of beer drinking and a lot of camaraderie. The Turners were like family to me, but they were the only thing keeping me at Mountain Home. It was a great location if you liked hunting, fishing, or snow skiing, but I hadn't joined the Air Force to see the deserts of southern Idaho. After putting in a request for an overseas long tour, I quickly received orders to Greece. Right before I was scheduled to ship out, Erik learned he and a group of other cops were headed to Saudi Arabia in support of Operation Desert Storm. I wanted to go with him and asked to have my orders canceled. My request was denied.

Iraklion AS

On 21 March 1990, after a six-thousand-mile flight, my plane touched down at Heraklion International Airport on the long, narrow Greek island of Crete. The taxi I hired sped along winding cliffside roads and rattled through tiny seaside villages before dropping me off at the gate of Iraklion Air Station. The base sat on a half-mile square of red earth coastline, surrounded by olive groves, artichoke fields, and vineyards. The perimeter was fenced on three sides; the fourth remained open to the Mediterranean Sea, the base beach, and marina. I reported to the 7276th Security Police Squadron and began in-processing. At a newcomer's briefing, a chaplain spoke to us and handed out a questionnaire asking for our names and other personal information. In the space marked "religious preference," I wrote "law enforcement." I was only halfway being a smartass.

Iraklion's facilities like the chow hall, dormitories, gym, and enlisted club were of typical Greek island construction: flat-roofed concrete buildings painted bright white with blue trim. We didn't have a flight line or aircraft. The primary mission of the 7276th Airbase Group revolved around a field of antenna towers and a large windowless concrete building where Air Force analysts intercepted foreign radio transmissions.

The 800 men and women stationed at Iraklion referred to the Airbase as Club Med. The atmosphere was so casual, the cop dorm had a vending machine that dispensed cans of Budweiser. I made friends with several fellow airmen and Greek nationals. I learned enough conversational Greek to order food and coffee at the downtown cafes and chat about the weather with the locals.

Our squadron was small; my flight consisted of about seven security specialists and three law enforcement specialists. I occasionally augmented security by guarding the antenna field, but primarily I manned the gate or patrolled the base. One night while writing a report in the patrolmen's room, I found a thick, black hardcover book hidden among regulation binders and training manuals on a dusty bookshelf. The bold white print on the cover read, *The Tactical Edge: Surviving High-Risk Patrol*, by

Charles Remsberg. The more I read, the more I realized I had found the book of secrets I was searching for. Remsberg had compiled the tactics and techniques necessary for surviving dangerous situations, using the experience of hundreds of police officers. His book taught me how to further develop my officer survival mindset.

The most important thing I learned from the book was the technique of mental rehearsal. In the same way an athlete trains by visualizing their performance, I began visualizing scenarios I might encounter and mentally practiced the actions necessary to survive them. Every night before I went to sleep, I'd mentally rehearse an incident, be it a traffic stop, a building search, an armed robbery, or a domestic dispute. I'd vividly imagine encountering a deadly threat and visualize myself successfully countering it. I also began critiquing my real-world tactics. After a traffic stop or any other interaction with the public, I'd return to my patrol car and ask myself: Did I leave myself vulnerable? What could I have done better? If I saw room for improvement, I'd work to correct it on the next encounter.

I finally felt better prepared to meet the challenges of the job. But I would discover that the hardest part of working law enforcement in the resort-like atmosphere of Iraklion was maintaining a survival mindset.

In his book, Remsberg points out that surviving a lethal-force encounter takes a combination of mental, physical, and shooting skills. Our Combat Arms Training and Maintenance (CATM) instructors did an excellent job of teaching us the fundamentals of marksmanship. As I grew more comfortable with the M9, I regularly achieved expert marksman status. I didn't like that we were only allowed to fire our handguns twice a year. I turned 21 while I was in Greece, old enough to own a personal handgun to practice with. But I would have to wait until I returned to the United States to buy one.

I spent three years at Iraklion Air Station. In April of 1993, I received orders to report to Fairchild Air Force Base. My home town of Port Orchard would only be three hundred miles away, and I looked forward to being closer to my family again.

A1C Andy Brown, Iraklion Air Station, 1992.

1991–1992 Air Shows

On 19 May 1991, thousands of Spokane area residents swarmed the flight line of Fairchild Air Force Base for the annual open house and air show. The US and its allies had just achieved an apparent victory in the Persian Gulf War, and thousands of US troops, including some of Fairchild's airmen, were still overseas. There was a strong sense of patriotism in the crowd as they were treated to several aerial displays, including one involving a bomber and a tanker.

Since 1958, Fairchild had maintained a nuclear-armed B-52 and a fully loaded KC-135 on alert status. Their crews slept and ate in an alert facility, ready to take off on fifteen minutes' notice. At the 1991 air show, crews delighted the crowd with a simulated alert scramble and minimum-interval takeoff of an unarmed B-52 and KC-135.

The B-52 made several low-level passes down the length of the airfield. If flown conservatively, the large plane would make a wide turn, taking it out of the spectator's view, as it set up for a return pass. The pilot of this B-52 banked the wings aggressively and made several of its turns directly over the crowd. In another maneuver, the bomber and the KC-135 flew a "loose visual formation," flying abeam of each other, passing low in front of the spectators before they peeled off right and left. The B-52 then made another low-altitude, high-speed pass down the airfield and pulled up sharply, performing a high-pitch-angle climb, gaining several thousand feet of altitude in a matter of seconds.

The maneuvers performed by the B-52 violated Air Force regulations regarding bank and pitch angles and flying over assemblies of people. The regulations specifically limited multi-engine aircraft to thirty degrees of bank unless flying at altitude. The B-52's flight profile also contradicted the guidelines laid out in the *B-52 Pilot's Flight Manual* (T.O. 1B-52G-1-11). The manual, known as the *Dash 11*, was the B-52 pilot's bible. The maneuvers performed by the B-52 would have required approval from Fairchild's major command headquarters, but permission was neither sought nor granted.

The pilot of the B-52 was Lt Col Arthur "Bud" Holland. Holland had been flying B-52s since 1972 and had amassed more than 5,000 hours in the heavy bomber, including sixty-one hours of combat time in Vietnam. Experienced B-52 pilots said Holland was the best they ever knew. B-52 Evaluator Pilot Maj Jay Slaughenhoupt said, "Lieutenant Colonel Holland probably had the best hands of anybody I have ever flown with … He had really good hands. He knew what he could do and what he couldn't do … His situational awareness was better than mine and his limits were farther out than mine."

According to his bosses, when they flew with Holland, he always flew by the book. Col Michael Ruotsala, the vice wing commander in 1991, said he "was probably the best B-52 pilot that I know in the wing and probably one of the best, if not the best, within the command." He was "very well aware of the regulations and the capabilities of the airplane."

There were a few among the ranks who thought Bud Holland could do no wrong. There was also an ever-increasing number of airmen who questioned Holland's airmanship, specifically his ability to exercise sound judgment regarding safety. Capt Alexander P. Brown, a B-52 Instructor Pilot, had flown with Holland on several occasions dating back to the mid-1980s. Brown said, "Virtually every time he flew, something would be done, apparently intentionally, that was not within the directives, that was not within the operating limits."

Capt Brett Dugue, a B-52 Aircraft Commander at Fairchild, said, "A lot of people on this base, including senior leadership, looked up to him … There were a lot of comments saying he's the best pilot on base … and personally, I did not agree … I don't think the best pilot on base or the best pilot anywhere would knowingly disregard regulations or aircraft restrictions."

Bud Holland's skill as a pilot was without question, but in a profession that demanded both precision and restraint, he was thought of as a maverick—the kind of man who considered becoming a crop duster when he retired. Holland thought flying for a civilian airline—a typical job of retired military pilots—would be boring.

For a pilot who knowingly disregarded regulations and restrictions, Holland held an unusual position of authority. He was the chief of Fairchild's pilot standardization and evaluation (Stan/Eval) program. In his position, Holland was responsible for enforcing flight regulations and evaluating B-52 pilots for competency. He was the top crewmember on base and was expected to set the example of safe flying.

Fairchild's senior leaders seemed unaware of the regulations covering flight safety. Perhaps they didn't understand the limitations of the aircraft, or maybe they were blinded by their admiration of the veteran pilot. Col Arnold Julich, the 92nd Operations Group Commander, was at the 1991 air show. When asked about Holland's performance three years later he said, "I don't remember any of the turn-outs being excessive or anything like that … We were still pretty sensitized by the Thunderhawks, you know."

The BUFF

The Boeing B-52 Stratofortress had been in the US Air Force arsenal since 1955. In the 1960s, during the Cold War, nuclear-armed B-52s served as a deterrent, flying routes that put at least one bomber within two hours of the Soviet Union at all times.

The B-52 could hold up to 70,000 pounds of conventional bombs and was used extensively in the Vietnam and Persian Gulf wars. As technology advanced, the B-52 received several upgrades, but it has always maintained its distinct appearance. Its swept wings spanned 185 feet. The fuselage stretched 159 feet from its dolphin-like nose to its four-story tail.

The B-52H is powered by eight turbofan engines that jut from its long, flexible wings. The engines are fed by 48,000 gallons of fuel from tanks in the top of the fuselage, including 10,000 gallons that slosh around inside the plane's *wet wings*. The fuel in the wings and the added weight of external ordnance cause the wings to droop, necessitating a single-wheel retractable outrigger to prevent the wing tips from dragging on the ground. When a B-52 rolls down the runway for takeoff, its wings rise into the air and begin flying well before they pull the rest of the aircraft off the ground.

The B-52 is a sluggish performer. A pilot can make a lateral control input and expect to wait up to three seconds for the plane to respond. The fuel in the wings tends to shift as the plane banks in a turn, requiring the pilot to anticipate the aircraft's changing center of gravity.

The B-52 is an impressive, well-loved machine, but it lacks the graceful lines of other aircraft. The hulking plane is proudly referred to as the BUFF—big ugly fat fucker. In polite company, the last word is rendered as *fellow*.

Operating the BUFF requires a team effort, what the Air Force calls *crew concept*. The crew accesses the plane by climbing through a hatch in front of the forward landing gear. The hatch leads to the lower deck, which reeks of urine, sweat, and motor oil, the product of decades of extended missions and the crew's primitive toilet. The lower deck is the cramped, windowless home of the navigator and the radar navigator-bombardier. The two sit side by side, lit by banks of red and green panel lights, switches, and buttons. Their only view of the outside world comes from the glow of their terrain-mapping radar and an infrared camera image on a monochrome screen. The navigator keeps the plane on course and the radar navigator delivers the appropriate weapons to the intended target.

A ladder leads from the lower deck to the upper deck. The narrow passageway is the only place on the B-52 where taller crewmembers can stand upright.

The rear section of the upper deck is also windowless. This is the station where the electronic warfare officer (E-Dub) sits facing the tail, surrounded by his instruments and controls. When the tail gunner position was phased out in 1991, the E-Dub became the sole defender of the B-52. He defeats potential threats with electronic radar jamming, frustrates enemy fighters and heat-seeking missiles by ejecting flares, and confuses enemy radar by dispersing chaff—bundles containing millions of aluminum coated fibers.

The passage between the E-Dub station and the cockpit holds a bunk and a small oven, providing the crew hot meals and catnaps during long missions.

Forward of the upper deck sit the pilot and copilot, whose cockpit is encircled with windows. Every available surface inside the cockpit is crammed with dials, gauges, switches, warning lights, and image screens. Some of the controls are only accessible by the pilot and some are only within reach of the copilot. But both fliers have a control yoke and access to the eight throttle controls that sit between them.

The crew communicates over the screaming noise of the eight engines via a helmet- or headset-mounted interphone. The copilot monitors the plane's instruments and warns the pilot whenever the altitude, airspeed, or bank angle exceeds recommended values. The navigator calls out airspeeds and headings to ensure the pilot keeps the plane on course and on time.

Additional seats can be mounted in the plane, but only the primary crewmembers are capable of independently ejecting from the airplane. Once ejection is initiated, a hatch blows and their seat launches explosively out of the aircraft. The upper deck crew leaves the plane out the top. The lower deck crew ejects downward. A successful downward ejection requires

600 feet of altitude, which significantly increases the risk of low-altitude missions for the navigator and radar navigator. For a BUFF crewmember, having trust in your pilot is essential.

Change-of-Command Flyover

On 12 July 1991, the 325th Bomb Squadron prepared for a change-of-command ceremony to formally recognize their new commander, Lt Col Jerry Schmidt. The event was to take place in Fairchild's Heritage Park, a treed triangle of grass where several decommissioned military airplanes stood on permanent display. The most prized of them, a B-52 bearing a red kill star, would serve as the backdrop for the ceremony. The plane earned the star in 1972, when its tail gunner downed a pursuing MiG-21 during a Vietnam bombing mission. The change-of-command ceremony included a B-52 flyover, piloted by Lieutenant Colonel Holland. Air Force regulations limited flyovers of congested areas or open air assemblies to 1,000 feet above the highest nearby obstacle.

Before the ceremony, Holland made several practice runs that barely cleared the tops of the trees surrounding the park. After one pass, Holland banked the plane's wings more than forty-five degrees and executed a tight right turn far exceeding the Dash 11 recommendations. After another low pass, Holland pulled the airplane up sharply, making an almost vertical climb. As the plane climbed and lost air speed, Holland performed a *wingover*, rolling the aircraft on its side, allowing the nose to fall below the horizon to regain airspeed. The Dash 11 recommends against wingover maneuvers, as the side slip may cause structural damage. As one pilot put it, "You don't really want to do a wingover in a B-52. You'd cut the tail off."

The change-of-command ceremony was presided over by several commanders assigned to the 92nd Bomb Wing. Rows of aircrew members wearing green flight suits and blue flight caps stood in formation, as Holland flew in from the north. The distant roar of the B-52's eight engines turned to a whistling scream as he approached and descended. Black smoke streamed from the engines as the bomber made a high-speed pass that some observers estimated was one hundred feet above the ceremony attendees. Holland wagged his wings slightly to the right, then made an excessively banked left turn and flew out of sight. Several who were in attendance were alarmed by the aggressive flying and looked to their senior leadership. B-52 pilot Capt Leland White said, "I remember looking at the expressions of the commanders up there on the podium. I'm not sure they were overly happy. … Maybe it made them overly proud, I don't know."

Col David Capotosti, the deputy commander of the 92nd Operations Group, was not proud of the "aggressive fly-by." When the ceremony ended, many of the attendees walked across the street to the Officers' Club. Colonel Capotosti said he approached his boss, the 92nd Operations Group commander, Col Arnold Julich, and said, "We can't have that. We can't tolerate things like that. We need to take action for two reasons: it's unsafe, and we have a perception problem with young air crews."

Colonel Julich had flown with Holland before. He said, "I always thought that Bud was the epitome of the professional B-52 pilot … He was the guy I regularly chose to fly with because he was so good."

Julich recalls talking to his boss about Holland. "I had talked to the wing commander"—Colonel Arnold Weinman—"after that fly-by, and he was concerned at that time that it had been too low. At that time, we did discuss the fact that we probably didn't want him doing any more air shows or any more flyovers for us." Julich said he discussed with Colonel Weinman whether Holland "should be grounded for a period of time or whether I should take any action, and I was not directed to take any action against Lieutenant Colonel Holland."

Colonel Weinman retired a few days after Holland's low flyover. It was part of an unusual trend involving the frequent turnover of Fairchild's senior leadership. Over a three-year period, the 92nd Bomb Wing went through four wing commanders, three vice wing commanders, three operations group commanders and three deputy operations group commanders. During the same three-year period, the 325th Bomb Squadron had five different squadron commanders. The lack of leadership continuity would play a part in allowing a rogue pilot to go unchecked. But even as commanders became aware of incidents of unsafe flying they took no action. There is no evidence to show that Holland was ever disciplined. There was no derogatory information in his performance file.

When Holland wasn't grounded for the blatantly low flyover, it sent a message to the members of the 325th Bomb Squadron. Capt Clem Countess said, "The power which was given to Colonel Holland to fly like this, I felt was fully approved after his fly-by of the change of command."

Capt Shawn Fleming noted, "That basically set the precedent, when he received no disciplinary action from that … The squadron was basically amazed that this was allowed to continue … There should have been something apparent to the crew force that that was not a condoned act. … He continued to fly, and it was business as usual."

1992 Air Show

Holland was chosen to fly in Fairchild's 1992 air show. Since witnessing the 1991 change-of-command flyover, the deputy commander of the 92nd Operations Group, Colonel Capotosti, had done some research and compiled a file of regulations covering flyovers and aerial displays. Capotosti voiced his concerns that Holland fly by the book for the 1992 air show. But other than "voicing concerns," nothing was done to prevent Holland from flying or ensure that he fly conservatively. The 92nd Bomb Wing commander at the time of the 1992 air show was Col Michael Ruotsala. Colonel Ruotsala had not seen Holland's performance in the 1991 air show but was told it was impressive. Ruotsala said the same profile was to be used in the 1992 air show–"What had been done before was all right, and it was going to be done again."

In the 17 May 1992 air show, Holland flew the B-52, making his usual low-level passes down the airfield and his signature high-pitch-angle climb. His low-altitude steep turns were dangerously aggressive. The crowd was awed at the sight of a B-52 with its wings stretched from ground to sky.

An aircraft commander with the 325th Bomb Squadron, Maj Don Thompson attended the 1992 Air Show with his visiting parents. Thompson said, "I remember seeing the B-52 in some, what they call, crowd-pleasing maneuvers … Yeah, it made the crowd cheer, but it was a little bit beyond what my comfort zone would be in the aircraft." A comment Thompson made to his parents was overheard by a *The Spokesman-Review* reporter. An article in the next day's paper read, "A 25-year-old man pointed his finger as a B-52 bomber roared past the viewing stand, then tilted its wings perpendicular to the ground. 'That guy is nuts. He's absolutely crazy.' … The pilot displaying his bomber's maneuverability and grace was Fairchild's Lieutenant Colonel Bud Holland."

The press likely boosted Holland's ego, and his maneuvers impressed the crowds. But those who knew the limitations of the B-52 knew that the further the airplane's wings banked from level flight, the less lift they generated. And when the wings approach vertical, the plane isn't flying anymore; it's falling.

Capt Derek Riggan, a 325th Bomb Squadron aircraft commander, had seen the bomber fly in previous air shows. What he saw that day didn't sit well with him. "I became nerve-racked watching the airplane flying for all the people out here because of my experience in the airplane, knowing how it handles, knowing how far you can push it. I felt very uncomfortable watching some of the maneuvers close to the runway, close to the crowd."

Holland's maneuvers were not only risky, they put undue stress on the airplane. The *Dash 11* says the B-52's maneuvering limit is 2 g, which Holland usually wouldn't admit to exceeding. The crews who flew with him during the high-pitch-angle climb said that it was the most 2 g they've ever felt. The force exerted on the B-52 during Holland's maneuvers was more than the aging airframe was built to withstand. B-52 pilot, Capt Eric Jones, recalled Holland, "discussed one of his air shows and that over five hundred rivets had been popped on one of the airplanes and there was potentially a cracked center wing tank. He had also stated somewhat proudly that while out doing one of his maneuvers an oven had come out of its mount and smashed what I believe was the E-Dub's [radar monitoring] scope and done forty some odd thousand dollars' worth of damage."

Capt Alexander Brown saw the 1992 Air Show from his off-base home. "I watched, and from fifteen miles away, I could see the climb quite clearly—an abrupt appearance of a B-52 to a very high pitch angle. The nose was at least seventy degrees, nose high—and in what appeared to be a stall at the top of a climb, with a falling of the nose forward, eventual recovery, and then flying away." Brown worked in the base command post and said that he spoke to Holland after the air show, and he admitted the maneuver put 3.75 g of force on the airplane. Brown said, a few days after the air show, "The operations group commander, Colonel Capotosti, came into the command post … We got to chatting about the air show, and I said to him that I felt it was unsafe, that I thought the maneuver was extreme, and that I felt he had stalled the airplane at the top of the arch and that something should be done about this. And he said 'I'll have a talk with him.'"

Capotosti had seen Holland's air show performance himself and was not happy. Seven days later, when he became the 92nd Operations Group commander, he was in a position to do something about it. According to Capotosti, he called Holland into his office and told him, "If you go out and do a violation and I become aware of it, I will ground you permanent-ly." Capotosti told his deputy commander, Lt Col Stephen Harper, and the bomb squadron commander, Lt Col David Bullock, "Lieutenant Colonel Holland will never fly another air show as long as I am the DO."

The vice wing commander during the 1992 air show, Col Larry Hinton, also voiced his concerns about Holland's maneuvers to Bullock, but no cor-rective action was taken.

Capotosti's warning to Holland went unheeded. Not long after the 1992 air show, Capt Eric Jones, an instructor pilot, flew with Holland on what was supposed to be instrument approach practice in a pattern around Fairchild. Once airborne, Jones relates, Holland contacted nearby Spokane International Airport. "He had requested from and gotten clearance from Spokane approach control to fly over Mead High School, where his daugh-ter was playing softball." Holland was given permission to descend to 4,000 feet. He told Jones he was going to make a sixty-degree bank turn over the school. But Jones said, "He rolled the airplane into about seventy to seventy-two degrees bank and began to pull. We exceeded 2 g. I told him 'watch the g's.' He said, 'Yeah, yeah.' As the nose began to track down a little bit, he applied more back pressure, even though we were over the g limit. The airplane seemed to tighten up the turn a little bit more. He made no attempt to roll out. The nose held it for a moment and then just fell through. We got into what I call the turning death spiral. We bottomed out of the maneuver once I got on the yoke and rolled the wings, right at about 3,000 feet." Spokane International saw the altitude drop and reprimanded Holland for not maintaining his given altitude. Holland responded, "I'm sorry, just a momentary deviation."

"Well, I just want to make sure we understand each other. When I give you an altitude to fly, I expect you to fly it."

"Roger, and we'll take it back to Fairchild at this time."

The incident was apparently never reported to Fairchild leadership.

Fairchild PMEL

Airman Mellberg flew into Spokane on 28 April 1993, and was met at the airport by two of his peers from the Fairchild Air Force Base PMEL. One of the airmen said, "He came off the airplane in full military blues. When we introduced ourselves, he mumbled something and came to attention. We had to tell him to relax." When new airmen arrive at their first duty station, they are often relieved to discover that life in the Air Force is a little more casual than what they experienced in basic training and tech school. The PMEL at Fairchild promoted an even more informal atmosphere in which a person's rank was overlooked to encourage airmen to seek help from the more experienced technicians. Most new airmen quickly conform to the change; but according to a sergeant who worked in the lab, Mellberg wasn't adapting. "My first impression of him was he is overly shy and quiet, even for an airman arriving fresh out of school. … One thing you noticed right away was he never relaxed. He was overly respectful to all people, especially NCOs and officers. He would stand at my office door and wait until I realized he was there and told him to come in. He wouldn't knock or interrupt in any way. When I was doing his initial interview, he sat at attention and was rigid even when I tried to calm him down."

His awkward demeanor extended into his off-duty time. Mellberg was two weeks into his assignment when a PMEL sergeant encountered him outside the Shoppette, the base convenience store. When the sergeant greeted him and introduced him to his wife, Mellberg stood at attention and muttered incoherently. The sergeant said, "Even in civilian clothes he seemed almost afraid of me."

Sgt Nathaniel Wilson was informed by his supervisor, TSgt Payton Kendall, that he was to be Airman Mellberg's trainer-supervisor. Wilson said, "He asked me to become his trainer because after meeting with Dean, he felt he would require a lot of patience and understanding."

In the Air Force, the PMEL is responsible for calibrating the complex machinery and equipment used to maintain aircraft and other resources. Like all new lab technicians, Mellberg started out calibrating torque

55

wrenches. It was a relatively simple process that must be mastered before moving on to the more complicated electronics. Wilson noted, "Training went very slow for Airman Mellberg. He seemed anxious to learn but didn't seem to comprehend what was being taught. … He seemed to have problems processing questions; and when he did ask questions, they normally couldn't be heard."

Mellberg struggled with the procedures and paperwork involved in basic tasks. After he failed his first quality verification inspection, the inspector sat him down and told him not to worry. "It happens to everyone." Even with this assurance, Mellberg was visibly upset. A co-worker noted, "You knew he was getting angry when he began breathing heavily and his face got red and he walked away from you before you were done talking to him."

Sergeant Wilson noticed Mellberg exhibited odd behavior. "During break periods and lunch, he would sit by himself and appear to talk and laugh to himself." Sometimes he would browse through a magazine, and when asked what he was reading, he would look up, smile, and laugh.

Mellberg's co-workers didn't exclude him from the typical lab hijinks. Wilson remembers when Mellberg got into the lab freezer and put distilled ice cubes in his drink. Wilson said, "Some of the guys told him that they were radioactive and even went so far as to pretend to check the radiation level in his body with a fake Geiger counter." A couple of airmen thought the prank freaked Mellberg out, but Wilson said, "He always seemed to take the jokes well. It almost seemed as if he felt like one of the guys."

Lois and Gary Mellberg traveled to Fairchild to see their son. One of Mellberg's co-workers said he "seemed to look for their guidance and approval during their visit." He went through considerable effort making sure his leave paperwork was in order and ensuring the lab looked perfect. When Mellberg brought his parents in for a tour, his co-workers noticed he had difficulty speaking as he showed them around the lab. They also noticed his father "was quiet, but his mother was very talkative and animated."

Although Mellberg didn't socialize with anyone from work, he participated in unit functions. At a unit picnic, he joined his lab mates in a volleyball game but ran "people over in his eagerness to return the ball."

He was the first to volunteer for weekly lab cleanup. During one cleaning session, Mellberg was asked to run three burned out light bulbs to the dumpster. He made three trips to the trash, each time running at full speed. When his co-workers teased him about it, he laughed and said, "I was just doing what I was told."

* * *

Mellberg shared a room in the 92nd Maintenance Squadron dormitory with A1C Erik Rayner. Airman First Class Rayner had also just recently arrived, and Fairchild was his first duty assignment. He was a maintenance troop; but unlike his roommate, he did not work in the PMEL. Rayner looked forward to getting to know his roommate. He introduced himself, talked excitedly about his fiancée and attempted to engage in other small talk. Rayner eventually gave up trying to get to know Mellberg. He said, "He never really talked and kept to himself … I respected that and tried to give him his space," but it "made it hard to be roommates." Mellberg recorded the event in his journal:

> Apr. 28—Entered Fairchild AFB after completing tech school, staying at the Arc Lite Manor room 315 with a roommate, Erik Rayner, who was there for two days before. Upon our very first discussion he indicated that marriage was his plan in four months.

Giving a roommate their personal space in a military dormitory wasn't easy. The rooms were considered small for a single airman, let alone two, and most of the space was filled with government-issue beds, dressers, chairs, nightstands and wall lockers. Their small bathroom was shared with the airmen in the adjoining room, which meant four people competing for the shower and toilet. Dorm life was a lesson in consideration and compromise.

Shortly after Mellberg moved in, he came home with a Big Ben windup alarm clock. The oversized clock ticked so loudly that Rayner struggled to fall asleep. He asked Mellberg to use the digital clock radio instead. When Mellberg refused, Rayner joked about throwing the clock out the window. Mellberg quietly took offense and recorded the threat in his journal:

> May 6—I was asked by Erik if I would put my clock away. I question if the power ever went out that I would need for that alarm to go off. He just wanted that clock gone or he would throw it out.

First-term airmen aren't highly paid and usually live from paycheck to paycheck. Mellberg was frugal. He rode his bicycle to the base gym and library, where he spent much of his free time. Without the expenses that come with cars and girlfriends, his bank account grew larger every two weeks. Rayner, on the other hand, wanted a car. When he found one at a good price, he asked Mellberg if he could borrow $400 until payday. Mellberg was unusually disturbed by the request and recorded the offense in his journal:

> May 12—After a day of looking for a VW Bug, to which he wanted very badly, he couldn't pay for the vehicle by the end of the month before it was planning to be sold. He offered at first for a lone of $400.00 dollar. He said that this deal would be a contracted and that he would want his Air Force career to be jeopardy because of this. My strong defense is that my parents would preferable like me not to partake in such deals of this kind. His reply to this is that he does better in life not to lesson to his divorced mother and even broke many ties with by not speaking with her on the phone do to money matter as well.

As soon as Rayner married his fiancée, Stacy, he would receive a housing allowance and be able to move off base. For now, when Stacy drove up on the weekends, she stayed with him in the dorm. Regulations prohibited overnight guests, but the rule was rarely enforced, and Mellberg didn't seem to mind the intrusion. Before introducing her, Rayner warned Stacy that his roommate was strange and quiet. On the night of her first visit, the couple were in the room talking when Mellberg announced he was going to bed. They offered to go down the hall to the day room, but Mellberg insisted it was okay if they stayed. Ten minutes later, Rayner laughed and whispered, "Don't look at the wall." Stacy said, "I looked … and saw the shadow of Dean lying on his bed with an erection and his hand on it. I got up to walk out and saw he was lying naked on the bed, masturbating."

The next day the couple planned a trip to nearby Medical Lake. Stacy invited Mellberg, hoping "to get him to lighten up a little by taking him out," and he seemed happy to get out of the room. The three walked halfway around the lake before mosquitoes made the outing unbearable. Stacy started running back to the car, and Mellberg ran with her. When she stopped to wait for her fiancé, Mellberg made a disparaging remark about Rayner's fitness and told Stacy, "You don't need to wait for him."

From that day on, whenever Stacy and Rayner went on a date, Mellberg felt entitled to join them. One evening when Rayner explained that he wanted to spend some time alone with Stacy, Mellberg stormed out of the room. Stacy found him in the day room and explained that Rayner wasn't trying to hurt his feelings. Mellberg changed the subject. He asked Stacy how she and Erik met. After she answered, Stacy said Mellberg asked her if "Erik was a virgin when I met him. When did we first have sex? How many girls has Erik been with? What kind of sexual things does Erik like?"

Stacy continued driving up from Oregon on weekends to spend time with her fiancé. On one occasion while Rayner was napping, Mellberg showed Stacy photographs in his *Playboy* magazine and asked her, "Do you think these girls are pretty? Would you do one?" When Mellberg refused to stop, Stacy woke Rayner, but he persisted in showing her the pictures until Rayner snatched the magazine away. Undeterred, Mellberg selected another magazine from his collection and read sexually explicit stories aloud until Rayner and Stacy left the room.

Rayner grew increasingly frustrated with Mellberg's obnoxious behavior and indiscreet masturbation. He and the airmen in the adjoining room were also irritated by Mellberg's monopoly of the shared bathroom, where he spent hours in the shower. Rayner came home one evening to find Mellberg sitting naked in a chair masturbating to a *Playboy*. He returned later and asked Mellberg to be more respectful and discreet. The talk seemed to help, but when he resumed his perverse behavior only days later, Rayner decided to get outside help.

On the first of June 1993, Rayner went to see the maintenance squadron acting first sergeant Chief Master Sergeant Hutchinson, who was filling in for the actual first sergeant who was away on a temporary duty assignment in Saudi Arabia.

Every squadron has a first sergeant, the squadron problem solver who reports to the squadron commander on matters of enlisted welfare and conduct. If an enlisted military member has a problem or is in trouble they will eventually find themselves in front of the first sergeant.

Rayner explained to Chief Hutchinson the problems he was having with Mellberg and asked the chief "to be easy on him because ... he's not a bad person." Rayner returned to work but was summoned back to the first sergeant's office twenty minutes later. Mellberg was in the office. Rayner said, "Dean denied everything that I said, even to my face. So the chief then said that one of us is lying and he needs to know who it is." Mellberg suggested Rayner had an ulterior motive for reporting him, which he later recorded in his journal:

> June 1—I was given a call by acting First Sergeant Chief Hutchinson. From there I was shook up with the fact that he was talking with me about masturbation. … He said my roommate said that I was in the shower masturbating. I explained on why he may have done this in order for him to have a lasting impression on my career and protect himself from any thing he might have do before this like the loan, and his girl friend staying the night.

The chief was unable to settle the dispute and dismissed the two airmen, telling them to return the next day with the truth.

Rayner said, "Later that night when I got home, around 1945, Dean had put all of his belongings into his closet and locked them up. Dean didn't come home until 2100. When he walked in, I said 'Hi.' He didn't answer. I asked him if he wasn't talking to me. No answer." When Rayner asked why he lied, Mellberg "blew up and started yelling." He denied that Rayner ever asked him to stop masturbating. Rayner said, "He kept saying that I was trying to hurt him and manipulate him and order him around." Rayner told Mellberg, "I'm not trying to hurt you I just want some respect." Rayner said Mellberg was unreceptive. "He didn't seem to care about anything, just that I'm trying to hurt him. He was acting so different compared to any other day that I lived with him."

Rayner asked, "Why are you yelling and acting like this?"

Mellberg began crying. "I don't know. I need some help."

Rayner asked Mellberg to sit down and talk but he went right back to yelling and name-calling. Rayner said, "It looked like he wanted to take a swing at me. I asked him if he wanted to hurt me. All he said was 'you'll see.' Then I got mad and started to say, 'Why don't you do it now, because I want to get you kicked out of the service.'"

Mellberg told Rayner he would have to wait and see. He hinted at harming him while he slept and said that they would both burn in hell because they both lied. Rayner told him, "Wrong. You lied, not me."

Around 2200 that evening, after Mellberg had calmed down, Rayner asked him about his past. "He seemed to really respect his family a lot. But when I asked him about his high school he told me that his schoolmates used to pick on him and that he wishes that he could shoot them all." Rayner told Mellberg, "Everyone gets picked on once in their life, even me. You just need to leave that in the past and get on with the present. Maybe find some friends or a girlfriend."

According to Rayner, Mellberg said that girls hurt him the most back in high school. Rayner cautiously probed Mellberg, asking him if he ever tried to hurt any of his other roommates. Mellberg revealed an incident involving lighter fluid in tech school but didn't go into detail. Rayner didn't need the details. He knew that having Dean Mellberg as a roommate wasn't just uncomfortable, it was dangerous, and he didn't "want to sleep with one eye open." He later wrote, "I don't think Dean is a bad person, he just needs counseling."

The following morning, Rayner and Mellberg returned to the first sergeant's office. Mellberg admitted that Rayner had been telling the truth and agreed to be more discreet. After the meeting, Rayner told the chief about Mellberg's threats and his desire to kill his former high school classmates.

Chief Hutchinson brought Mellberg to the office of the maintenance squadron commander, Maj Stephen Dawson. As the chief briefed the commander, Mellberg waited outside the door. A passerby stepped into the office and reported that Mellberg was in the hall shaking profusely.

Major Dawson brought Mellberg into his office. He later wrote, "Mellberg was acting extremely abnormal. He was using the word *sir* every fourth or fifth word and had difficulty completing sentences and conveying his thoughts." Dawson had Mellberg wait in another office while he called the base psychologist, Capt Alan London, who agreed to see Mellberg the following day. Dawson said, "I called Mellberg back into my office to inform him that I was sending him over for an evaluation. Mellberg's reaction to the news really surprised me. He was very apprehensive about going to mental health and thought that his going over there was going to end his enlistment in the military." Mellberg recorded the exchange in his journal:

June 2—Hearing my request at that point I spoke to him that I didn't wish to be in anyway have this being done. I was evaluated before and they came back with negative statement of how I was stressed and wasn't fit.

Immediately after learning of Mellberg's threat to harm his roommate, Chief Hutchinson arranged for Rayner to move to a different dorm room. Rayner was moving out when Mellberg returned to the dorm room. Rayner shook Mellberg's hand and told him he was sorry things didn't work out between them. He told Mellberg he should stop by his new room and talk sometime. Mellberg didn't respond.

Fairchild Mental Health

The Medical Group sat just outside of Fairchild's west perimeter fence on land leased to the base from Spokane County. The main hospital, hospital annex, and dental clinic sat on a ten-acre square between two Air Force housing areas.

The main hospital was a multi-wing three-story building that took up the southern three quarters of the grounds. It was surrounded by manicured lawns, hedges, and evergreen trees. The single-story dental clinic was wedged in the northwest corner, and the three-story hospital annex sat in the opposite corner.

The annex was a long, narrow building built in 1958 as a dormitory for medical personnel but had since been converted to office space for doctors and administrators. The first floor of the annex was occupied by flight medicine and the mental health center. Flight surgeons are specially trained doctors who exclusively treat flight crewmembers and their families. The mental health center was staffed by the base psychiatrist and psychologist and a team of social workers and mental health technicians.

Having the Medical Group located off base meant hospital personnel and patrons didn't have to pass through entry screening at the base gate. But what they gained in convenience they lost in their sense of security.

On Friday, 3 June 1993, Chief Hutchinson drove Airman Mellberg out the Offutt gate, down Graham Road to the hospital annex, where he was seen by Capt Alan London, chief of psychological services.

Dr. London had been born at Fairchild's hospital thirty-nine years earlier, the firstborn of a young Air Force family. By the time his dad retired from his career of data processing, Alan had become the mentor, coach and confidant to three sisters and a brother. The Londons settled in Montana and, after graduating from Bozeman High School, Alan joined the Navy. In 1985, after twelve years as an enlisted man, he returned to the Northwest to pursue a degree in psychology, telling his siblings he wanted to work in "a helping profession." In 1991 he received his PhD from Washington State University. He joined the Air Force as a captain and interned at Wilford

Hall Medical Center at Lackland AFB before coming to Fairchild. He was every bit a military man. His shoes were always shined and his uniform always pressed. He was equally devoted to his wife Kathy, whom he met during his internship at Wilford Hall. Kathy London now worked as a maternity nurse in Fairchild's hospital across the parking lot.

Dr. London had a PhD in clinical psychology but had not yet completed the one year of supervised practice in Washington to meet the state licensing requirement. He worked under Dr. Brigham, the base psychiatrist, but also ran his cases through his clinical supervisor, Dr. James Mitchell, the staff psychologist at Fairchild's Survival School. Dr. London evaluated Mellberg over a period of three days and found him to be anxious, guarded, and evasive.

Mellberg was inexplicably incensed by Dr. London's line of questioning. He later wrote in his journal:

> Jun 3—I though that after my roommate had left all that I was only going to be evaluated on the accusations of a sexual nature or stress nature, but from the first few questions I became very suspicious. I was asked if I like to kill things or if I would go to my high school and kill people.

Dr. London arranged for Mellberg to take the Revised Wechsler Adult Intelligence Scale test and the Minnesota Multiphasic Personality Inventory (MMPI), a psychological test consisting of 567 true or false questions. Mellberg took an inordinate amount of time to complete the tests, despite having a normal IQ, and had to return the following Monday to finish them.

On 14 June 1993, Dr. London prepared a memorandum to Major Dawson saying that Mellberg "was evaluated at your request due to his demonstrating aggressive and destructive attitudes toward himself and others. … He adamantly denies any expression of any destructive thoughts or conflicts with his peers, but when pressed will admit to a minimal amount of the behaviors which brought him to the attention of his commander and this clinic." Dr. London listed his diagnoses of Mellberg as "generalized anxiety disorder" with "strong obsessive-compulsive features." In the memo, Dr. London noted:

> Mellberg, both upon initial presentation and later during psychometric testing, demonstrated a significant level of

anxiety. He appeared tense and addressed both officer and enlisted personnel as *sir* innumerable times, and was even observed saluting officers who passed by on the opposite side of the street when he was taking breaks from his testing. Further, he took well over twelve hours to complete a test battery that typically takes about three hours to complete, and the data provided from that testing proved to be invalid, primarily because of his efforts to skew testing in a favorable direction ... At the present time there is evidence of a definite mental health abnormality and/or personal history of mental disease.

Dr. London's memo to Dawson went on to say that Mellberg had been previously evaluated during basic military training, where he had been strongly recommended for an administrative separation. The memo continued:

The issues and behaviors that created problems for him then have not subsided, and are likely to continue to create friction between him and the military environment. This individual is clearly unsuited to further military service due to the behavior he has demonstrated, which is compatible with the diagnosis given above. Prompt administrative separation from the US Air Force is strongly recommended. While not currently suicidal or out of touch with reality there is a potential that he could rapidly decompensate under the stresses of facing an administrative separation. While hospitalization is not warranted at this time, I recommend that he be monitored closely until a decision has been made and that decision has been fully implemented.
Alan W. London, Capt. USAF, BSC
Chief, Psychology Services

Dr. London could only recommend Mellberg be separated from the military. The final determination fell to his commander, Major Dawson. Dawson would later say he believed Dr. London "was probably giving an accurate recommendation from his perspective." However, he said, "I was leery about pursuing a discharge because Mellberg had only been assigned to us for a couple of weeks and the Air Force just spent thousands of dollars training Mellberg for the last nine months while he was going through technical school … I wanted to wait a little while to see how he was performing in his duties. I also wanted to get more information on Mellberg to try to help him adjust to the military and better understand his background."

Dawson telephoned Lois Mellberg, whom he described as "extremely helpful," to see if she had any information that might help her son adjust to the military. According to Dawson, Lois talked at length about her son, revealing that he had difficulty making friends and had been made fun of by other kids while in school. Lois told Dawson that Dean was not unlike his father at that age, who had come into his own after she married him.

After speaking with Lois, Dawson felt that "with a little help from Mellberg's co-workers, we could help him adjust." He informed Mellberg that although he had been recommended for discharge, he had decided to retain him and make an effort to integrate him into the unit's social structure. Mellberg interpreted the situation differently, writing in his journal:

> Called back into the commanders office about eval to just be told that my parents had made a call and finally he heard what my roommate did, he didn't hear this from the acting first sergeant to which didn't care about all that. His last words were that they would be watching me from now on.

Mellberg was a frequent customer of the base barbershop. His regular barber couldn't recall ever having a conversation with Mellberg that made sense. "You would ask Dean a question, and instead of answering … he'd have a conversation of his own going. So, you'd try to join in on his." The barber recalled a day when Mellberg came into the shop and was visibly upset. He asked him, "What's wrong?"

Mellberg replied, "Roommates are fucked. They don't know who they are messing with. They're always messing with me. They can't do this to me." The barber said Mellberg acted like "a little kid who felt picked on. He seemed to have a lot of self-pity."

Mellberg had avoided discharge and received no disciplinary action other than a memo warning him not to have any contact with his former roommate. As far as his commander was concerned, the incident was in the past. But Mellberg obsessed over the derogatory information in his mental health record and worried it would ruin his career. Not long after his mental health evaluation, a co-worker drove Mellberg to an appointment at the dental clinic. When the airman arrived to pick him back up, Mellberg walked out of the main hospital, holding his medical records. The airman asked Mellberg why he had his records and said Mellberg told him he wanted to review them. He said Mellberg told him that "if there was something in them that he didn't like, a friend at tech school had told him that he could lose it out of his records." The airman told Mellberg to return the records to the hospital and reported the incident to Sergeant Wilson, who put a Memo for Record in Mellberg's personnel file.

After his roommate's complaint led to his mental health referral, Mellberg's co-workers noticed his mental health and work performance began a steady decline.

Sergeant Wilson recalled, "Maybe a month after his assignment to Fairchild, Dean missed his first appointment. The very next week he missed another. He also failed to turn in his first volume of his CDCs [Career Development Course—a mandatory correspondence course of continued learning]. ... I gave Airman Mellberg a formal written Letter of Counseling. During his counseling session ... I noticed his face turn bright red and his lip quivering. I thought he was going to cry. I took Airman Mellberg to a private room. ... I told him it was his responsibility as a member of the USAF to meet all obligations, such as appointments and CDCs. I also informed him that he wasn't being punished and that letters of counseling are only used to document trends, whether good or bad."

Sergeant Wilson told Mellberg to take whatever measures were necessary to ensure he didn't miss future appointments and suggested he purchase a watch with an alarm or an alarm clock. Before he left the room, Wilson told Mellberg to add any comments he wanted included in the letter and sign it. An hour and a half later Wilson saw Mellberg was still sitting in the room staring at the letter and had to order him to sign it. Later, one of Mellberg's co-workers saw he was still visibly upset and told him, "Cheer up, tomorrow might be a better day."

Mellberg replied, "There might not be a tomorrow."

Sergeant Wilson closely monitored Mellberg, and his concern for him steadily increased. He remembers watching from across the lab as Mellberg electrocuted himself by applying a high voltage to a meter and placing his hand across the positive and negative terminals. Wilson said he came to his aid and, "after seeing he was all right, I instructed him to take a break and re-lax. After his break, I noticed that he seemed almost furious. He told me he was upset because I wouldn't let him stay and work." On another occasion, as Mellberg was leaving for his lunch break, he stopped at a soldering station and held the hot iron in front of his face, staring at it intently. Wilson said, "I often wondered, and even posed the question to my branch chief and supervisor, how someone like Mellberg could make it through tech school and even basic training." Wilson was concerned about Mellberg's well-being. "I felt he might be suicidal, so I always kept a close eye on his actions."

Others feared Mellberg might be homicidal. On 6 May 1993, in two separate incidents, postal workers in Dana Point, California and Dearborn, Michigan used firearms to kill and wound their co-workers at US Postal facilities. There had been several other incidents of workplace violence committed by postal employees in the 1980s and 1990s. One occurred in Royal Oak, Michigan, ninety miles from Mellberg's home, while he was still in high school. The apparent trend of postal worker violence received wide media attention, prompting a discussion in the lab about who among them would most likely go on a shooting spree. Mellberg laughed when everyone agreed it would be him. He also laughed when he saw what someone in the lab had drawn on a dry erase board—a caricature of Mellberg holding a machine gun.

Most airmen are required to qualify annually with the M16 rifle. When Mellberg and a few of his co-workers went to the base firing range, he did better than qualify; he shot well enough to earn expert status. Upon seeing his skill with a rifle, one of Mellberg's co-workers no longer saw him as "quiet and meek." He said, "I had no reason to suspect anything different until he qualified expert on the M16. This suggested to me that there was more to him." Other lab personnel voiced a similar intuition. "After we found that out, there were jokes and comments about 'of all the people who could shoot expert it had to be Dean.'" They were concerned enough to ask Mellberg if he owned any firearms and were relieved when he said that he didn't. Their concern intensified during a break time discussion in the lab. "One time the guys were talking about guns, and Dean piped up and asked where one would go to buy a gun. Everyone cringed when an airman told him Sportsman's Surplus had good prices. The airman said he really regretted saying it as soon as it left his lips."

PMEL leadership employed a variety of training techniques and assigned Mellberg to several different trainers in an effort to improve his work performance. There was a glimmer of hope when Mellberg scored ninety-five percent on a closed-book volume review exercise. When Wilson commended him for the achievement, Mellberg revealed that he had memorized the answers but hadn't really learned anything.

Wilson thought sleep deprivation might have contributed to Mellberg's problems. "During many training sessions with Airman Mellberg, I noticed he had problems holding his eyes open, even at attention." He also fell asleep during his break time.

Wilson said, "after a substantial amount of time," he "determined that Airman Mellberg was practically untrainable." Wilson and his supervisor notified their leadership. "It was our considered opinion that Airman Mellberg needed professional help to improve his almost nonexistent social skills."

Mellberg obsessed over his roommate's accusation becoming a part of his mental health records and appeared to resent Dr. London and his probing questions. He received multiple reassurances that the complaint was not a threat to his military career, but he fixated on seeking justice. He wrote in his journal:

> Aug 3—I want to see if there was any action that I could take against Captain London from the legal office, and they referred me to the patient advocate office. From there I was filing out critics about the treatment to which I received.

Mellberg made an appointment with Dr. London's boss, thirty-one-year-old psychiatrist, Maj Thomas Brigham. Tom Brigham was a brilliant and disciplined man who had completed his schooling and residency at the age of twenty-nine before joining the Air Force with the rank of major. He was tall and athletic, with the southern drawl and calm demeanor acquired from growing up in Mobile, Alabama. At times, his dark blond hair was disheveled and his uniform in need of ironing, but as social worker Krista Pierson put it, "He didn't really care so much for the particulars of the military. He was there to be an outstanding psychiatrist, and that he was."

In a series of memos, Dr. Brigham documented the 12 August 1993 meeting with Mellberg:

> Mellberg stated that he did not feel he had received appropriate treatment thus far. My impression at that time was that he might have generalized anxiety disorder, as had been diagnosed in basic training. I also noted obsessive-compulsive

and passive-aggressive traits during the interview. … He denied any of the specific symptoms of generalized anxiety that were enumerated for him, although he appeared to demonstrate some of them during the interview. Instead of answering many of the questions appropriately, he frequently answered them with questions to the interviewer. He uttered many platitudes such as "There are no problems, just challenges." He adamantly denied any intention of harming either himself or other persons, even when careful probing was performed. He also denied any psychotic symptoms such as hallucinations or delusions. Airman Mellberg declined follow-up treatment at that time.

Mellberg journaled his version of the meeting with the psychiatrist:

Aug 4—Made another appointment with the physic to see if this person would do anything as far as coming up with something to. From that meeting I found him very uncaring as well and he even commented that sometimes they work for two masters, one being the patient, one being the commander.

Mellberg was undeterred in his pursuit of justice. In late August of 1993, First Sergeant Jones had returned from his temporary duty assignment. Mellberg went to the first sergeant and demanded to know what was being done about Erik Rayner's threat to break his alarm clock. The first sergeant told him nothing could be done since Rayner hadn't broken the clock and suggested Mellberg pursue further counseling sessions at mental health.

Mellberg met with Major Dawson and lobbied for the punishment of his former roommate. Dawson was perplexed and asked Mellberg what punishment he thought would be appropriate.

"Should I give him an Article 15?"

"No."

"Should I give him a Letter of Reprimand?"

"No. I would like to see him talk to someone in mental health just like me."

Mellberg's frustration and persistence are reflected in his journal entry:

Aug 30—I went to the office of the first sergeant. This time it was Senior Master Sergeant Jones. I spoke with him about the treatment to which I received the beginning of Jun. I had also some concern over the training record and how I was being affected. I also wanted to see social actions and if through the military I could find legal action. All he could come up with is to just for me to see Major Brigham. Then later that day I spoke with the commander over the lack of attention I received from the sergeant earlier that day. The commander even asked me if I wanted out. I told him a strait no and that for him to ask is not your in his position to even ask that question of me. To the end of that he told me that he spared me my life, but I added no action was taken for Erik.

When Dawson refused to punish his former roommate, Mellberg elevated his complaint to Fairchild's inspector general's office as well as the wing commander.

*　*　*

Erik Rayner and his fiancée got married and moved into an off-base apartment. Rayner hadn't seen Mellberg for months, although Stacy was sure she had spotted him riding his bicycle outside their apartment.

*　*　*

On 31 August 1993, Mellberg walked to the maintenance squadron and hid in the parking lot waiting for Rayner to get off work. When he saw Rayner walking toward his vehicle, Mellberg emerged and began yelling as he walked toward him. He held his briefcase to his chest and reached inside as he demanded to know if Rayner intended to break his clock. Mellberg continued ranting and blocked Rayner's path, all the while keeping his hand inside his partially closed briefcase. Rayner's co-workers and supervisor came to his aid. His supervisor said, "I was sure a gun was in his hand and positioned myself to put Dean at a disadvantage if it was true." The supervisor sent everyone away except Mellberg and asked him what was going on. "Dean was very rigid in body and facial movements. … He stayed at attention during the whole conversation and consistently started and ended each sentence with *sir* even after I told him I was not an officer." Mellberg produced his alarm clock from his briefcase and repeatedly claimed that Rayner had threatened to break it. The supervisor tried to reason with Mellberg to no avail. He said, "When I knew I couldn't change the course of the conversation, I advised Dean to not confront Erik again and to forget the incident with the clock."

Immediately after the parking lot incident, Mellberg was called before his commander and first sergeant, where he insisted Rayner had violated the Uniform Code of Military Justice (UCMJ). He told Major Dawson that Rayner had communicated a threat and needed to be punished. When he was told that threatening to break a clock is not a violation of the UCMJ, Mellberg pursued a different angle. Since Rayner said he was going to break the clock but didn't, he should be punished for lying.

Dawson was concerned for Rayner's safety and directed Mellberg to undergo another mental health evaluation. After conferring with Mellberg's supervisors in the PMEL, the major wrote in a statement, "He was also making several mistakes in the shop. Mistakes that most people learn after their first few weeks in the shop. It was then clear to me that Mellberg was unsalvageable and I was either going to pursue discharge through mental health or through failure to progress."

By now, all of the mental health center personnel were leery of Dean Mellberg, as he had been prone to "dramatic emotions" and "fits of anger" in previous sessions. SSgt Gary Johnson, a mental health tech, wrote in a statement, "The more times he came in, the more guarded we got about him. We even asked our civilian [receptionist] who was pregnant, to not be in the office when he had a visit scheduled."

Mellberg routinely carried a briefcase to his appointments, and when he opened it, he was careful not to let anyone see inside. As a precaution, the staff began taking custody of the briefcase when he arrived for an appointment. Staff Sergeant Johnson wrote, "We did search it once and found that it was almost empty, only a couple pens and pencils." The empty briefcase didn't help alleviate their fears. "We were all frightened of him. We even said, 'Watch out for him—he will meet you in the parking lot someday!' The comment seemed innocent at the time—stress relieving."

Dr. Brigham reevaluated Mellberg on 1 September 93, and prepared a memorandum for Major Dawson:

Airman Mellberg was evaluated at your request today in response to his somewhat frantic efforts to file a legal charge
against his former roommate. ... During this interview he
was slightly less guarded and more open, his affect was less
intense. He acted surprised to hear that his former roommate had accused him of implying threats to harm him.
This was the only subject that caused Airman Mellberg to
raise his voice. Careful probing was again performed to
elicit a possibility of suicidal or homicidal thoughts, but
Airman Mellberg refused to endorse such ideas.

Dr. Brigham arrived at a new diagnosis of "rule out brief reactive
psychosis, history of generalized anxiety disorder, and probable paranoid personality disorder in addition to his history of generalized anxiety
disorder."

Dr. London conferred with Dr. James Mitchell, staff psychologist at
Fairchild's Survival School, regarding Mellberg's case. Months later in a
written statement, Dr. Mitchell said he remembered the case because it
was the only one he and Dr. London discussed, "involving such strong
concerns for homicidal acting out."

Dr. Mitchell said, "Mellberg's thought content was marked by persecutory beliefs involving Airman Rayner. He characterized Rayner's complaint
as a horrible injustice. I recall Dr. London saying Airman Mellberg compared his treatment to the Holocaust. These beliefs had a delusional quality,
but my recollection is that Dr. London did not see them as frankly psychotic. When challenged, Airman Mellberg would refer to these comments
as figures of speech. Dr. London and Dr. Brigham suspected the possibility
of psychosis, but the diagnostic picture, though emerging, was not clear.
My impression was that by September they were struggling with whether
Airman Mellberg had a generalized anxiety disorder superimposed over
paranoid personality features or whether he was in the early stages of a
psychotic disorder with paranoid features."

On Friday, 3 September 1993, Dr. Brigham arranged for Mellberg
and Rayner to attend a conflict resolution meeting at the mental health
center. Thirty minutes before the meeting took place, Dr. London called
Dr. Mitchell, who later wrote, "Dr. London expressed concerns about the
potential danger to Airman Rayner and stated that he hoped the session

would clarify the potential risks." Dr. Mitchell said the meeting had two objectives: one was to defuse Mellberg's anger toward his roommate, and the second was to assess Mellberg's mental status in order to reach a clearer diagnosis. Dr. Mitchell was not comfortable with the idea of a conflict resolution meeting, saying, "While it is not unusual for clinicians to bring conflicting parties together for the purpose of conflict resolution, it is, in my opinion, risky to bring together someone who has homicidal ideation with the person on which that ideation is focused—particularly if psychosis is suspected." Dr. Mitchell expressed his concern to Dr. London and suggested canceling the meeting. Dr. London told him he had already approached Dr. Brigham with his concerns but was told the meeting would take place as scheduled.

Dr. Brigham had hoped the meeting would last thirty minutes, but Mellberg spoke at length and in excruciating detail about his roommate's attempts to ruin his career.

Mental health technician SrA Jeff Cook was asked to sit in on the meeting in case Mellberg became violent. Mellberg was unreasonable, argumentative, and hostile. Senior Airman Cook said, "I remember that he would always sit straight up, with his palms facing downward, in the position of attention. Whenever someone would ask him to relax, he would get angry and tell us he was relaxed and that people needed to stop telling him to relax."

Mellberg told his side of the story without incident. When it was Rayner's time to speak, Mellberg fidgeted and constantly readjusted his position. At one point, Mellberg yelled, "Don't you think I'm right to complain?" and lunged out of his chair toward Rayner. He stopped short when Dr. Brigham raised his voice, asking, "Think you're in control of yourself?" Mellberg whispered, "Yes, sir," and returned to his seat. Dr. Brigham described the meeting in a memo to Mellberg's commander:

> Airman Mellberg was called to the mental health clinic on 3 September 1993 to participate in a conflict resolution session with A1C Rayner, First Sergeant Jones, Dr. London and myself. Despite A1C Rayner's apparent true expression of regret for the discomfort he had caused Airman Mellberg with his allegation, Airman Mellberg was unfazed. He called the allegation against him a "crime against humanity." He felt just compensation for it would be 1

million dollars, because he believed his life was ruined as a result of it. At one point in the interview he appeared as if he would attack A1C Rayner as he rose out of his chair yelling loudly and moving toward A1C Rayner. Several times in the interview Airman Mellberg's thought processing was noted to be rather loose. Many times he assumed the affect and speech of an Elizabethan pastor pronouncing statements from the King James Bible in a rather inappropriate context.

Dr. Mitchell clarified his concerns about the meeting in his written statement. "If Dr. Brigham did in fact allow the patient to demonstrate what he suspected to be more severe pathology, it was most likely done as part of a multifaceted approach to differential diagnosis and treatment, a byproduct of his appropriate treatment plan rather than a contrived attempt to increase his patient's discomfort. He was not a devious or unethical physician."

After Mellberg left the hospital, he went to the base barbershop where he was greeted by his regular barber.

"Hey kid … Bad day?"

Mellberg replied, "No shit. … That fucking London."

"What's the matter?"

"They can't do this to me, they are messing with my future. They don't know who they are messing with."

"Who are you talking about?"

"The hospital, this place is fucked."

During the haircut, the barber said, Mellberg muttered repeatedly, "My mom knows what they are doing to me. I told her. She knows. They can't do this to me."

That evening, Dr. Brigham went home to spend the three-day Labor Day weekend with his wife and two young children. He dug out his heirloom Winchester rifle and a shotgun and, against her protests, showed his wife how to load the firearms. Then he stashed the shotgun in the closet and the Winchester under the bed. Susan Brigham wasn't comfortable having guns in the home, but her husband insisted. He sat down with her and without mentioning his name, he warned her about Mellberg, "This is the type of patient that could come back and kill us, two weeks, two years, or twenty years from now."

Susan was alarmed. She had never seen her husband react like this. She asked, "What does he look like?"

Her husband replied, "He looks like a short, fat, red-headed Hitler. … If anybody comes to the house who looks like that, just get the gun."

On Tuesday, 7 September 1993, Dr. Brigham met again with Mellberg to determine if the conflict resolution meeting had any effect on his obsession for justice. It had not. According to a statement written by mental health technician, SSgt Karl Anderson, "Dr. Brigham had come to the determination that Dean Mellberg had to be hospitalized." Staff Sergeant Anderson saw Dr. Brigham talking with Mellberg in the hall. He approached them and stood behind Mellberg in case there was any trouble. Anderson said, "Dr. Brigham was explaining to Dean that if the sheriff had to take him to the hospital, that procedures required he be handcuffed. Dean's demeanor changed suddenly from passive to one that had all the indications that he was about to attack Dr. Brigham. He stepped up to Dr. Brigham, almost nose to nose. … He fixed Dr. Brigham with a direct stare. He told him, 'Well Dr. Brigham, why don't you just gag me while you're at it?'"

Anderson prepared to physically subdue Mellberg but Dr. Brigham intervened. "Dean, this is just the type of behavior that brought you to the clinic."

Anderson said, "Dean took a full step backward and acknowledged the truth of the statement. Dean conceded to going to an inpatient facility." There was no psychiatric inpatient facility on the base, so Dr. Brigham arranged for Mellberg to be admitted to Sacred Heart Hospital in Spokane, while he worked to convince Wilford Hall Medical Center, a military hospital at Lackland Air Force Base, to accept him.

Dr. Brigham contacted the chief of inpatient psychiatry at Wilford Hall, and described Mellberg's symptoms and behavior, hoping to get him into their inpatient ward, one of only two in the Air Force. Initially, the inpatient chief didn't think Mellberg sounded any worse than a number of others with his psychological profile and refused to accept him. Dr. Brigham enlisted the help of Maj Gen Edgar "Andy" Anderson Jr., the commander of Wilford Hall. Major General Anderson contacted the inpatient chief and convinced him to accept Mellberg.

Dr. London also made a call to Wilford Hall. He contacted a colleague and asked her to do everything she could to make sure Mellberg received a medical discharge and a transfer to a civilian or VA inpatient psychiatric hospital.

In downtown Spokane, Mellberg told the staff at the Sacred Heart psychiatric unit that the only reason he was there was because he was complying with the orders from the doctors at Fairchild. He denied any history of psychiatric problems.

The Sacred Heart staff acknowledged in Mellberg's chart that he could not be forced to stay against his will, but they worked to convince him to stay overnight until Fairchild personnel could pick him up in the morning. Mellberg used the hospital telephone to make several calls for help. He reached out to the PMEL, where a supervisor told him he should cooperate with the doctors at Wilford Hall and they would be able to help him. Mellberg attempted to contact Fairchild's base commander, chaplains, military attorneys, and his congressman. He telephoned his mother, who contacted a Spokane law firm. In a teleconference with Lois and her son, an attorney advised Mellberg to claim Article 31. In essence he told him to remain silent during his psychiatric commitment. Air Force Chaplain David Knight said he spoke at length with Mellberg and was under the impression that his involvement with mental health stemmed from his roommate complaining about a single incident of masturbation. Chaplain Knight said he called Dr. Brigham and tried to convince him to allow Mellberg to stay at Fairchild and continue out-patient counseling. According to Knight, Dr. Brigham responded, "Chaplain, by coming to you he is grasping at straws. He is going to Wilford Hall and that's final."

When the PMEL personnel learned that Mellberg was going to be committed to a psychiatric ward, one of them admitted, "Most of the personnel in PMEL were scared of him because of his size and mental attitude. … Everyone here was relieved when he was transferred to Wilford Hall for evaluation."

The next morning, SrA Jeff Cook arrived at Sacred Heart in an ambulance. He would escort Mellberg to a medevac aircraft at Fairchild that would take them to Wilford Hall. The previous evening, Dr. Brigham had warned Cook to be careful, telling him, "This is the kind of patient who thinks you're his friend, but then one day he's going to decide that everything is your fault, and then he's going to come back and kill you." When Cook arrived, Mellberg was on the phone with his mother. Cook said, "She insisted on talking to me, and her question wasn't about what was wrong with her son, but rather that he didn't have a mouthpiece. Her son is about to be flown to Texas for a mental health issue and she wants to know where his lawyer is." Cook finally convinced Mellberg to end the phone call, and they raced to Fairchild to catch their flight. When it came time to board the aircraft, Mellberg became uncooperative. Cook took comfort in knowing he had a set of leather restraints and 300 mg of intramuscular Thorazine. He wrote, "I was scared and very nervous about what Airman Mellberg might attempt to do during his transportation to WHMC. I then made a deal with Airman Mellberg that as long as he was cooperative with me during his transport to WHMC and did not try to escape, I would make sure he had the telephone numbers to the Area Defense Counsel office at Lackland AFB before I left him on the unit at WHMC." Mellberg agreed, and according to Cook, the only thing unusual about the flight was the reactions of the crew as they learned they were transporting a dangerous mental health patient.

The aeromedical flight made an overnight stop at Travis AFB, California, where Cook and Mellberg stayed the night at David Grant Medical Center. Cook said that during a tour of the Medical Center, Mellberg ran ahead of the group, smiling and smirking like a mischievous child, apparently delighted that Cook had to chase after him.

On 9 September 1993, Cook and Mellberg arrived at Wilford Hall Medical Center and rode an elevator to the fourth floor of the nine-story, one million-square-foot facility known affectionately as Big Willy. They walked to the end of a white-tiled hallway through two large, solid wood doors to Psychiatric Ward 4D.

Cook turned Mellberg over to the staff and handed off Mellberg's records, including a transcript of the conflict resolution meeting and a three-page narrative written by Dr. Brigham which read in part, "We are referring Airman Mellberg for an extensive psychiatric evaluation to rule out reactive psychosis or treat it as well as possible if it does exist. We consider this patient dangerous ... he is totally involuntary—he has no insight into his problem."

1993 Air Show

In May 1993, Colonel Capotosti, the man who forbade Lieutenant Colonel Holland from flying another air show, was reassigned to another base. Fairchild's new operations group commander, Col William Pellerin, arrived a month later. Capotosti didn't have an opportunity to brief his replacement. He gave his folder containing flight regulations to his deputy operations group commander, Lt Col Stephen Harper, telling him, "Stephen, this is your bible; this will keep Bill's butt out of trouble."

92nd Logistics Group Deputy Commander, Lt Col Richard Day, described Pellerin as a very sharp man who exuded professionalism, but was sometimes overbearing in his opinion. The atmosphere promoted by Holland's bosses initially dissuaded several officers from complaining about his unsafe flying. Aircraft Commander Capt Shawn Fleming said of the operations group commanders, "Colonel Capotosti was known to be very, 'You don't go against the wishes of the colonels'. And, I know that Colonel Pellerin sometimes was that way" too. Holland seemed untouchable. Fleming said, "He was a good ol' boy, a member of the colonels' club." Speaking out against him could be career suicide.

Not long after Pellerin took command of the ops group, Bud Holland was selected to pilot the B-52 in the 1993 air show. Pellerin said of the decision, "It was kind of an accepted fact that Bud was Mr. Air Show."

By 1992, the Cold War had ended, SAC was retired, and Fairchild now fell under Air Combat Command (ACC). The bombers and tankers were no longer on alert, and the nuclear weapons had been returned to the weapons storage area (WSA) on the south side of Fairchild's flight line. Along with Fairchild's reorganization, Lieutenant Colonel Bullock, the commander of the bomb squadron, proposed some changes to the standards and evaluation program. Bullock said, "I wanted the Stan/Eval crews to move down to my area. … I felt that there was too much aloofness. … They weren't a part of the squadron itself, the organization." Bullock said Holland resisted the move. "We had some disagreements on several occasions, very verbal, about this. I had ended up alienating myself from

Colonel Holland at that point … and we had not really been very friendly with each other ever since then." Bullock intended to fly the air show with Holland, perhaps believing he could curtail Holland's aggressive flying if he was on the plane. He flew as the copilot on one of Holland's air show practice flights. "Bud and I had not gotten along … we did not speak very much at all … other than to read the checklist. He objected to my presence on the airplane that day."

During the flight, Bullock noted that Holland had a tendency to over-roll the airplane. Bullock said Holland, "made a couple of figure eight patterns around the field, simply flying down the runway at, oh about a hundred feet on a low approach type of a thing. … At one point he made a left going south. … When he did that, he pulled the nose up into a close left turn. … He over-rolled it to almost ninety degrees. … At that point, the only time that I touched the controls, and concurrently with him, rolled the airplane back, almost at level flight. And then he re-rolled it back into about sixty degrees."

Bullock attempted to address the safety issue with Holland. "I told him to be careful with the bank because of his speed. … He didn't have the speed to be rolling that airplane beyond, you know, the standard thirty degrees." Holland didn't acknowledge him, but Bullock knew he was aware of the restriction. Bullock said, "You are talking about a guy that had six thousand hours, I think, in the airplane, not somebody you could talk to."

When Bullock was unable to fly in the air show, the operations office started making a list of people who were willing to fly with Holland. One of the pilots they asked was Aircraft Commander, Capt Clem Countess. Countess said, "I didn't really feel comfortable with going on the flight, but I told them that I would. I also informed them that if he put that plane in a position that I did not like, that I would be using my seat to leave it. Amazingly enough, my name did not come up on the schedule to go fly the air show with him."

They eventually found a crew, and on 8 August 1993, Holland flew the B-52 in Fairchild's air show. According to one crewmember, he flew the maneuvers with extreme aggressiveness. The navigator on the flight said that during the pitch-up maneuver, Holland pulled about three and a half g, with the nose eighty degrees high, almost vertical.

Countess took his family to the 1993 air show. He said Holland made what looked like "an eighty-five-degree bank turn, flaps down, right over the top of the crowd." When the B-52's nose started to slice down through the horizon, Countess thought, "Oh great. I got out of the airplane so I wouldn't die, and now he is going to kill me and my whole family on the ground."

Capt Stephen Coppi, a B-52 navigator, also saw Holland's tight banked turn over the crowd. Coppi said, "I remember distinctly looking up and seeing a B-52 standing on its wing over my head."

Lt Col Stephen Harper, deputy operations group commander, had flying experience. He was appalled at Holland's maneuvers, calling them "far too aggressive." He saw the "max performance banks past the crowd-line" and explained how dangerous they were. "The airplane aerodynamically is going to slice in that maneuver. There are only two ways to avoid it. You either over-g the airplane or you roll out of the maneuver in the slice and accept the fact that you are going to lose some altitude." He said that type of flying was a last-ditch maneuver you might see in combat, "at high speed and relatively higher altitude, but not something you would do for an air show. … I remember being very upset about that, and as I remember, I said so to Colonel Pellerin at the time."

Regarding the plane's maneuvers, Pellerin said, "It was part and parcel of the mindset—it had been done before, however right or wrong it was."

The wing commander at the time, and Pellerin's boss, Brigadier General James Richards, was an experienced B-52 pilot. Harper explained Pellerin's mindset, saying Richards had "much more B-52 time, of course, than Pellerin had himself, and I think he was basically deferring to Richards."

Before the 1993 air show, Harper didn't consider Bud Holland's flying to be dangerous. "He was more aggressive than the average flier. But I never considered him to be unsafe in the type of procedures that he used." But Harper apparently reprimanded a junior pilot for emulating Holland's maneuvers. B-52 Instructor Pilot Alexander Brown said Harper was the site commander on a deployment to New Mexico. When a pilot performed a low-level, flaps-down turning maneuver with sixty degrees of bank, Harper grounded him. When asked why he grounded the pilot, according to Brown, Harper responded, "If someone wanted to kill himself, that was his own business, but if he wanted to perform maneuvers that were going to kill *his* crewmembers and destroy *his* airplanes, that was something else entirely." When Brown asked Lieutenant Colonel Harper why he thought the pilot performed the maneuver, Brown said Harper responded, "I think he's been watching too much of Bud Holland."

Not long after the 1993 air show, Harper left Fairchild for another assignment. Harper said, "When I left, I believed in my own mind … that Colonel Pellerin and I had discussed the fact that under no circumstances would Bud fly [another] air show." But Fairchild's senior leadership made no overt attempts to curtail Holland, and his aggressive flying continued. Captain Countess said, "After the 1993 air show, it seemed like more instances of his continued lack of concern for anybody that flew with him continued to pop up. … It would seem like once a month you would hear a Colonel Holland incident."

After the 1993 air show, Brigadier General Richards left for a new assignment and was replaced by Col William Brooks. It wasn't long before another "Colonel Holland incident" arose that both Brooks and Pellerin were reportedly aware of. When Holland flew over the small town outside the base, a civilian complained. Captain Fleming recalled, "I was flying with Colonel Brooks, and we landed and basically got a call from Colonel Pellerin. … Someone had complained to the TV news that someone was banking sixty, seventy degrees bank over the Super Buy grocery store in Airway Heights. … they had a PR nightmare."

Stateside

And he that hath no sword, let him sell his garment, and buy one.
—Luke 22:36

In May of 1993, I drove down a stretch of Highway 2 through the small town of Airway Heights on my way to Fairchild. Trailer parks, bars, and restaurants clung to the two-lane highway like thorns on a long-stemmed rose. I showed my ID at the gate and entered Fairchild Air Force Base, where I reported for duty at the 92nd Security Police Squadron. I was assigned a room in the cop dorm and processed into the base. I met my new flight, spent a few days in training, and began working patrol.

Not long after arriving, I went to a Spokane gun shop and looked through their display cases. As an E-4, my basic pay was $1,213 a month. After taxes and living expenses, I couldn't afford the civilian version of the Beretta M9, but I wanted to ensure my off-duty practice would enhance my on-duty performance.

The best gun I could afford that met that need was a used Taurus PT92, a clone of the M9. Taurus handguns were made in Brazil. They didn't share the same reputation for quality as the Italian Berettas, but the PT92 was otherwise identical. Mine was a stainless steel model with a set of Hogue black rubber grips.

We were not authorized to keep firearms in our dorm rooms, and if anyone asked I told them I stored mine at a friend's house. I obtained a Washington concealed pistol permit, kept the Taurus PT92 loaded with hollow-points, and carried it whenever I left the base.

I liked the double action/single action of the Beretta design. The long, deliberate first pull of the trigger made them inherently safe to carry; and the relatively light pull of their single-action trigger made them capable of precise shooting.

A few of my co-workers and I would go target shooting in the woods near the base. Most of the time, we challenged each other to hit cans and pinecones at a distance. But when we could afford it, we shot paper targets.

On one excursion I boasted that I could shoot the head of a silhouette target and make a smiley face with the bullet holes. From several paces away, I fired a series of shots into the head of the target. It was a nice grouping of hits, but looked nothing like a smiley face. I joked that I was a good shot but a terrible artist.

When I couldn't live fire, I unloaded the pistol and practiced dry firing while keeping the sights aligned. My marksmanship skills continued to improve. As I would later tell detectives, I shot my best qualification score to that date on 17 May 1994, putting all thirty-six shots in the nine-inch circle of the cardboard silhouette target.

My flight worked swings and mids: three days working from 1400 to 2200, followed by three days working from 2200 to 0600, followed by three days off. The constant change in our sleep cycle was taxing, but I preferred working while most everyone else on base was off duty.

Between radio calls, I drove around familiarizing myself with the base. The summer breeze rolled off the flight line, carrying with it the kerosene smell of jet fuel and the roaring whine of jet engines, a sound that would become as imperceptible as music in a department store. Not long after arriving at Fairchild, I discovered the seatbelt buckle of our new patrol cars was hitting the ambidextrous safety lever of my holstered Beretta. I got into the habit of thumbing the lever upward whenever I exited the car to ensure it was in the fire position.

I incorporated the new base into my nightly mental rehearsals. One scenario I visualized involved me walking in on an armed robbery at the Shoppette. I envisioned shooting the perpetrator from a kneeling position so the trajectory of my bullet would be less likely to endanger innocent bystanders. Mental rehearsal was not the only ritual that followed me to Fairchild. Like many police officers, I was plagued by the occupational nightmare. I frequently dreamed that my firearm malfunctioned while I was in a life-or-death fight. In my dreams I would encounter someone shooting at me, and when I returned fire the bullets came out of the gun in slow motion, bounced off the perpetrator, or fell harmlessly to the ground as soon as they left the barrel. At other times the trigger wouldn't pull or the hammer fell without discharging a round.

On 8 August, I was among several security policemen tasked with the additional duty of working crowd and traffic control for Fairchild's 1993 air show. I was on foot patrol among the crowd that had formed alongside the flight line, and had a good view of the demonstration aircraft. One of Fairchild's B-52s lumbered down the runway and took to the sky. The whistling scream of its eight jet engines was unmistakable as the bomber circled back. It made a low pass in front of the crowd before pulling up and rocketing skyward in a nearly vertical climb. I had never seen aerobatics performed by such a large plane. Like most spectators that day, I felt reassured that the stunt must have been safe or the pilot wouldn't have received approval to perform it.

Wilford Hall

Wilford Hall Medical Center. Credit: Andy Brown

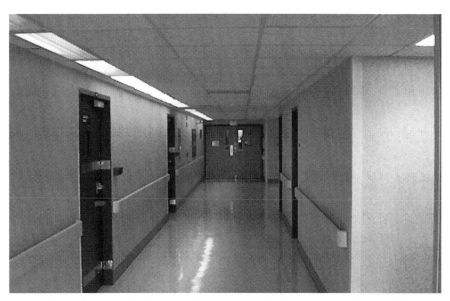

Doors of Psychiatric Ward 4D, Wilford Hall Medical Center. Credit: Andy Brown

On 9 September 1993, Amn Dean Mellberg waited anxiously in a room on ward 4D, wearing a pair of hospital-issued pajamas. Capt Elizabeth Keene, the assistant chief inpatient psychiatrist of the twenty-eight bed unit, read through Mellberg's case file. Dr. Keene hoped an intake interview would elicit further information from Mellberg, but he appeared angry and suspicious of her questions. He refused to talk about his psychological history and what brought him to the unit. What he did say was nearly inaudible. When asked about his career he told Dr. Keene, "The Air Force is a great way of life and I am proud to serve my country." He refused to offer any new information other than to say he "was sent here for a reason I don't know," and it was an "unjust act." Mellberg said he felt "accused of something" but was unsure what it was. When Dr. Keene probed further, Mellberg said, "I would like to see an attorney before I answer any questions."

At the end of the interview, the psychiatrist noted in Mellberg's medical record that he demonstrated paranoid and schizoid traits. She planned to rule out bipolar disorder, organic mood disorder, organic mental disorder, schizophreniform disorder, adjustment disorder, and delusional disorder. Her treatment plan included further observation, obtaining collateral history, routine labs, head imaging, psychology review, and testing. Dr. Keene considered prescribing Haldol and Ativan for Mellberg's violent behavior but ordered, "Hold standing meds for now to assess his symptoms." She planned for Mellberg to attend facilitated morning group meetings, goal-setting meetings, and one-on-one counseling. She also annotated the possibility of a medical evaluation board (MEB) to consider his discharge from the military.

Wilford Hall Medical Center served as a training hospital as did its psychiatric unit. Psychiatrists in training were paired with, and mentored by, experienced psychiatrists. The residents offered diagnosis, but the definitive diagnosis was the responsibility of the attending doctor.

Being a military psychiatric unit, the staff didn't see a lot of serious mental disorders. The inpatient non-commissioned officer in charge of ward 4D said, "Most of the people I talked to were not 'crazy,' but had found themselves in some overwhelming life situation. Most had probably tried to kill themselves or at least made some gesture."

In addition to the psychiatrists and psychologists, Air Force mental health technicians staffed the ward. They frequently interacted with the patients, observed their behavior, built therapeutic relationships, and encouraged them to work on their goals.

New patients were watched closely until they demonstrated they were participating in therapy and weren't a danger to themselves or others. Over time, they could apply for an increase in their privileges, including wearing civilian clothes and obtaining passes to leave the ward. Mellberg was initially put into Category A status, restricted to the ward and required to wear hospital pajamas and a robe. Until the staff could determine he wasn't a risk, he was given the special precaution of *eye contact*—requiring a staff member to keep him under constant observation even during bathroom breaks and shower time. He would take his meals separately from the other patients and was limited to eating with a spoon.

Mellberg spent the first few days lying in his hospital bed or lurking outside his room. At times he paced the halls, drinking frequently from a gallon jug of water. When approached by the staff, Mellberg showed no emotion other than to smile "inappropriately." The technicians tried to engage him in conversation and encouraged him to interact with his peers and verbalize his fears and anxiety. After a few days, Mellberg was moved out of eye contact status, but his unwillingness to talk or participate in therapy kept him in the precautionary status of *close observation*. The staff checked on him every fifteen minutes and noted their observations on Progress Note forms which became part of his medical records. Many of their entries shared a similar theme. "Patient would not discuss any of the issues that brought him here. When asked about his job, patient appeared to brighten as he explained his AFSC [career field]." Medical Technician SSgt Cedric Dunmore noted Mellberg "seems confused at times. He appears to be slightly slow educationally. … He still doesn't know why he's here: 'I have no comment about my situation as I have not seen the orders yet!'"

After several days of encouragement, Mellberg began attending group meetings but participated minimally. He sat erect in his chair as his peers discussed their personal situations. He smiled silently when the other patients confronted him about his aloof behavior and was unresponsive even as they expressed their concern and fear of him. His behavior made the group so uncomfortable they unanimously voted to remove him from the group meetings.

Capt Joseph Buzogany, a resident psychiatrist who was paired with Dr. Keene, noted, "Patient is completely non-participatory in group" and exhibits "superior facial expressions and at times staring down doctors and other patients." According to Dr. Buzogany's notes, Mellberg was likely hearing voices or experiencing auditory hallucinations. He noted "nursing staff is concerned that patient may be attending to some internal stimuli. … Numerous staff members have related their feelings of uneasiness with this patient. Despite this, patient is continually being encouraged to participate in ward activities. He chooses otherwise."

According to Dr. Buzogany, the staff vetoed the patients' vote to exclude Mellberg from attending future group meetings. He still participated minimally, silently observing as his peers discussed their situations. His only self-disclosure was to say that he intended to "work on anything to complete his order to be here." A med tech noted Mellberg's singlemindedness: "Patient unable to set goals at this time and focuses on remaining in the military. Patient stated he wouldn't know what to do if he were discharged from the service: 'I just can't think about anything like that now.'" During one-on-one counseling, "he refused to disclose any new information, stating, 'I don't trust anybody here. Until I do, I can't talk to anyone.'"

On his ninth day on the ward, Mellberg sat alone in the day room, listening to music. Later, he anxiously paced the hallways until he found a female patient alone in the laundry room/gym. He stood staring at her as she rode an exercise bike and asked her if she liked to sweat and make her heart beat fast. When she retreated to her room, he followed her, repeatedly asking to read her journal and wanting to know what she was going to do with her husband during her weekend day pass.

When the woman returned to the ward later that evening, Mellberg pursued her down the hall and resumed questioning her. She slipped inside her room and slammed the door. Mellberg pounded on the door, demanding to know what she had done with her husband. When the staff confronted Mellberg about his inappropriate behavior, he maintained his fixed smile and whispered, "I don't have to talk to you about this." Citing patient safety reasons, Mellberg was relocated to a room near the nurse's station and was again placed on eye contact status.

While he was on eye contact, the staff noted, "Patient has been staring at other female patients and has been laughing for no apparent reason." He displayed antisocial behavior and a "preoccupation with sexual themes." A doctor who worked on the ward said, "Dean would masturbate anywhere and everywhere. We would put him in a chair in front of the unit desk so we could keep an eye on him—but that didn't stop him."

The technicians who were tasked with observing Mellberg were concerned about him spending hours in the shower, prompting them to limit his bathroom time to ten minutes. He refused to discuss his inappropriate behavior, telling one staff member, "I don't really have anything to talk about. I don't ever think I'll get off eye contact. Ha ha." After three days, Mellberg was upgraded to close observation but continued to laugh spontaneously and exhibit "silly behavior." He entered the seclusion room and stuck his face directly into the camera that was monitored at the nursing station.

One of Mellberg's fellow patients said, "The staff would tell us he was a little kid in a grown man's body. The women there were very scared. ... Just about everyone on the floor wrote in their journals that they were scared to death of this guy. ... I kept saying he should be in the state hospital. Everyone did." In private, some of the staff referred to Mellberg as Hellberg, "like an iceberg where you only see the tip but what you do see is hell."

Two weeks into his stay, Mellberg began attending discharge planning meetings where the staff noted, "Patient is not responding to treatment because he chooses not to take an active participative role. Patient states that his family is fully supportive of his decision not to speak of the specifics as to why he is here."

The staff advised Mellberg that his refusal to participate in therapy would likely end his Air Force career. They explained that his case would soon go before a medical evaluation board (MEB). Mellberg's MEB would be composed of three physicians who would evaluate his medical history and make a recommendation as to whether or not his medical condition would impede his ability to continue serving in the military. The findings of the MEB would be referred to the physical evaluation board (PEB), which would review the MEB's documentation and formally determine if he was fit for continued military service or eligible for disability compensation. A doctor noted, "Mellberg is worried about his career and seems happy to hear that an MEB has not yet been initiated." Another doctor noted his dilemma. "He wants to remain on active duty but does not want to talk."

During the course of his stay on the ward, staff members noted, "Mellberg was easily startled, often found leaping off his bed and straightening his clothes when staff would enter his room." On the evening of Mellberg's nineteenth day on the ward, despite his being on close observation, a mental health technician found him sitting in bed, holding a sharp piece of metal he had removed from his hospital bed. A search of his room uncovered another sharp piece of metal wrapped in the torn sleeve of a hospital robe. When Mellberg refused to disclose what he planned to do with the sharp objects, he was placed on eye contact and transferred to a room near the nurse's station.

Dr. Keene updated her assessment, diagnosing Mellberg with anxiety disorder and personality disorder with paranoid and schizoid traits. She suspected an organic mental disorder or psychotic disorder and wondered if he might be attending to internal stimuli. She wrote that Mellberg was "noted to smile and laugh inappropriately at times and staff reports that he appears to speak to himself." She recommended further observation and referral to an MEB. She again considered psychotropic meds, but Mellberg refused to be medicated.

On 30 September 1993, day twenty-two, with the approval of Dr. Keene, and using her latest diagnosis, Dr. Buzogany prepared a five-page narrative summary for Mellberg's MEB report. The narrative summarized Mellberg's history at Fairchild as well as his behavior on the ward and refusal to participate in therapy. It also noted that Mellberg demonstrated an expectation of being exploited or harmed by others without sufficient basis and that he often read hidden or threatening meanings into benign remarks or actions. At the end of the summary, Dr. Buzogany typed a recommendation: "In light of patient's dramatic demonstration of paranoid behavior with regard to his roommate and his inability to perform his job secondary to worrying about the activities of his roommate, the patient is not recommended to continue on in the US Air Force." The report did not contain a recommendation for follow-up care if the board approved the discharge recommendation.

It would take several weeks for the board to meet and make a determination. During that time, Mellberg submitted a handwritten letter to the MEB:

> Dear, Medical Board
> I am not disabled in any way. It was only the situation that put me down here. If you add in all the events that happened at Fairchild AFB then you would understand.

I am going to list to you the events. Number one event is the asking for the loan by my roommate is a clear stresser for both of us, for me it was a large break in trust to ask for money, for him it was a break in trust for friends should loan money. Second stresser is the clock to which I owned and needed was certainly a seemingly simple task of working around, but yet my roommate so disterbed by the ticking insisted to threaten to break it. Thirdly a girl friend of his stayed knowing against dorm regulations this is a clear violation and action should have been take toward him and not me. He even admits to this fact in the taped conversation to which was taken on Sep, 3 93. So as far as any action it should have been handeled anmistratively by my commander Major Dawson. Fourly being called into my First Sergent office for something to which no one knows or even cares is my masterbating in the shower. This is a false accusation and also should have been handled administarively. Clearly I don't and did not be in any way have to this action and any libles to be taken out that this took place. I am only a victom in this situation and the victomizer is left to get away!

On day twenty-seven, Mellberg met with a resident doctor in one-on-one counseling and appeared to begin to accept his probable discharge from the military. "Patient voiced concerns about differences between military and civilian life and how he would be treated in civilian life. … Concerned that he would always be judged based on past behavior."

On his twenty-ninth day on the ward, Mellberg met with Air Force social worker Capt Nancy Weingartner. According to an entry she made in Mellberg's medical record progress notes, he told her, "I just got some bad news. I read my MEB. Dr. B said I should be transferred to another hospital because I'm not cooperating. He also said I may be a danger to others. I'm not a danger to others."

Mellberg sounded and appeared afraid of the situation he was in and expressed concerns about being in trouble and believing he was going to be court-martialed. He told Weingartner that he believed he was sent to Wilford Hall to be "out of everyone's hair." He thought he was there for them to find his faults and pursue a trial if indicated. He claimed this was why he was resisting staff. "I wasn't going to fall on my own sword. … If I was going to be judged, I wasn't going to give anyone anything to help that process." When it was explained that he was not there to be punished, Mellberg said, "You mean I'm just here to be changed? What do I need to change?"

As the meeting progressed, Mellberg shared his family history, describing his dad as an "Earth man" who worked hard and always provided. Mellberg said his dad thought he should get a simple job. He said his mom was who he went to for support. Weingartner's notes continued:

> Mellberg described an incident when at age nine or ten he was riding his bike in a park when he was approached by a teenage boy with a gun who took him away on his bike. Mellberg reports he was let go when he started crying. He claims his parents found the boy and his parents. He does not believe they went to court but states ten thousand dollars was given to his parents in a settlement.

A later entry in Mellberg's medical records shows there may have been more to the incident than Mellberg revealed. "Collateral history obtained from the patient's mother does indicate, however that the patient was sodomized at gunpoint when he was seven. … The patient's mother stated that the patient did seek counseling for several months thereafter." Mellberg adamantly denied being sexually assaulted.

According to Weingartner's notes:

> Mellberg revealed that this is his fifth command-directed evaluation and is unsure what we want. Mellberg claimed he will cooperate with mental health, now that he understands. However, he held on to the hope of returning to Spokane to complete his duty assignment. When asked about his support system he said, "My work center is helpful … I believe they wish I would return. … I feel I am ready to return to duty."

On Mellberg's fortieth day on the ward, the MEB convened and agreed with Dr. Buzogany and Dr. Keene's recommendation to discharge Mellberg from the Air Force. They referred his case to an informal PEB that would conduct a records-only review and determine the compensable percentage of Mellberg's disability. Mellberg would then have the option to accept the informal PEB's decision or dispute its findings and appear before a formal PEB with legal counsel.

By day forty-four, Mellberg appeared to open up even more. He confided in Staff Sergeant Dunmore that he was admitted to the hospital after his roommate complained about him masturbating. Dunmore noted, "Patient states that he sees nothing wrong with his behavior. Patient states that he has recently asked for a change of room (and received it) because of the same complaint from his roommate on the unit." The next day Mellberg approached Dunmore again. "Patient requested that the following become a part of his inpatient record: 'I request that no one else ask me any questions pertaining to my masturbating or other sexual issues that may exist with me! Any further probes into this area of my life will be considered as sexual harassment by me!'" Dunmore explained he wasn't trying to make him uncomfortable yesterday, and Mellberg replied, "Yesterday it didn't bother me to talk about it."

On day fifty, during a group meeting, Mellberg revealed he was tired of fighting to stay in the military. Dr. Steven Cathey made a note in Mellberg's record:

> Patient revealed that his mother would be greatly disappointed that he was not making his best effort to return to duty. Patient states that his mother believes one can do anything if they work hard enough. … In summary, patient is experiencing great anxiety about being perceived as a failure by mother.

Mellberg later told his social worker, "I failed because I can't go back to duty. My mom will be disappointed. She invested so much."

Later that day, Mellberg spoke with Dunmore, who observed that his previous guard was somewhat relaxed and his mood appeared to be happy. Dunmore noted, "Patient reported to me that he has now decided to accept that he is going to be separated from the military. Patient states that his plans are to return home to live with his parents and return to school."

Dr. Keene noted that Mellberg "continues to improve with increased interaction in group and more disclosure of past difficulties and enmeshed relationship with parents. He continues to deal with issues of trust."

The staff noted Mellberg was "becoming much more involved in unit activities" and he was "initiating one-on-one interaction with staff and other patients." The patients on 4D had a party with music and refreshments. Mellberg let everything go and was dancing and talking to everyone. He was later observed in the unit kitchen, smiling and animated. He appeared happy as he gestured with a hand puppet he made from a gym sock, causing other patients to laugh.

Mellberg began to willingly participate in group meetings and was upgraded to Category B status. He could wear civilian clothes or his uniform and could participate in supervised off-ward activities like occupational or recreational therapy. Mental health technician SSgt Sarah LaPoint noted:

> Patient attended group and was very tentative as another patient spoke of her son and their relationship. Patient stated at the end of the group that he wanted to break away from his mother but it was hard. ... Patient appears much more willing to talk in group, but needs to work on asserting himself.

In early November, the informal PEB reached a decision and determined that Mellberg should receive a twenty percent disability rating and be discharged with severance pay. Dunmore noted, "Patient reported that he has been in touch with his family, keeping them abreast of any changes to his situation here. 'My mother thinks that I should get more and my dad just wants me to come home!'"

In mid-November, Lois arrived in San Antonio and took advantage of visiting hours, spending a lot of time on the ward and staying at the nearby Fisher House.

Lois Mellberg was forty-three, but doctors said she "looked worn out and older than her stated age." The staff noted that Mellberg appeared excited about his mother's arrival, though he "has not interacted with others ... and continues to isolate himself." According to a report, Lois "promptly established [her son] in an adversarial relationship with medical and mental health teams." One doctor said Lois Mellberg was distressed that her son "was stuck on a psychiatric ward. ... She challenged the basic premises about Dean having any mental illness and responded to [our] findings with skepticism." Her "denial that he may have some bona fide problems led her to reject any labels for her son from the Air Force and view the organization as punitive." She "allegedly made some negative remarks to other patients in our day room about what she perceived as our limitations. ... I believe the other patients thought she was rather odd, and I never feared that she could ferment any uprisings on the unit." However, "she definitely annoyed some of our staff."

Coinciding with the arrival of his mother, Mellberg contested the findings of the informal PEB and requested a formal hearing.

On day sixty-nine, psychiatry intern Capt Gia-Evita Lanzano met with Dean Mellberg. Lois sat in on the interview and answered many of Dr. Lanzano's questions on behalf of her son. Dr. Lanzano noted Mellberg appeared scared and noted in his record, "Patient able to articulate some in the presence of his mother, however exhibited continued evidence of halting, whispering responses combined with possible blocking process with some evidence of loosening in his responses," meaning he was not staying on topic or making sense. He resisted divulging too much information, saying, "You know me too much. If you know me, you can control me." Dr. Lanzano asked Mellberg, "What do you want at this time to help you with your confused thinking?" Mellberg maintained his singular focus. "I want to be calibrating." Throughout the interview, Dr. Lanzano noted, "patient exhibited progressive discomfort and became tearful, acknowledging that he needed help." Dr. Lanzano noted Mellberg maintained delusions of a persecutory nature. She gave a diagnosis of psychotic disorder (schizophrenia prodrome)—a period of decreased functioning prior to the onset of psychotic symptoms usually occurring in adolescence. She noted a parent-child problem and indicated she suspected obsessive-compulsive disorder with schizoid traits. She suggested a plan to pursue continued family intervention and examine options for transport to a group home setting for continued care after discharge from the military.

Mellberg met with social worker Nancy Weingartner to plan for life after the military and "reduce risk for patient to be segregated in community." Mellberg said he wanted to stay in the local area, get a job, and be independent. Weingartner noted:

> He has $14,000 in the bank and feels he can do okay. ... Unsure what his real plans or motivation is. Tends to walk hallways and be indirect with requests. Mood remains aloof—avoidant. Patient at times appears to attend and then at others appears lost. Relationship with mom appears

extremely close, almost constricting. Patient appears un-
certain how to deal with relationship or any relationship.
Psychotic behavior appears to be smoldering.

On day seventy-one, Mellberg sought an upgrade in category and, according to some of the staff, resorted to manipulative playacting to achieve
it. Whenever the staff considered a category increase, they encouraged the
patient community to provide input based on their observations of the
individual. Dunmore noted, "Patient states that he is receiving a lot of
positive feedback on his going up for category increase to C. 'I feel good
because people actually believe and trust in me. Now we can bridge some
of our gaps!' Patient states that he is becoming closer to many of his peers
and is trusting them and staff more. … He wants to change from the person he used to be to someone who loves others and wants to be loved by
them."

Patients' complaints about Lois Mellberg were noted in her son's medical records. "I've never been so uncomfortable in my life. That woman over
there is making me upset. She is so negative. She's calling us all crazy. One
of the other patients told her off. I don't want to be around her." Another
patient agreed. "She's upset me. I wish you'd ask her to leave."

About a week after Lois arrived, Dean spoke with Staff Sergeant
Dunmore. "Patient states that he is really ready for his mother to leave.
'I appreciate her taking the time to come to see me, but I really need to
start to depend on myself and develop relationships outside of my family.'"
Later, Dr. Lanzano noted, "Patient expressing desire for independence. Has
not discussed this with his mother as yet. States he is willing to consider
assistance in this matter." One doctor later said, "Unconsciously, I think
he did resent mom's control, but I don't believe he would own or verbalize
his rage, because he was not ever allowed to. … I think that was one of his
main problems: owning and validating his anger and other emotions and
then learning how to express them in healthy ways."

During group meetings, Mellberg became agitated when asked if he
had changed his mind about limiting his mother's intrusion into his life. He
responded, "No I don't think I am dependent on my mom. You're leading
me again." Social worker Nancy Weingartner noted that Lois "continues
to sit extremely close to Mellberg and hold him in ways that make patients
and staff uncomfortable." The "relationship remains enmeshed and appears
inappropriately close. Mom has been told of our concerns in reference to

her enmeshment previously, and no adjustments have been made." The "relationship with mom continues to present additional therapeutic concerns and at times appears to be impeding patient's treatment. Patient's mom denies all of above and appears hostile and resistant." Weingartner noted, "If concerns continue and/or increase, request patient and mom to visit off unit to decrease potential negative impact to others."

Mellberg continued in group therapy meetings. He was tearful at times and on one occasion he squirmed in his chair while another patient talked about a lack of hugs and kisses as a child. Mellberg made several hand gestures as though he wanted to speak, but remained silent.

At other times he opened group by proclaiming, "I'm enthusiastic, and I don't want to come down." Dr. Lanzano noted, "Patient in a 'pretend' mode of 'feeling great' and reluctant to discuss his concerns. ... Patient enumerated his reasons for desiring to continue in the Air Force—avoidant in focusing on his changed thought processes" since his mother's arrival.

Mellberg was upgraded to Category C status and was granted weekend day passes to leave the hospital with his mother. It was around this time that he wrote a letter requesting the help of his Michigan congressman, Dave Camp. Mellberg also filed a written complaint with the inspector general's office at Lackland AFB, requesting "an investigation into the steps, processes, and procedures which have resulted in my current stay and status at Wilford Hall Medical Center." Lois also filed complaints with the IG's office alleging that her son had not been afforded dermatology or dental appointments during his stay at Wilford Hall.

On 30 November 1993, a letter arrived at the Pentagon addressed to Air Force Lt Col Walter "Mark" Washabaugh, Office of Legislative Liaison for the Secretary of the Air Force:

> I have been contacted by my constituent who has a concern with the United States Air Force.
> I would appreciate you reviewing this matter, and addressing my constituent's concern. Please direct your written response to me at my Midland District Office.
> Sincerely
> Dave Camp, Member of Congress

Mellberg's typed complaint was enclosed in the letter:

I am an airman who has served my country with both honor and pride. I am presently in the psychiatric ward of Wilford Hall USAF Medical Center. I am here as a result of unfounded and unsubstanciated accusations made against me by my former roommate. I have never hurt myself or anyone else nor have I threatened to hurt myself or anyone else. My former roommate made requests of me that I did not fulfill such as; lending him $400.00, staying out of our joint room from Thursday evening until Sunday evening when his girlfriend came to visit him on base, and getting rid of a windup alarm clock. Because I did not comply Airman Rainer requested a roommate change and when Sgt Jackson didn't comply told him that I was taking hour showers and he found me asleep in our room naked and that I was continuously masturbating. From this there was an air of homophobia throughout the barracks. I have continued being punished for unfounded accusations and now find my career in jeopardy. I believe that the mental health department is being used to punish or dismiss serviceperson.

* * *

The doctors rotated on and off of the psychiatry ward every three months. On 1 November 1993, Capt John Campbell III took over as Mellberg's staff attending psychiatrist. Dr. Campbell had received additional schooling in neuropsychiatry. He noted that Dr. Keene "had been impressed" by Mellberg's "persistent symptoms of anxiety and paranoia" but felt "we had not yet arrived at a diagnosis that accurately reflected Airman Mellberg's unusual personal style."

Throughout the month of November, Dr. Campbell worked to rule out the possibility of schizophrenic prodrome. On 1 December 93, the day after the Air Force received the congressional inquiry, Dr. Campbell noted, "Patient's difficulties with reciprocal social interaction, verbal and nonverbal communication, and repertoire of activities suggested a diagnosis of autism."

Dr. Campbell reviewed Mellberg's CT scan and noted Mellberg's brain had an asymmetrically enlarged left front ventricle (the hollow, fluid-filled center of the brain), suggesting something developmentally awry with his brain. He ordered a neuropsychological evaluation with specific attention paid to the possibility of autism.

A technician administered a battery of tests on Mellberg that measured his IQ, attention, concentration, and memory, as well as his language and communication skills, learning, abstract reasoning, and problem-solving abilities. Maj Randy Robinette, a clinical neuropsychologist, interpreted the test results and met with Mellberg for approximately ninety minutes to review his general history.

On 7 December 1993, Mellberg's ninetieth day on the ward, Dr. Robinette gave Dr. Campbell a report on Mellberg's neuropsychological evaluation. According to a statement written by Dr. Campbell, the report "documented several deficits associated with left hemispheric functioning, which supported the findings of the CT scan." Dr. Campbell wrote that he and a colleague were "intrigued by the potential of autism but we agreed that this diagnosis would be unusual and of low interrater reliability" (having others agree with them). Dr. Campbell asked two other colleagues who had experience treating patients with autism to review a videotaped interview he had conducted with Mellberg. According to Dr. Campbell's statement, "They supported the idea that Airman Mellberg may have autistic disorder."

Not everyone agreed with the diagnosis of autism. A doctor who worked on the ward said, "Dean had significant antisocial traits ... the rules didn't apply to him. He never admitted hearing voices but many of the staff observed him attending to internal stimuli and it would explain all the inappropriate laughing and several other odd behaviors. He seemed as if he had developmental delays, especially in regard to social behavior (which is probably why he got the autism label)—but I don't think that was the problem. He was extremely paranoid and had significant anger issues. He really fit the paranoid schizophrenia diagnosis, but he seemed to be more in touch with reality than most schizophrenics. But I have very little doubt about the antisocial personality traits, as he never experienced guilt, remorse, concern for others ... nor did he ever accept responsibility for his actions."

A female doctor who worked on the ward suggested Dr. Campbell didn't see as much of Mellberg's odd behavior as the women did. She suggested this was because Mellberg respected Dr. Campbell more because he was a male. She said, "Dean had major issues with women."

On 8 December 1993, Mellberg's ninety-second day on the ward, he was to appear before the formal PEB. After conferring with legal counsel,

Lois Mellberg demanded a second opinion from a psychiatrist of her choosing. She succeeded in getting the board to defer their decision until after she arranged for the independent evaluation.

Dr. Campbell and his intern, Dr. Lanzano, sat down with Mellberg and his mother and informed them of their "current working diagnosis of autistic disorder in presence of high intelligence, well compensated by supportive structure provided by patient's mother." Dr. Campbell wrote, "I also shared with them my feelings that this condition explained his inability to perform the mission of the USAF. … They were not pleased, but not opposed to the idea." Dr. Campbell also informed Mellberg that he was recommending he be separated from the military.

Dr. Campbell wrote an addendum to the narrative summary submitted to the medical board offering a sole diagnosis of autistic disorder. The narrative listed Mellberg's hospital course. It revealed that the CT scan of Mellberg's head "demonstrates left ventricle dilation suggesting early developmental pathology for left hemisphere. This is supported by neuropsychiatric testing which displayed obvious lateralized impairment in left hemisphere functions of verbal memory, word attack, etc. It was noted that the patient had above average right hemisphere functioning. … It was further noted that beyond evidence of attention, memory (verbal), and academic skills deficits, the patient's history suggested a pattern of limited interpersonal relationships. … The patient has definite impairment in areas of reciprocal social interaction, verbal communication and repertoire of activities. … It is clear that the patient has a strong sense of duty and patriotism, however his significant social impairment interferes with his ability to function in the organizational structure of the United States Air Force."

Dr. Campbell's summary indicated Mellberg had a marked military impairment and that he was "non-worldwide qualified." The final paragraph of the summary listed Dr. Campbell's recommendations:

> The patient is to be discharged to the patient squadron where the patient has been assigned starting 9 December 1993, awaiting formal evaluation of activities of daily living to ascertain feasibility for follow-up arrangements post separation from the military. The patient is contesting formal PEB. The patient is to follow up with Captain Weingartner of Social Work to arrange for possible group home placement after discharge from the military.

Based on the new diagnosis of autism, Mellberg's PEB was canceled and a second MEB was scheduled for January.

Back at Fairchild, Dr. Brigham learned that Mellberg had been diagnosed with autism and thought the doctors were missing the point. He believed Mellberg was manipulating the system. His fear of Mellberg returning to harm him or his family led him to consider buying a handgun. His wife, Susan, had acquiesced to him keeping a knife under his mattress, pepper spray on her nightstand, and a shotgun and rifle in the bedroom. But she drew the line at him owning a handgun.

Mellberg's discharge from the hospital was delayed by one day so he could have a final meeting with social worker Nancy Weingartner. On 10 December 1993, Weingartner met with Mellberg and his mother. She noted that Mellberg "remains avoidant and schizoid in behavior." She discussed his needs after his inevitable discharge from the military and noted that his "goal orientation, task completion, abstract decision making remain poor. He is unable to make plans and follow through with plans without help. ... With Mom's intervention, appropriate plans can't be made. She is unable to see patient's ineptness for what it is. She believes he will go home with her while patient remains undecided and unwilling to let social work help. Patient wants to throw a dart at a map to decide where he will live." He "feels he is capable" but "when asked how to follow through with specific tasks is unable to. ... Ability to interact with people is severely hindered. Wants a relationship but unable to appreciate his negative effect on others and why they distance from him. Overall insight and judgment is poor at best."

Weingartner believed a group home was the most appropriate setting for him. She provided the Mellbergs with local referrals and advised them she would make more available on request to any area in the US or overseas. Mellberg resisted, saying "If I can't be in the Air Force, which I am going to fight to, I'll be out and want no help or benefits." Weingartner made her final entry in Mellberg's records, "Both plan to fight Air Force ... and have limited insight and abstract skills to appreciate big picture."

On 10 December 1993, after ninety-three days on ward 4D, Dean Mellberg was discharged from the hospital. He was assigned to the patient squadron of the 59th Medical Wing. The patient squadron is a work center where military members perform clerical and administrative duties while receiving long-term medical care or while they await the results of a medical board.

Patient Squadron

When he was released from the psychiatric unit, Airman Mellberg moved into a Lackland AFB dormitory reserved for personnel assigned to Wilford Hall's patient squadron.

While he awaited the MEB's decision, he was assigned duties in the inpatient records section of Wilford Hall. His co-workers initially described him as quiet and distant. He eventually opened up to a few of them but spoke mostly about sports and his desire to stay in the Air Force. A co-worker who invited Mellberg to a dorm room party said he "did not associate with anyone, but simply danced in a corner by himself."

The records section personnel were familiar with Lois Mellberg, who regularly demanded copies of her son's records while he was in the psychiatric ward. According to an inspector general report, when her son was transferred out of the psychiatric ward, Lois immediately shifted her "attention to, and interest in the operations of the 59 Medical Wing Patient Squadron." The patient squadron personnel described Lois as "pushy" and noticed Dean withdrew even further when she was around.

Mellberg's job consisted of making photocopies of patient records. This gave him access to his own medical records. He was observed photocopying his records as well as sneaking them out of the section by hiding them in his briefcase. A doctor who dealt with Mellberg while he was at Wilford Hall said, "If he read his medical record … he would have found a number of unflattering reports from the Fairchild mental health clinic."

When there weren't any files to photocopy, Mellberg rummaged through people's desks, linked paperclips into a chain, or fell asleep. He made some of the women he worked with uncomfortable, often asking them for hugs and smiling inappropriately while staring at them.

Mellberg flew home around Christmastime. On 29 December 1993, Lois took him to Michigan State University to see psychiatry professor Dr. Jed Magen for an independent assessment. Dr. Magen talked with Mellberg and his mother for forty-five minutes. He noted, "It became immediately apparent that Dean has a very formal and somewhat stylized speech pattern. He was also slightly circumstantial in terms of telling me about his difficulties." Mellberg described his first encounter with military mental health, telling Dr. Magen that he was diagnosed with an anxiety disorder and paranoid personality disorder after complaining that his basic training instructor had sexually harassed him. As Mellberg spoke, Dr. Magen noted, "It was difficult to understand exactly what had happened, since he laboriously seemed to want to inform me of every detail about his difficulties."

Dr. Magen noted Mellberg struggled to communicate. "At times his mother would intervene when he was trying to describe something to me." Lois told the doctor that her son was "extremely moralistic … taking very seriously various injunctions he may have read or heard on television." She said he was a normal child with no developmental delays, an above-average student who had "normal social relationships" and "played with many other children." She "denied any problems with teachers, with other students, with retaining friends or any other school difficulties."

The Mellbergs provided Dr. Magen a selection of psychiatric records, which he used in conjunction with the brief interview to compose a narrative assessment. In the narrative, Dr. Magen acknowledged that Mellberg had "difficulties with a roommate who alleged that he has some inappropriate sexual behaviors as well as threatening behaviors." He noted Mellberg's assertion that his roommate had committed a "crime against humanity" and his desire to sue the roommate for causing him so much distress. Dr. Magen saw, "nothing which would make me think of a thought disorder or a psychosis at this time." He didn't agree with Mellberg's latest diagnosis. "I frankly think that labeling him as having autistic disorder is somewhat over-calling the situation."

Dr. Magen preferred the diagnosis of pervasive developmental disorder and suggested an "additional diagnosis which may fit … is that of Asperger syndrome … This syndrome is usually applied to individuals who have autistic-like impairments but are quite high functioning."

Dr. Magen noted, "Mr. Mellberg appears to be an individual who is quite rigid and has a quite rigid way of interacting with other individuals. His stylized speech, his moralistic bent and his perseverative quality, in terms of both speech and his fixation on one task or attitude at a time, all fit with this kind of style." He also said, "He was quite fixated on staying in the Air Force and did not seem to be able to consider other possibilities or alternative career pathways." Dr. Magen believed Mellberg's ideal work environment would be a solitary one that did not involve a lot of variability. Dr. Magen ended his written assessment saying, "I do not think that Mr. Mellberg will be able to develop a tremendous amount of insight into his behaviors nor that he will be able to change his pattern of interaction very much at all. These phenomena should be considered strongly when contemplating any sort of work or social environment for Mr. Mellberg."

Toward the end of December 1993, Mellberg returned to Lackland AFB to await a decision from the MEB.

He was sitting on a washing machine in the dormitory laundry room when a woman walked in and said hello. Her name was Faith, and she was also assigned to the patient squadron. Faith asked Mellberg why he was sitting in the laundry room, since most people put their clothes in the machine and then go back to their room. Mellberg said, "I don't want someone stealing my clothes." Faith suggested they sit in the day room and talk.

Over the next several weeks, the two spent a lot of time together, but Mellberg revealed little personal information. Faith got the impression that Mellberg was close to his family, that he had a strong camaraderie with his brother but was especially close to his mother. Mellberg told Faith that he was picked on a lot in high school and was a loner most of his life. He eventually told her he was being evaluated by mental health. Faith said, "He felt embarrassed and ashamed of the diagnosis they gave—autistic. He didn't want people thinking he was crazy."

Faith said that Mellberg seemed to be in a daze at times, as if he were daydreaming. She would ask him where he was during these times, but he wouldn't say. She said Mellberg didn't socialize with anyone other than her, and his only interaction with others was when her friends came to visit. She said he was interested in electronics but did not have any other interests. "He stayed in his room a lot, slept, and played video games." He slept a lot, day and night. He could lie down after work and sleep until the next morning. But he never fell asleep when he was with Faith.

Mellberg would sit with Faith while she watched television in her room, but he refused to look at the screen. He told her that his mother had once told him he was watching too much television, so he had stopped watching entirely.

On one occasion Faith was watching *MacGyver*, and Mellberg listened to the show with her. When the program was over, Mellberg asked Faith if she ever thought about blowing things up. He said he really liked the way

MacGyver used electronics and blew things up, but he didn't like the idea of rescuing people like MacGyver did.

Faith said that Mellberg was obsessed with death. "He would ask me if I ever thought about dying. … He would ask me if I ever thought about killing someone or going out with a 'big bang.'" According to Faith, Mellberg said he wanted to go out with a big bang and that "they would have to take him down." Faith said, "I understood this to mean that he would get into a confrontation with the cops somehow, but it didn't make any sense to me."

Faith felt protective of Mellberg and thought of herself as a mother to him. She said he didn't even know how to dress himself, and she had to tell him what clothes to wear. Mellberg wanted to take their relationship to another level. Faith said he badgered and bullied her to have sexual intercourse with him. He "begged and pleaded" for sex "almost like a little kid would beg for something." Faith protested and even slapped Mellberg when he would not let up, but she eventually gave in to his demands. Faith said she did not find the sex satisfying. She believed she was his first sexual relationship, and she had to constantly assure him that he was sexually capable. Mellberg became smothering and suffocating in their relationship and demanded that they spend all of their time together. He told Faith he thought she was special, beautiful, and smart and that he wanted to marry her.

On 4 January 1994, the MEB convened to consider Mellberg's case. After reading Dr. Campbell's narrative and his recommendation to discharge Mellberg from the military, the board enigmatically recommended that Mellberg "return to duty for appropriate administrative disposition." A doctor familiar with the case said the board used this phrase when someone didn't qualify for medical separation but was unfit for military service.

Mellberg's diagnosis of autism was not characterized as a psychiatric or medical condition. Autism is classified as a developmental disorder. Unlike mental disorders, developmental disorders can result in an administrative discharge only if the condition interferes with a person's duty performance. According to an inspector general report, "The patient squadron first sergeant interpreted the MEB recommendation to allow reassignment as an appropriate disposition." The investigators who authored the report believe the first sergeant interpreted the MEB paperwork as he did so he would not have to deal with Lois Mellberg. Their report indicated the first sergeant was aware of the complaints Lois had filed against the psychiatric ward and noted, "He was undoubtedly aware that had an administrative separation been initiated, the patient squadron would have become the focal point for [her] complaints." The first sergeant determined that Mellberg satisfactorily performed his job copying medical records. Using this as justification, he initiated the paperwork to have Mellberg reassigned to another Air Force base. When Mellberg and his mother learned of this, their complaints stopped.

In January of 1994, according to a statement written by the Fairchild PMEL section commander, she passed by Dr. London's office and asked if there was any word from Wilford Hall. Dr. London replied, "I guess you didn't hear, they decided to retain him." Dr. London went on to explain that he believed there had been some error in the paperwork. The PMEL section commander said, "Dr. London added that the board probably felt pressure from the congressional investigation and IG complaints and did not want to make a decision that would not line up to these agencies' reviews. … Dr. London stated that Mellberg would probably act up again, and his new base's only recourse would be to discharge him administratively. In this case, Mellberg would not be entitled to any medical help."

Reassignment

On 24 Jan 94, the day after his birthday, Airman Mellberg went to the Lackland AFB library and typed a letter to his family.

Dear Mom, Dad and [brother]. Yes I am typing this letter to you on a louse typewriter. Every once in a while the ink carbon will catch and not print clearly ... This is your tax dollars at work ... I received the card in the mail today ... It was so real that I could smell the flowers on it. Since I am now twenty years of age I do feel as though I did grow older in a way. I am quite sure life is different now that I am out of that ward. I ask the I.G. if you resubmited the right list to them and all they know is the one in December and the one they gave you as a congressonal responce. Other then that there is nothing they have. Now I would like to present to you the most magnifisent check made out by your's truely. That was like the most thrilling thing to do this bright and lively Monday morning. I've always gotten the same teller every time for the two times I've used the bank before this. She reconized me and didn't ask for my I.D. at first ... I think that is because I only withdrew less then 10 dollars the last two times ... Then she looked at the dollar amount and changed her mind. It shocked the hell out of her because she labled me as a tight wade. ... May I please know about the funds and what is happening to that CD moola. I would also like to know how much is there please. I sapose that Muicual Funds are out of it is that hard to keep track of the money and if they are not insured by the government ... I would like for the orders to get here soon for this sucks rocks being in inpatient records just copying things part of the day. The other part of the day I go off to lunch and sit on my ass. I might get to study for part of the day there. ...

The Air Force Military Personnel Center received Mellberg's MEB paperwork and the request for his reassignment from the 59th Medical Wing Patient Squadron. The staff at the personnel center apparently did not notice the disparity between the MEB narrative recommendation and the request for reassignment. They stamped the paperwork "Return to duty." On 26 January 1994, Mellberg received orders to Mountain Home Air Force Base. He was to report no later than 20 February 1994.

Mellberg booked a flight for 19 February 1994. According to his notes, he called Mountain Home three days before his departure date. When he spoke to the maintenance squadron first sergeant, he received some disturbing news. They were aware of his problems at Fairchild. The first sergeant suggested it would not be in his best interest to come there. He attempted to convince Mellberg to accept another assignment and offered to help him get his orders changed. Mellberg was insistent. He told the first sergeant he liked the northern part of the country and looked forward to working in Mountain Home's lab. The first sergeant seemed adamant that Mellberg not come to Mountain Home but took down his flight arrival information anyway.

Mellberg may have suspected that Fairchild's mental health center warned Mountain Home about him. In reality, a PMEL airman from Mountain Home AFB had recently traveled to Fairchild AFB for a medical appointment and stopped by the PMEL to visit a former co-worker. The airman said, "During this visit I talked with the branch chief briefly about an inbound airman to Mountain Home who was assigned to Fairchild AFB PMEL. He told me the airman had some problems and if it was possible to get his assignment canceled, he would advise it. The airman would require special attention, was a slow learner, had a short attention span, and had problems in the dorms." When the airman returned to Mountain Home, he notified his superiors of the potential problem.

Fairchild's PMEL section commander remembers they contacted Mountain Home after learning Mellberg was headed there. She said Fairchild's maintenance commander called his counterpart at Mountain Home "to let them know Mellberg's history. The intent was to forewarn them that Mellberg was not 'normal' and to closely evaluate him. Mountain Home's commander accused us of pushing off our dirty laundry instead of handling it ourselves. We tried to make them understand that we did everything in our power to have him discharged."

Mellberg was not pleased to learn that his assignment to Mt. Home was in jeopardy. He confided in a co-worker at inpatient records that he was concerned about being sent back to Fairchild Air Force Base. He was rightly concerned. Shortly after he left Fairchild, the maintenance squadron commander began preparations to separate him from the Air Force and planned to initiate the discharge if he ever returned.

As it turned out, Mellberg wouldn't return to duty at Fairchild. He later told his mother it was because Fairchild's lab was transitioning to civilian contractors and phasing out most of the military personnel slots. Someone at Mountain Home must have called in a favor. Mellberg's orders were amended, assigning him to Cannon Air Force Base in New Mexico. He was to report no later than 28 February 1994. Fairchild's maintenance squadron learned Mellberg was headed to Cannon AFB but opted not to warn them. The PMEL section commander said, "We elected not to call Cannon because of Mountain Home's reaction."

Mellberg confided in Faith that he was angry about his Mountain Home assignment being canceled. He told her, "somebody did him wrong and he was going to pay them back." She said he was "really ticked off that Fairchild had screwed up the privacy act." He was "just plain ticked off that Fairchild was spreading rumors about him."

Mellberg accepted his orders to Cannon AFB but didn't want to leave his "girlfriend." Faith was relieved to hear Mellberg was leaving. She saw his assignment to a new base as an easy way to end the relationship. Although her phone number was listed, she purposely didn't give it to him, hoping to never hear from him again.

* * *

On 14 February 1994, Lt Col Thomas Shubert, from the Congressional Inquiry Division of the Office of Legislative Liaison, wrote a letter in response to Congressman Camp's inquiry. In the letter, Shubert explained that Mellberg "was accused by his roommate of indecent acts and behavior" and that "no disciplinary action was taken." The letter went on to say:

> As a result of interviews with several different doctors, Airman Mellberg was air evacuated to the psychiatric inpatient unit at Wilford Hall Medical Center. ... On

November 1, 1993, a physical evaluation board considered Airman Mellberg's case in an informal hearing and
recommended that he be found physically unfit for further military service and discharged, with entitlement to
disability severance pay. ... He did not concur with the
recommended findings and requested a formal hearing of
his case. The formal physical evaluation board was scheduled for December 8, 1993, but never convened. The case
was recalled by Wilford Hall Medical Center on December
27, 1993. On January 4, 1994 Airman Mellberg's records
met another medical board, which recommended he be returned to duty for appropriate administrative disposition.
Airman Mellberg was briefed on January 5, 1994, and
concurred with the recommended findings. He will be returned to duty upon his release from Wilford Hall Medical
Center.

Upon receipt of the letter, Congressman Camp sent a letter of his own
to Lois Mellberg:

Dear Lois: Thank you for contacting me requesting assistance. ... As I am sure you are aware, the USAF states
Dean will be returned to duty in the very near future. I am
sure this was good news for both you and Dean, and I am
pleased to have been of assistance. If Dean encounters any
further difficulty at his new duty station, please contact me
and I will inquire further with the USAF.
Sincerely,
Dave Camp
Member of Congress

Black Rock Desert

In February 1994, two of Fairchild's B-52s flew a tactical cell formation to Nevada, along a route known as IR 300, to practice a low-level bomb run. Although the B-52 was designed for high-altitude flying, pilots were trained to fly low to penetrate enemy radar. In mountainous areas like the IR 300 route, the B-52 was restricted to no lower than 600 feet above ground level.

The two planes flew over mountains, fields, and hills headed to the Black Rock Desert. Lt Col Bud Holland was in the lead plane, giving Capt Brett Dugue a check ride to recertify him on the low-level bombing maneuvers. Col Robert Wolff, the vice wing commander of the 92nd Bomb Wing, was also being recertified and flew behind Holland's plane with two instructor pilots, Captain Countess and Captain Fleming.

Countess observed the flight of the lead plane change drastically as it traversed terrain. The crossovers were obviously lower than they had been a few minutes before. Countess remarked, "Well, Colonel Holland is flying now." Countess said, "Then, as we descended into the Black Rock Desert, he was sending up rooster tails, going through the dirt and the dust. … I don't know what rooster tail altitude is—fifty feet, possibly—but there was a nice dust trail behind the aircraft." According to Countess, when he pointed out the lead plane's low altitude, Colonel Wolff replied, "Oh, that's just Bud."

Fleming had just returned from weapons school and had a number of tactics he wanted to share with the crews. He had planned several simulated threats along the route for the crews to detect and evade. Countess relates, "Colonel Holland seemed to blow all that off. He didn't fly the preplanned route to defeat any of the simulated threats. … He tried to fly as many ground tracks as he could … to have as much fun as possible."

After the planes returned to Fairchild, Fleming confronted Dugue, the pilot of the lead plane, asking him why he allowed Holland to fly as low as he did.

According to Countess, Dugue replied, "You got to be kidding me. If they allow him to fly a fifty-foot fly-by at a change of command, do you think me telling anybody about him flying low at IR 300 is going to do any good? … I had my hands ready and was concerned only about my life and getting back safe on the ground."

Countess agreed. "A point well taken … when the whole wing staff sees a guy, basically tree-top level, and doesn't do anything about it, you have just given him the ability to steal."

Bud Holland's reckless flying had troubled Fleming for some time. He saw Holland as "a bad cop in a position of power." The Stan/Eval office was supposed to be "setting the standards and flying by the book." But Fleming said the other Stan/Eval pilots emulated Holland. "The office was corrupt. … The people there had an attitude that that's how they could fly. … And with a leader like that there to protect them," they weren't setting a good example. Fleming had unsuccessfully complained to his squadron commander and ops officers in the past. One ops officer asked Fleming if he, as a captain, really wanted to tell the operations group commander that his chief of Stan/Eval shouldn't be flying. Fleming was frustrated. "You got, 'He's about to retire,' or 'That's Bud Holland. He has more hours in a B-52 than you do sleeping.' … Yeah, he might have that many hours, but he became complacent, was reckless, and willfully violated regulations."

Fleming worked in the training flight, where he taught tactics and maneuvers. "For us in training flight, he undermined our authority, he undermined what we wanted to do with tactics because, in the debrief, when we tried to teach them something, he'd be saying, 'That's all bullshit; all you need to do is fly low.' … Colonel Holland liked to say that you weren't a man if you didn't fly below the clearance plane and basically espoused that attitude. … I often openly expressed to crews that he was not an example to follow and that he would end up killing himself."

Fleming had become a sounding board for crew complaints. He said, "Everybody had a Colonel Holland scare story." Fleming related a story of an Electronic Warfare Officer (E-Dub) who flew on one of Holland's aggressive flights. From his seat on the upper deck, the E-Dub "saw that the g meter was vertical and said, 'Hey … Sir, I think we have over-g'd the jet; I think we need to go back.' And he basically was told that you're just an E-Dub; you don't know anything. And when he looked back up, the needle had been cleared."

According to Fleming, Holland acted as "a single entity in a crew aircraft." He ignored the crew's inputs to climb or fly more conservatively. "I had several people come to me, especially radars and navigators, who would complain about that. … He seemed to enjoy making them uncom-fortable. … The nav teams came to me, expressed fear, and didn't want to fly with this person. … All of us in training flight actively subverted the schedule. We weren't gonna let him fly with our guys."

After the Black Rock Desert flight, Fleming was determined to do something about Lieutenant Colonel Holland. He conferred with several aircrew members and decided to make another push to ground the reckless pilot. He approached Maj Mark McGeehan, an ops officer who was about to put on the rank of lieutenant colonel and take command of the 325th Bomb Squadron.

Mark McGeehan had only been at Fairchild for about a year but was well liked by the air crews. They saw the young ops officer as a straight shooter, someone they could trust. Fleming said, "I went in one morning and talked to him for a couple of hours and said, 'Sir, I'm speaking for all the weapons officers here and for basically the entire crew force, and we don't think Colonel Holland should fly anymore. … The crew force really doesn't question his ability but his judgment. He's reckless.'"

Mark McGeehan was aware of Holland and the risk he posed. He as-sured Fleming he would put a stop to it.

There wasn't much time left. Fairchild was making yet another transi-tion and would soon fall under the Air Mobility Command. The 92nd Bomb Wing would become the 92nd Air Refueling Wing, the largest tanker wing in the Air Force. The 325th Bomb Squadron was scheduled to deactivate on 01 July 1994, and Fairchild's bombers, along with most of its support crews and pilots, were already in the process of moving to other bases.

Yakima Valley

In late February of 1994, at the age of 38, Lt Col McGeehan realized his dream of leading a B-52 squadron. He would only be in charge a few days before yet another "Lieutenant Colonel Holland scare story" occurred.

Capt Eric Jones had been at Fairchild for five years and was familiar with Holland. He had worked with him in Stan/Eval and flown with him on several occasions. Jones said, "Colonel Holland was an extremely aggressive pilot. He had the tendency to deviate from regulations. He was a very competitive individual who liked to demonstrate his superior capability to fly the B-52. ... He was very aggressive and was more aggressive at terrain avoidance flying than I cared to fly." After Jones unsuccessfully complained to his superiors about Holland's unsafe flying, he took other measures to protect himself and his crew. "I had gone over and kind of worked a deal with the schedulers not to schedule Colonel Holland to fly with us."

In March of 1994, Jones and his crew learned they were slated to fly a low-level bomb run in the Yakima Valley and were surprised to discover that Holland would be flying with them. Jones's concern grew when he learned why Holland had been put on their flight. The mission would double as a photo opportunity for civilian photographer Jim Benson. Benson was a well-known photographer of military aircraft and was working on a project he called "The Big Bomber Book." Benson wanted some close-up shots of a B-52 in flight, and according to Jones, "Bud told me that that's why he was going along, to be in the seat for Yakima and to make sure that he got the pictures." A Spokane news crew would also be on the ground to get footage for a documentary on Fairchild's B-52s. Jones was worried because those who knew Holland said he "was a showman—anytime a photographer was there he was going to give them a show. Just like the air shows. He was going to give them the best show he could."

On 10 March 1994, Jim Benson, the news crew, and a ground crew from Fairchild stood on a ridge overlooking the wide, flat desert of Yakima Valley as the B-52 came into view. Holland was in the pilot seat, and Jones was in the copilot seat. Before the photo session, the flight plan called for the crew to make three passes over a target, dropping one BDU-48 training bomb on each run. Holland was eager to start the photo op. As soon as he located the group on the ridge, he flew toward them and told the radar navigator to open the bomb doors. Jones recalls the radar navigator told Holland, "Not with weapons on board, I'm not going to do it."

Jones said, "I think Colonel Holland called him a pussy at that point." Holland flew over the ground crew and then set up for a pass over the bomb target. He convinced the radar navigator to drop all three BDU-48s on one pass.

According to Jones, Holland wanted to "get rid of the weapons and do the fly-bys." During mission planning, the minimum altitude for the valley was briefed at no less than 500 feet with 200–250 foot momentary crossovers as they flew by the camera crews. But Holland brought the plane down to within fifty feet of the valley floor. Jones recalls, "I told him that that was well below clearance plane, that we needed to climb. He ignored me. I told him as we approached the ridge line—I told him in three quick bursts, 'climb, climb, climb!' It appeared to me that he was fixating on the people on the ground. They were about a quarter of the way down from the top of the mountain and we were aimed right at them and, at the time, below their level." Jones didn't see how they were going to clear the mountaintop. "It appeared to me that he had target fixation. I said, 'climb, climb, climb' again. He did not do it. I grabbed hold of the yoke, and I pulled it back pretty abruptly."

Jones estimated they cleared the ridge by about fifteen feet. The crew on the lower deck yelled over the interphone, reprimanding Holland, telling him there was no need to fly that low. Jones said, "His reaction to that input was, he was laughing, I mean a good belly laugh." As Holland set up for another pass, Jones said, "Look, you know, I don't want to go that low. It's far too low, and I'm telling you I'm not comfortable there."

Holland laughed and said, "Well, if you've been doing this as many years as I have, you'll get used to it."

Jones tried a different tactic. "This is almost making me sick. Why don't you let me fly?"

Jones made a couple of higher passes over the ridge before relinquishing control back to Holland, who continued making lower and lower passes in spite of his crew's continued objections. Jones said, "The radar had told him that his scope had gone down to a dot. He was talking about how low and senseless that was." The radar altimeter had bottomed out, leading the lower deck crew to believe the aircraft was about to impact. Since they eject out the bottom of the aircraft they would have had no chance to escape.

As Holland passed over the ridge, he didn't make wide conservative turns to set up for another pass. Instead, Jones said, Holland "pulled the aircraft up aggressively to, I think the highest we reached was maybe forty-five degrees nose-high attitude. He would roll the airplane over on its side in excess of ninety degrees of bank."

Jones again asked for control of the airplane, and Holland said, "No, I'm going to fly this last pass." At that point a couple of A-10s came into the area, and Holland asked them if they wanted to join on his wing for a low pass. The A-10 pilots responded, "Well, we haven't briefed formation with you, but we'll hang off loose on your right side."

Jones said, "Holland asked them how low they could go, and they said, 'Five hundred feet is our minimum.' He goes, 'Five hundred feet? I'm going to be down at about fifty feet.'"

Holland flew toward the ground crew. As he climbed up the side of the valley, Jones again doubted they would clear the ridge. "Again I said, 'climb, climb, climb' ... it was like we were playing chicken in the airplane. ... He was going to push it as far as I would actually let him before I got on the yoke. ... I grabbed the yoke again. I pulled the airplane back. I told him I had the airplane. He was still attempting to fly it. ... I feared for my own life as well as the lives of the crewmembers on the airplane." Jones estimates they cleared the ridge by three feet. "Even with my action, I was unsure as to whether or not we had struck the bomb bay doors on the side of the ridge line." Holland didn't acknowledge Jones's attempt to take control of the airplane. "All he could do was laugh."

Jones's fears were well justified. Even when they were flown conservatively, it was not uncommon for B-52s to crash during noncombat missions. In 1984, a B-52 out of Fairchild flew a nighttime low-level training flight in a remote Arizona valley. The plane lost control when its right wing skipped off the top of a mesa. The plane momentarily pitched upward, giving six of the seven crewmembers a chance to eject before the plane impacted the rocky ground. Five of the crewmembers were injured and two were killed. Col William Ivy, the 92nd Bombardment Wing deputy commander of operations, was in the non-ejecting instructor pilot's seat and went down with the plane. The tail gunner, Sgt David Felix, died when his chute failed to fully deploy.

Eventually Captain Jones managed to get Lieutenant Colonel Holland out of the pilot seat by telling him that his copilot, 1st Lt Steve Hollis, needed some flying time. Jones said, "When Colonel Holland went downstairs, I leaned over, off the interphone, and I told Lieutenant Hollis that he was not to get out of that seat again, and I didn't care if Colonel Holland ordered him out." Jones said that as he and Hollis flew back to Fairchild, Holland wanted to get back in the pilot seat. "Bud made some kind of noises about wanting to get in for low-level." Jones insisted his copilot needed the training and reminded Holland, "He was just on there for Yakima and that Yakima was over with, and that he wasn't flying. He didn't press the issue any further."

Jones and his crew brought the B-52 back from the Yakima mission and landed safely at Fairchild. During their post-mission debrief, Jones talked about how they had deviated from the mission plan and violated regulations. Before he could confront Holland, the ground crew returned from Yakima, and everyone gathered in the training room to watch a video of the mission. On some of the passes the E-Dub had jettisoned chaff, and Jones said, "You could clearly see on the tape that the crossovers were very low. When you had chaff coming out of the airplane, it didn't have time to open. It was just hitting the ground as a full box. ... Colonel Holland watched the tape. He was very proud of his work. He commented that he would have had a lot lower crossovers had not 'Jonesie'—as he was referring to me—been pulling back on the yoke."

Jones said Holland indicated that the tape should probably be kept from public view until after he retired.

Holland and the photographer got into an extended conversation about the photography session. Holland was pleased to hear that Jim Benson had finally gotten the pictures he had lain awake dreaming of.

Jones waited for a chance to confront Holland. "Since I knew him on a personal level, it was my intention to pull him aside and tell him exactly what I thought." That chance never occurred, but Jones assured his wary crew, "I vowed to them that never again would they or I be subjected to flying with him."

A copy of the Yakima video circulated through the 325th Bomb Squadron. When it was played in the crew lounge, several experienced airmen couldn't believe the extremely low flying and even lower crossovers. After Navigator Captain Coppi saw video footage of the low crossovers he said, "There's no reason for that. Not in peacetime, not even in wartime with an F-86 flaming up your butt."

The day after the Yakima flight, Jones reported the incident to one of his ops officers, Maj Don Thompson. Major Thompson had also seen the video and had several questions. Jones spoke in detail about Holland's maneuvers and told Thompson, "I did not ever want to fly with Colonel Holland again, even if it meant that I couldn't fly anymore as an Air Force pilot."

Thompson didn't think it would come to that. Jones was joining a growing list of pilots who refused to fly with Holland.

Jones next met with the new squadron commander, Lieutenant Colonel McGeehan. "I not only told Lieutenant Colonel McGeehan everything that had happened on that flight; I went into some of the past history of flights I'd had with Lieutenant Colonel Holland, and I said that in my opinion, although I was a new instructor pilot, Lieutenant Colonel Holland was a dangerous pilot."

Jones was concerned about Holland flying in the upcoming air show and spoke with McGeehan for over an hour. "It was my intention to provide my commander with as much information as I possibly could, so that they could take steps to prevent him from flying in the air show." Jones went on to say that if Holland was to fly in the air show, he would not be anywhere near the airfield. "The best-case scenario is that he is going to crash and kill himself and the crew, and worst-case scenario, he's going to take out a bunch of spectators. And I didn't want to be a part of that."

Jones said, "Lieutenant Colonel McGeehan accepted everything I had to say. He agreed with me." McGeehan had seen videotapes of some of Holland's previous flights. Jones said, "He commented a couple of times about how he couldn't believe that he was making those types of maneuvers." McGeehan was also aware of, and hadn't forgotten, the deadly lesson of the Thunderhawk tragedy.

McGeehan interviewed the rest of Jones's crew and held a meeting with his operations officers. They all agreed that Holland should not be allowed to fly anymore; he needed to be grounded. McGeehan didn't have authority over Holland. Being the chief of Stan/Eval, Holland fell under the command of Colonel Pellerin, the commander of the 92nd Operations Group.

Jones said McGeehan assured him that he would make every effort to keep Holland from flying with his crews or on his airplanes again. "He vowed to me that he would take it up with the operations group and work the situation out."

Cannon AFB

The town of Clovis began as a railroad terminal in the early 1900s, when the Santa Fe Railway laid its tracks through New Mexico's high desert prairie. By 1994, Clovis had grown into an agricultural community of 30,000 residents and become a major railroad hub.

Clovis was also an Air Force town. If you were to stand in the railyard and look eight miles to the east, where the blue sky meets the treeless expanse of farm and grassland, you might see a fighter jet landing at Cannon Air Force Base. Cannon was the home of the 27th Fighter Wing, with its F-111 tactical strike aircraft.

Cannon's 2,500 military members and their families were isolated compared with those at other Air Force bases. The nearest big cities, Amarillo and Lubbock, were a hundred miles east, across the Texas border. Albuquerque was two hundred miles to the west. The area didn't offer much entertainment, especially for single airmen. But small bases like Cannon fostered a camaraderie not found at larger Air Force bases. Like the small town it neighbored, Cannon was a place with a strong sense of family.

No one at Cannon received any warning about Dean Mellberg's history. In the final days of February 1994, Cannon's PMEL received a last-minute notification that an airman who had been a patient at Wilford Hall had been assigned to their unit. MSgt Roberto Leal, the lab superintendent, telephoned Airman Mellberg to coordinate his arrival. He advised Mellberg that Cannon was not a good location if he was in need of long-term medical care. Master Sergeant Leal hoped Mellberg would volunteer the reason for his hospital stay, but instead he simply replied that he was no longer in need of medical care. Before getting off the phone, Leal took down the arrival time and date of Mellberg's flight and assured him that someone from the PMEL would be at Clovis Municipal Airport to meet him.

When an airman met Mellberg's plane, he wasn't on it. At 2300 that evening, Mellberg telephoned Leal at home asking to be picked up at the Albuquerque airport. Leal refused to send anyone that late in the evening, and besides, a 400-mile round trip was too far to drive. He instructed

Mellberg to get a room at nearby Kirtland AFB and fly into Clovis the following morning. On 1 March 1994, Mellberg arrived at Clovis Municipal Airport wearing his dress blues. When he was approached by the PMEL airmen who were there to meet him, Mellberg snapped to attention. The airmen found the unnecessary military demeanor strange, since they were both enlisted and Mellberg had been in the Air Force long enough to know better.

Mellberg stood out when he attended a newcomer's briefing. Maj Sally Whitener, the Commander of the 27th Component Repair Squadron (CRS), first noticed him as she welcomed the new arrivals to her squadron. She had a distinctly uncomfortable feeling that there was something wrong with Dean Mellberg. It was more than the way he looked at her with his yellow-encrusted, bloodshot eyes. Major Whitener's father had been a World War II Marine veteran and taught her to trust her instincts, and there was something about this airman that gave her the heebie-jeebies.

Mellberg moved into a room on the second floor of the CRS dormitory. It was an old dorm, with typically small rooms and a community bathroom and shower down the hall. Mellberg's roommate remembers he "smiled a lot, for no apparent reason, as if he was thinking about something." When his roommate asked him, "Where are you from?" Mellberg replied, "When I first meet someone, I try to get to know them for other reasons than where they are from." When asked "Where do you work?" he responded similarly: "I don't like to talk about those things until I get to know people."

Soon after he moved in, a few dorm residents were headed out for a beer and knocked on the "new guy's" door to invite him along. Mellberg stood silently in the doorway as they introduced themselves. When they asked if he wanted to go to the NCO club, he grunted, snorted, and closed the door in their faces. Mellberg continued to close himself off from his peers. Eric Kervina, an avionics technician, lived in the room across the hall from Mellberg. Like many of the dorm residents, Kervina worked the night shift and slept during the day. Mellberg worked the day shift and played his music loudly while his neighbors were trying to sleep. Each time Kervina knocked on Mellberg's door and asked him to turn his music down, Mellberg closed the door in his face and turned the music louder. When Kervina complained to the dorm manager, Mellberg accused him of lying.

Mellberg had few possessions besides his IBM computer, a stereo, and a chess set. His side of the room was sparsely decorated with a first-place chess trophy from Waverly High School and an unpainted model of a German Messerschmitt. On his dresser, he displayed a stuffed animal and a

Valentine's Day card from his mother. The only pictures adorning his walls were *Playboy* centerfolds.

Mellberg kept the room dark. He loosened the fluorescent tubes in the room's light fixture, causing them to emit a dim flickering glow. He used his computer to study his career development courses, and to play video games. He played Wolfenstein 3D, where he assumed the role of a US soldier navigating a maze of corridors and rooms, killing Nazi soldiers. He played video games until 0100 or 0200, even if he had to work in the morning. On weekends he played through the night and into the next day.

Mellberg's civilian attire appeared to have been purchased several years before he joined the military. His clothes were mismatched and out of style. At one squadron activity, he wore gray striped pants and a brown and green shirt, both several sizes too small.

He slept in the nude and often didn't put on clothes before trudging down the hall to the community bathroom staring silently at the floor. He frequently spent forty-five minutes in the shower, singing loudly in an operatic style.

Mellberg went through a series of roommates, who all asked to be relocated due to his indiscreet masturbation.

After one roommate discovered him performing his lewd activity in front of his girlfriend, he burst into the dorm manager's office complaining loudly. Mellberg denied the accusation and called his roommate a liar. Not long after Mellberg arrived at Cannon, all of the women on the first floor of the dormitories were moved to rooms on the second- or third-floor. The official reason given for the move was that it was for their safety. The rumor was that Mellberg had been detained by security police for peeping at women through their first-floor windows.

Despite Mellberg's aloofness, some of his fellow airmen continued to show him compassion. An airman who knew Mellberg from technical school saw that he always sat by himself in the chow hall. Remembering how it felt to be the new guy at a base, the airman sat and attempted to talk with him, but Mellberg's one-word responses made for an uncomfortable, one-sided conversation. Mellberg continued to push people away. He rejected invitations to play cards and join in other social activities. Aside from playing on the PMEL volleyball team he didn't socialize with anyone.

At work, Mellberg was described as a quiet person who mumbled to himself. He wore taps on his boots like a TI. They clicked on the tile floor as he walked through the lab, and they clacked when he snapped to attention, which he did whenever his co-workers approached. It was such a distraction that he had to be ordered to remove the taps.

During one of his shifts, Mellberg cut his finger with a razor blade. He stood in the lab watching his finger bleed until he was ordered to report to the emergency room.

Mellberg's supervisor, Sgt Patrick McGowan, said, "Mellberg was a substandard technician who daydreamed and laughed to himself a lot. ... As part of PMEL formal and on-the-job training, it is expected that at some time one will graduate to working on more complex equipment. The only task that he was certified on was calibrating torque wrenches."

On Mellberg's Enlisted Performance Review (EPR), McGowan rated Mellberg a 2—not recommended for promotion. The EPR showed Mellberg's work was untimely and of poor quality. His equipment labels were misspelled and illegible. His work area was messy and disorganized. He didn't understand the process of equipment accountability. He misplaced parts, equipment, and hand receipts. He misidentified equipment, he condemned equipment that was functioning properly, and sent tools out into the field that had not been calibrated. The EPR also showed that McGowan counseled Mellberg to speak up and to speak more clearly.

In addition to having limited skills, Mellberg also made unusual errors. On one occasion, instead of calibrating a torque wrench, he took it apart to see how it worked. Ball bearings flew out of the wrench and scattered across the lab floor. Mellberg lay on top of a rolling chair and scooted around the lab collecting ball bearings as his co-workers looked on in concerned amusement. McGowan said, "Soon after this incident, he was decertified on torque wrench calibration. I had him in a room one-on-one while I briefed him on his decertification. He said nothing. His eyes became bloodshot and teary and he looked distant. It was then that I left the room and requested supervisory back-up to finish my decertification discussion. I did not trust his demeanor."

Mellberg's behavior caused some of his co-workers to be leery of him. Others thought he was downright dangerous. During a squadron cookout, Mellberg took a kitchen knife from a picnic table and smiled as he strode through the family gathering, silently tapping the blade against the palm of his hand.

One of Mellberg's co-workers, Sgt Sam Prescott, predicted he would come to work with a gun, intent on killing. When he saw that Mellberg was scheduled to qualify with the M16 rifle, Prescott got approval from a supervisor to cancel his weapons training. Prescott's fear increased daily. He warned his co-workers not to be alone with Mellberg and to avoid gathering in groups while at work. Prescott made sure to sit near a door during lab meetings or stand in the hallway outside the room. Prescott's co-workers told him he was paranoid, but he was undeterred and reiterated his concern. "That kid's got postal worker's syndrome, and it's just a matter of time. When he goes, it's going to be at one of these meetings, and I'll be the only one to make it."

Prescott recalls a day in which he thought his prediction was coming true. He was working at a desk near the entrance of the lab when he heard the airlock door open. He looked up to see Mellberg holding a four-foot-long torque wrench case as if it were a rifle. Prescott backed into a corner and ducked behind a workbench. According to Prescott, Mellberg wore a "wicked grin" as he walked methodically through the laboratory tapping the side of the case with his hand. When he reached the end of the lab, he turned and slowly retraced his steps, leaving the lab with his surrogate rifle in hand.

Prescott said there was a group of people standing around in a "bullshit session" who hadn't noticed Mellberg. Prescott jumped out from behind the workbench and yelled, "Every one of you fuckers is gone! That was a practice run, he's gonna get you all!" Another co-worker who had taken Prescott's cue to hide ran across the room asking, "Did you see that? Did you see that?" Prescott responded, "Postal syndrome! Just wait. You and I will be the only ones to make it."

Prescott also feared Mellberg was stalking him. During a lunch break, Prescott drove to the base car wash. He was washing his car when Mellberg stepped around the corner into the bay, holding a sponge, asking if he needed help. Prescott later recalled, "This scared the shit out of me, because he had no car and no reason to be there."

Mellberg was failing at his job and had alienated himself from his co-workers and peers. The only thing he had going for him was his "girlfriend" back at Lackland AFB. On 17 March 1994, Mellberg sent a handwritten letter to Faith:

> To my sweet English girl
> I hope thee is well. It has been to long since we've seen one another. I miss you dearly. You're the joy in my life. The summer in my seasons. When we parted I felt a great

loss in my heart. I've been left to count the days from when I last set eyes on you. So beautiful I remember for all time. No other can compare to yours. Yours is a sight to which if you were in the heavens above it would shine brighter then the sun. And yet so gentle the moon fails in compareison. I wish we could be together forever. Oh! why is life so cruel. I can only hope that one day we will be together once more. I think I deserve your love more then ever for it is so empty without you. My life has little meaning now. If you come please tell me. I must arrange for your coming. Just let me know so I put more of you in my day. How soon till we meet again. I hope for the shortest time. A very very short time till we meet. I must be with you. Please come soon I'll be so patiently awaiting. May I say and this will not be the last. I love you.

On 25 March 1994, Mellberg sent Faith a postcard of a Pueblo Indian village. He wrote a short note asking if she was doing well, telling her everything was fine at Cannon "except it would be better if you were here. … I still need you Faith. … Enjoy your time in the big city, I wish I was still there. I love you, Dean."

Mellberg had only been at Cannon AFB for about a month before he found himself in trouble again. On Monday, 4 April 1994, at approximately 1530, the security police commander, Lt Col William Ruark, and Mellberg's first sergeant, CMSgt David Walker, were playing golf at the base golf course. They saw someone riding a bicycle across the back nine greens, taking a shortcut to the post office. It was Mellberg. Lieutenant Colonel Ruark was concerned that the bicyclist had damaged the greens and radioed the law enforcement desk, asking them to dispatch a patrolman. SSgt Mark Young made contact with Mellberg at the post office and detained him for suspicion of vandalism. He transported Mellberg to the 27th Security Police Squadron building. Young said Mellberg looked like a "deer in the headlights" as he got him settled in a chair in the interview room. When Young emerged from the room he told the desk sergeant, "There's something weird about this guy."

Lieutenant Colonel Ruark conferred with the greenskeeper and determined the golf course was not damaged. He advised the law enforcement desk to release Mellberg. Staff Sergeant Young entered the interview room to tell Mellberg he was free to go. Young emerged from the room looking perplexed, telling the desk sergeant, "He wants a lawyer." Young's flight chief went into the interview room and tried to convince Mellberg he was not being detained or charged with a crime. Mellberg stared silently at the wall.

Mellberg's first sergeant, CMSgt David Walker, responded and told Mellberg, "I am the component repair squadron first sergeant. You are not in any trouble and are going to be released. Do you understand?" Mellberg sat silent, staring blankly. After a while, Chief Walker emerged from the interview room and told the SPs, "That son of a bitch told *me* he wants a lawyer!"

Chief Walker called the CRS commander, Major Whitener, at her home and explained the situation. Based on Mellberg's behavior, they suspected he might be under the influence of illegal drugs or medication. Whitener advised the chief to take Mellberg to the 27th Medical Group emergency room for a urinalysis. The ER staff were concerned Mellberg was either on drugs or in need of medication. They noted his eyes were glazed over and that he stared at the walls and was unresponsive to their questions.

The ER staff went to pull Mellberg's medical records, but they were gone. In their place was a note indicating his records had been checked out to family practice, although he had no recent medical appointments. Chief Walker went to Mellberg's room looking for medication or other signs that Mellberg may be suffering from a medical condition. The chief found Mellberg's missing medical records strewn across his bed. All records pertaining to mental health had been removed and set aside. Chief Walker gathered what records he could find and returned to the ER.

Mellberg refused to provide a urine sample and remained silent other than asking for the phone number of the ADC. Major Whitener arrived at the ER to find Mellberg lying on a hospital bed staring at the ceiling. She asked Mellberg, "Do you know who I am?" Mellberg sat up as if at attention and stared straight ahead replying, "Yeah, you're my commander." Whitener said Mellberg was "totally out of it ... like a zombie," and she thought he was "on something." She assured Mellberg he was not in trouble, that they just wanted to help him. She said, "I am ordering you to submit to a urinalysis." When Mellberg refused, Whitener picked up a nearby catheter, telling him he could voluntarily provide a sample or they would stick it up his penis and get one. Mellberg's voluntarily-provided urine sample showed no indications of illegal drug use.

Maj Deborah Garrett, a social worker with Cannon's mental health center, responded to the ER at about 2000, but Mellberg refused to speak to her without a lawyer. The ER contacted the Area Defense Counsel (ADC), Capt Melinda Davis-Perritano, who advised Mellberg to talk. Mellberg spoke minimally to Garrett, saying he was afraid he was in trouble and refused to talk with the security police. Although he continued his evasive, defensive behavior, the ER doctors couldn't find anything physically wrong with Mellberg. At 2300, he was released from the ER, and Chief Walker dropped him off at his dorm room.

The following day Major Whitener began making phone calls, hoping to learn more about Mellberg's background.

Whitener contacted the PMEL superintendent at Fairchild AFB, who explained that Mellberg was sent to Cannon from Wilford Hall because Fairchild's PMEL was transitioning to civilian contractors. Whitener said the superintendent warned her that there were two things she needed to understand about Mellberg. "One is this guy scared me. Two, you gotta be careful; his mother knows people."

Whitener called Fairchild's mental health center and Wilford Hall's psychiatric ward. In addition to providing her with Mellberg's mental health history, Whitener said the physicians at Wilford Hall warned her about Lois Mellberg's influence with her local congressman.

When Whitener finished her phone calls, she had a better understanding of Mellberg's mental state but she could not understand why people were apparently so afraid of his mother as to allow her to influence their decisions.

Whitener called Mellberg to her office. Now that she knew his background, the way he looked at her scared her even more. She verbally reprimanded him for riding his bike on the golf course and for refusing to speak to her and the first sergeant on the previous night. She ordered him to go to mental health for an evaluation and assured him, "We're here to help you, not hang you."

The first sergeant, Chief Walker, called the PMEL superintendent, MSgt Roberto Leal, into his office and informed him of Mellberg's mental health history. When Master Sergeant Leal left the office, he wondered why the PMEL hadn't been notified of Mellberg's problems. He also wondered why Mellberg was still in the Air Force. Leal returned to the lab and called a meeting of the supervisors. He told them he did not want Mellberg left alone with anyone, especially the females.

The next day Mellberg went to his command-directed mental health appointment, where he met again with social worker Major Garrett. He denied being suicidal or homicidal but otherwise refused to cooperate with Garrett, telling her that he didn't want to be evaluated. At a follow-up appointment, he met with psychologist Capt Lisa Snow, chief of mental health services. Dr. Snow noted Mellberg "exhibited a rather stiff, defensive posture." He refused to answer many of her questions and when he did respond, his answers were cryptic. Dr. Snow had acquired Mellberg's mental health records from Fairchild and Wilford Hall, and when she tried to get him to clarify something from his records, "He refused to talk about anything in his past." Dr. Snow noted she was "unable to fully ascertain the existence or nonexistence of delusions or thought disorder due to patient's uncooperativeness."

At a follow-up appointment on 20 April 1994, Mellberg was administered two psychological tests, the MMPI-2 and MCMI. According to his records, the results of the testing "were almost identical to the results of the ones given to him by Dr. London at Fairchild AFB." The test results were invalid and distorted, suggesting Mellberg intentionally presented only his "good side."

With Mellberg refusing to talk, Dr. Snow was forced to use his "mental health records and discharge summaries from his previous evaluations, as well as psychological testing" to reach a diagnosis. On 05 May 1994, Dr. Snow wrote a memorandum to Major Whitener. The memo parroted the last diagnosis Mellberg received from Wilford Hall—autistic disorder and paranoid personality disorder. Dr. Snow wrote, "Administrative separation should be considered if this condition manifests in behavior which interferes with military service." Dr. Snow wrote a narrative summary of Mellberg's involvement with military mental health and ended the memo with a warning:

> This individual's behavior is evasive and unpredictable. His communication skills are marginal, at best. His history suggests long-standing psychopathology that is highly resistant to change, especially with his lack of insight into his inappropriate behavior. It is strongly advised that this individual be separated from the Air Force.

This was at least the fifth time mental health professionals had recommended Mellberg for discharge from the United States Air Force. Whitener intended to heed the advice of Dr. Snow and was aware that previous attempts to discharge Mellberg had failed. Over the next several days, she worked closely with the base legal office to ensure the discharge paperwork was done "by the book."

On 10 May 1994, a co-worker observed Mellberg sitting in the dining hall by himself. The co-worker said, he "appeared really happy about something; he was sitting at a table eating a banana and appeared to be elated with it."

His demeanor was about to change. On 11 May 1994, Major Whitener prepared for a meeting with Mellberg by borrowing a bullet-resistant vest from the security police and making sure several members of her staff would be on hand. When Mellberg arrived with his briefcase, she feared it might contain a weapon and told him to leave it outside the room. Whitener read Mellberg a Letter of Notification informing him that based on the mental health report of 5 May 1994, he was found to have an autistic disorder and paranoid personality disorder, and she was recommending he be discharged from the Air Force. She advised him that her recommendation and supporting documents would be forwarded to the separation authority, who would make the final decision. She informed him of his right to military counsel and that she had made him an appointment with the ADC. She told him he was to report immediately to the separation section to pick up an out-processing checklist and complete it by 13 May 1994.

Mellberg stared silently at the major. When she finished the letter she asked, "Airman Mellberg, do you have any questions?"

Mellberg replied, "You're doing this to me? Why are you doing this to me?"

Whitener responded, "Airman Mellberg, I'm not doing this to you. You're doing this to yourself. I am only recommending your discharge to the separation authority."

Whitener didn't tell Mellberg that the separation authority was the base commander, to protect him from becoming a target. After the meeting, Whitener warned the security police, the base legal office, and the mental health center that Mellberg had been served with the Letter of Notification.

Discharged

During his separation process, Airman Mellberg worked in the component repair squadron orderly room. This allowed Major Whitener and Chief Walker to keep an eye on him; it also afforded him time to work on his rebuttal letter to the separation authority. And it kept him away from the PMEL. Mellberg not only wrote his rebuttal letter, he wrote another letter to his congressman and filed yet another IG complaint.

In his complaint to the office of the inspector general, he alleged that a Department of Defense (DoD) directive requiring advance written notice of mental health referrals was violated. He hoped that by claiming the Air Force hadn't followed the rules, they would be obligated to retain him. On 11 May 1994, Mellberg typed out an Inspector General Action Request form to "seek redress for violation of Public Law 102-484." His complaint continued:

> On April the fourth 1994 I was brought to the Cannon AFB emergency room by my First Sergent Chief Walker of the CRS Squadrun. I was addmited and examed by the staff on duty that night. Once done with the physical exam I was seen by a mental health professional which is a violation of Public Law 102–484 for my commander did not direct any evaluation to take place in writing. The day after I had to see a mental health professional virbally, but not in writing. This is twice this regulation was violated. I request that no reprisal upon me will take into affect by the mental health or by the CRS Squadrun for thier inappropriate actions taken.

Along with the complaint form, Mellberg attached a four-page typed letter addressed to the "Inspector General of the Department of Defence:" He wrote:

First of all it would be an extreme pleasure to have you look in to this action request. Your duration as Inspector General has brought an improved Air Force for its members and the American people as well. For that reason I am certain many people are indebted to you and I am quite certain that you will continue accomplishing monumental events for many more people.

I've in the process of receiving a discharge. … This possible discharge has taken place in an inappropriate manor and has falsely discredited my career. My rights under Public Law [and the] Rights of the Mentally Ill have been violated.

Mellberg listed the names of his current and previous commanders and first sergeants as well as the names of his doctors at Fairchild, Wilford Hall Medical Center, and Cannon. He quoted multiple laws and regulations and alleged numerous violations, specifically Public Law 102-484, enacted to protect military members from mental health referral in reprisal for blowing the whistle on fraud, waste, or abuse.

Mellberg also typed a letter to the separation authority, who would decide whether to retain or discharge him. The separation authority was Brig Gen William Guth, the commander of the 27th Fighter Wing, Cannon Air Force Base. In the first part of the rambling eight-page letter, Mellberg listed fifteen individuals by name and described what he perceived as violations of his rights made at basic training, Fairchild, Wilford Hall Medical Center, and Cannon. He complained that he had not been notified in writing prior to his many referrals to mental health. He complained that he was not afforded an opportunity to consult with an attorney or chaplain prior to his mental health evaluations. He alleged that he had not been informed of the reason for the evaluations. He also alleged that he was refused the right to be evaluated by a mental health professional of his own choosing while at Wilford Hall. He quoted sections of "Public Law" the "Rights of the Mentally Ill" and the "Whistle blower protection act." He wrote, "None of the areas mandated aloft were furnished to me when analysis at mental health were conducted for these periods. If these details were obeyed then I would desire to petition for duplicities of this information."

As the letter went on, Mellberg alluded to his commitment to die seeking revenge for his perceived injustices. He claimed that his request for a complete copy of his medical records had only been partially fulfilled. Mellberg wrote, "If these records are refused me for any purpose I have asked that they be supplied to my next of kin."

The letter continued with Mellberg complaining that "multitudinous things have been transcribed in my records which are rumor, hearsay, errors, slander and/or libelous." Mellberg attacked Dr. Snow's report extensively, pointing out minute errors such as being transported to the ER by his first sergeant as opposed to the security police. Mellberg listed several examples of statements that Dr. Snow copied from his records to justify her recommendation for discharge from the Air Force. He was particularly distressed that Dr. Snow quoted his Wilford Hall records "and again his administrative separation from the Air Force was recommended." Mellberg refuted this:

> The only statement which the medical board goes on to say is 'Return to duty for administrative disposition.' … I will add as a last note as far as Captain Snow's report of me does not say that I need treatment of any sort from now on and she does not even go into what sort of an environment might be best suited to myself. … There is nothing to indicate I need further treatment and so there is a good possibility that I am functioning well and have the ability to do as others around me. I am being retaliated against and punished for invoking my Fifth Amendment rights against self incrimination.
>
> As for any Paranoid Personality Disorder I was Medical Boarded on that and found to be perfectly alright. After more than three months of being evaluated … I still remain in the Air Force after all the evaluation that was done. … Now one evaluation has brought me to the Separation Authority again over Paranoid Personality Disorder and Autism. This shouldn't even be a consideration for separation because a medical board of psychiatrists found me fit for duty.
>
> Even if this possible discharge end process were to return myself back to duty I will still seek redress under PL102–484 and DoD Directive 6490.1 for this has greatly harmed not only my career, but has put me under great distress.

Mellberg went on to blame his poor work performance on the stress of being hospitalized: "I am still recovering from my stay at Wilford Hall Medical Center."

Toward the end of the letter Mellberg wrote, "All that I needed for help in get over the stay in a psychiatric ward was the love and affection to which I have seen very little of in the beginning of my career. You could help me now if this decision at all and help me see that there is caring and understanding left."

Mellberg's IG complaint was forwarded to Major Whitener. In a detailed narrative, she effectively refuted the allegations using several attachments, including mental health referral letters signed by Mellberg.

On 12 May 1994, Mellberg began out-processing. Master Sergeant Leal escorted him to the separations section, where he received a checklist and listened to an out-processing briefing. He would need to attend a transition assistance briefing, which would help him write a résumé and prepare him for interviews in the civilian job market. He would need to obtain a temporary ID card and receive a final medical examination. The briefing was a reality check for Mellberg. He sweated profusely and his eyes were big and wild as he stood at attention listening to the instructions. Afterward, he was silent except to say, "I did not know my commander had that much power."

The next several days were stressful for Leal as he escorted Mellberg to his appointments. He was afraid of the younger and stronger airman but accepted the responsibility and worked to build a rapport with Mellberg. He encouraged him to focus on life outside of the Air Force. He asked about his plans after his discharge. Where would he go? What kind of work would he look for? Mellberg always answered, "I don't know."

The more time Leal spent with Mellberg, the more uncomfortable he felt. He was afraid to turn his back on him. No matter how hard Leal tried, Mellberg always managed to slip behind him as they walked to his appointments. Leal noticed Mellberg had frequent and sudden mood swings. He transitioned from happy and joking to staring blankly to laughing out loud. Leal said one thing that never changed was his lack of a plan for what he would do when he got out of the Air Force.

Mellberg hoped his military legal counsel would fight his discharge. On Friday, 13 May 1994, he met with the ADC, Captain Davis-Perritano, and gave her a stack of documents, including medical records. A typical separation takes three days, and Davis-Perritano claimed her schedule prevented her from immediately reviewing the documents and researching the law. She requested and received a delay of discharge from Major Whitener until close of business on 24 May 94.

Master Sergeant Leal knew that every appointment was one step closer to the end of Mellberg's military career. Yet the whole time he escorted him he sensed that Mellberg never believed he would be discharged. It was as if Mellberg were waiting for someone to put a stop to it. Leal knew Mellberg had called his mother several times, and he got the impression she was going to help him somehow. On 16 May 1994, as they were about to leave for an appointment, Leal got a glimpse of Mellberg's plan. He was anxious to send a fax, and when Leal asked if it was for official business, Mellberg smirked and proudly showed him a three-page letter he had written to Michigan congressman Dave Camp. As Leal read the letter, he sensed that Mellberg had asked for the congressman's help in the past, and he wondered if that was why Mellberg was still in the Air Force.

Along with the letter, Mellberg faxed a privacy release form to his congressman. On it he scrawled a note reminiscent of a message in a bottle:

> I have been falsely discredited and am being wrongfully discharged from the United States Air Force. I was evaluated by mental health on April 20th 1994 and was not informed of my rights ... On Jan 4, 1994 a medical board recommended return to duty. Now I am being administratively discharged. I have only 3 days to respond.

In Mellberg's letter to Congressman Camp, he referred to him as a senator:

> Dear Honorable Dave Camp: First of all it is a extreme pleasure to have you as Senator of Michigan. Your duration in office has brought an improved way of life for Michigan and it's residents. You have not only the abounding interest of Michigan, but the United States of America as well. For that reason I am certain we're all indebted to you and the public in general knows you will continue accomplishing monumental events for our state.

The remainder of the three pages was similar to the letter he wrote to the separation authority. He alleged that his records contained "many things … which are hearsay, errors, slander or libelous" and expressed a desire to have his records corrected. He again requested copies of various records and again intimated his intent to die for his cause. "If these records are denied me for any reason I have asked that they be supplied to my next of kin."

Mellberg never received a response from Congressman Camp. While he waited to be discharged, his behavior grew increasingly bizarre. He knocked on dorm residents' doors late at night, and when they answered he stood silently smiling in the hall. Mellberg's frustration with his legal counsel's apparent inaction manifested in stalking behavior. On three occasions he was observed standing outside the base legal office staring at the building for extended periods.

On 23 May 1994, Brigadier General Guth signed off on Airman First Class Mellberg's discharge. He issued a memorandum stating, "Based upon A1C Mellberg's Personality Disorder, he will be discharged from the US Air Force with an Honorable Discharge. A1C Mellberg will be discharged at the earliest possible date under the provisions of AFR 39-10 … for Conditions that Interfere with Military Service … A1C Mellberg is not a suitable candidate for probation and rehabilitation and, as such, it will not be offered to him."

Whitener gave Mellberg his discharge package in a sealed envelope and directed him to take it to the separations section for final out-processing. When Leal escorted Mellberg from her office, she called the separations section and warned them that Mellberg was on his way. She cautioned them not to leave anyone alone with him. Leal recalls the discharge struck Mellberg as a complete surprise. On the way to separations, Mellberg asked Leal if he could re-enlist in a different branch of service. Leal responded evasively. "Maybe not in the Air Force, but I don't know about the other services."

Mellberg was issued a temporary ID card that granted him sixty days of medical care and two years of Base Exchange and Commissary shopping privileges. He refused to give an address where he wanted his household goods shipped. The separations personnel used his parents' address listed on his emergency data card to finish their paperwork. Leal couldn't understand why Mellberg didn't offer his parents' address; after all, Mellberg had been in contact with his mother several times. When Mellberg repeatedly asked, "What if I don't want to go there?" Leal got the impression he was afraid to go home. Mellberg gave Leal power of attorney authorizing him to oversee the packing of his household goods. When he was finished out-processing Leal offered to take Mellberg to the scheduled airline ticket office to pick up his tickets home. Mellberg refused. Leal asked where he was going to spend the night and Mellberg said he didn't know. Leal picked a motel out of the Yellow Pages and drove Mellberg to the Motel 6 on Mabry Drive in Clovis. When Mellberg was settled in his room, Leal offered to pick him up the following day so he could get his tickets home and offered to take him to the airport or bus station.

The next day, Leal was at the dorm preparing to have Mellberg's household goods shipped. He went down to check on Mellberg's Murray eighteen-speed bicycle and saw Mellberg riding by on another bicycle. Mellberg rode behind a brick wall and hid. When he peeked his head around the corner, Leal called him over and asked what he was doing on the base. Mellberg said he was going to see his legal counsel. Leal told him to be sure to return the bicycle to its rightful owner, and Mellberg rode off.

Mellberg called Leal later that day and asked if he could help him move out of the motel. Leal was relieved, thinking that Mellberg was finally going home. But when he picked him up, Mellberg revealed that he had checked into billeting (the base temporary lodging facility, similar to a motel). During the ride back to base, Mellberg asked Leal about used cars for sale on the base. He also asked if Cannon had a campground. As Leal dropped Mellberg off at billeting he told him he needed to go home and find a job. He needed to get on with his life. Before he drove away, Leal wished him luck in the civilian world and resolved to cut himself off from Dean Mellberg.

Mellberg had no intentions of leaving Cannon. He had declined his plane ticket home, opting instead for the equivalent value in cash. Leal said, "The entire time I escorted him was very stressful for me. Just turning him loose on the streets did not make me feel any better." Master Sergeant Leal grew increasingly concerned for the safety of his family and his troops. He had read Mellberg's records and knew he was an expert shot with the M16. He also knew that at one time Mellberg had access to a recall roster listing all of his co-workers' home addresses. He warned the lab personnel to be on the lookout for Mellberg. Leal also voiced his concerns to his superiors, telling them, "Mellberg should have been treated differently since he was a mental case and not your average problem child. … He should have been given his plane tickets and escorted to the airport. Maybe a chaplain should have contacted his parents and explained the situation so they could try and convince him to come home." Leal said, "My impression was they simply wanted to wash their hands of the entire situation. Mellberg was no longer their problem. I told them I didn't think we had heard the last of Mellberg."

Mellberg spent the next two days hanging out in the dormitory. He hung out in the dorm room of two airmen, watching movies late into the night until they eventually asked him to leave so they could get some sleep. He asked several airmen to take him into town, offering to treat them to dinner and movies and pay for their gas. Most declined, but one airman took pity on Mellberg and drove him to Clovis where they played miniature golf.

On 25 May 1994, Whitener asked the base commander to issue a letter barring Mellberg from Cannon Air Force Base. The security police went to Mellberg's billeting room to serve him with the debarment letter, but he was not there. The dorm residents were asked to be on the lookout for Mellberg and contact the base police if they saw him.

Deployed

In November 1993, word came down that our flight needed to provide an E-4 for a temporary duty assignment to Riyadh, Saudi Arabia. The only E-4s on our flight were me and the woman I was dating. So naturally I volunteered and was sent to Riyadh. We worked twelve-hour shifts guarding an air base and other resources in heat that I had never experienced and never got used to. There was no off-duty entertainment to speak of, and the US military didn't allow us to consume alcohol since it was against Saudi law. I spent what free time I had in a tent that served as our gym, lifting weights and riding an exercise bike. When we returned to Fairchild ninety-nine days later, I discovered the woman I had been dating was seeing someone else. In hindsight I should have let her go to Saudi Arabia. But I was better off without her, and the time I spent in the desert allowed me to reach a new height of physical fitness.

The next four months were relatively uneventful. In mid-June I took a week of leave and returned to Port Orchard to catch up with my family and friends. I met up with a longtime friend, Morgan Johnson, and we got in some target practice just before I returned to Fairchild.

The afternoon of 20 June 1994, was my second day working our squadron's newly developed bike patrol. Instead of the usual uniform, I wore black athletic shoes, black shorts, and a black nylon duty belt, which held my radio case, holster, spare magazine, handcuff cases, and a three-cell Maglite that I carried day or night. Over my bullet-resistant vest, I wore a white polo shirt with a security police badge embroidered on the front and the word POLICE in large black letters on the back. The vest was hot and uncomfortable. But as I told my co-workers, you never know when you are going to need it, and they don't work if you're not wearing them.

I couldn't wear our beloved blue beret on bike patrol. Instead I was issued a bicycle helmet. The helmet was ridiculously bulky, consisting of about four inches of styrofoam covered in blue nylon fabric. It was the same styrofoam that cheap six-pack coolers are made of, and I probably would have looked just as professional if I strapped a beer cooler on my head. But I wore the helmet.

At about 1300, I stepped out of my dorm room and met up with A1C Dan Singer. We walked across the parade ground to the 92nd Security Police Squadron. The squadron building housed our armory, confinement cells, interview rooms, and administration offices. It was also the location of the law enforcement desk which was our communications center. Once at the squadron we headed to the armory window and got in line for equipment issue. When I approached the window, the armorer placed a radio and two fifteen-round magazines of ammunition in front of me. I put the radio and one of the magazines in their cases on my belt while the armorer disappeared among the racks of M16 rifles and M9 pistols. When he returned, he told me my assigned handgun had been tagged for maintenance and that I would be issued a temporary firearm, one identical to mine but one I had never fired. I reluctantly accepted the unfamiliar handgun, its slide locked to the rear, and carried it muzzle up to the clearing barrel. After conducting a function check of the pistol, I loaded and holstered the Beretta. I flipped the safety lever to the fire position and fastened the thumb-break strap, saying, "Well, I guess it would shoot somebody."

After everyone armed up, we fell in for guard mount to receive our duty assignment and any pertinent information from our flight chief, MSgt John Shenk, whose call sign was Police 1. I was assigned the call sign of Police 6 and told to concentrate on patrolling the housing areas. We watched a training video on how to respond to mass casualty incidents before being released to go to our assigned posts and patrols.

I met up with the off-going bike patrolman in front of the squadron. I inspected the bicycle, put on my helmet, and rode off. It was about 1400 when I headed to the on-base housing areas to begin my patrol.

The radio was quiet, a welcome relief. Bike patrol was a new concept to the Air Force, and the desk sergeant on my previous shift hadn't considered my mode of transportation when she dispatched me. I was sent to relieve a gate guard for a latrine break on one side of the base before being sent miles away in the opposite direction to run another errand. My legs were pretty worn out. So for more reasons than just the pleasant weather, I was enjoying the quiet day.

As I rode down the sidewalks and streets of the housing areas, I greeted residents who were watering lawns and washing cars and waved to kids who were running through sprinklers. After patrolling the on-base housing, I rode down a path to the Offutt gate, located at the intersection of Offutt and Graham Road. I intended to patrol south on Graham in the area of our base hospital and the two housing areas on either side of it. But first, I ducked into the air-conditioned gate shack. I visited with my friend A1C Herb Simpson as he checked the ID cards of vehicle occupants seeking entry to the base. Simpson and I were discussing plans to go to the gym that evening when a call came over the radio.

Senior Airman Brown, Riyadh, Saudi Arabia 1994.

Mister Mellberg

On 26 May 1994, Dean Mellberg was spotted on Cannon Air Force Base. He was holding a briefcase, standing at attention in the pouring rain staring at the legal office building. The Security Police had not yet served Mellberg with his debarment letter but by the time they were notified, he had disappeared. At midnight Mellberg was spotted inside the CRS dormitory, but left after he heard a resident calling the security police.

The SPs found Mellberg at about 0430. He was walking up and down a side road talking to himself with his arms outstretched to the cold desert sky. The SPs noted his T-shirt and jeans were soaking wet and he was shivering and dazed. They detained him and advised him that he had been barred from the base. Mellberg refused to accept or sign the debarment letter. The SPs were concerned for his welfare and feared he was unable to care for himself. They placed him in the back of a patrol car and headed to the base emergency room. As they drove, Mellberg refused to speak other than to object to being called "Airman Mellberg." As he was no longer in the Air Force, he requested they call him "Mister Mellberg." At the emergency room, one of the SPs noticed Mellberg kept eyeing his gun.

The ER was unable to provide Mellberg with long-term care. The SPs transported him to Clovis High Plains Medical Center where he was uncooperative, refusing to answer most of the civilian medical staff's questions. He told a nurse that he had a grievance with the Air Force for being wrongfully discharged. He would not talk to anyone in a military uniform and communicated with the SPs through the nurse. He told her he intended to return to Cannon to retrieve a bicycle, suitcases, and other property. When the SPs told Mellberg they would bring him his property, he declined. The physicians at High Plains said they could not admit Mellberg since they did not have a psychiatric ward.

When the SPs offered to take Mellberg to a motel, the nurse asked him if he had money to pay for a room. He angrily told her his finances were none of her business. The SPs had exhausted their available options and could do nothing but stand idly by as Mellberg was released from the hospital. They watched as he walked away from the hospital and disappeared into the streets of Clovis.

Sgt Sam Prescott feared barring Mellberg from Cannon wasn't the appropriate way to handle the situation. He warned Master Sergeant Leal, "We ought to at least call his parents. We got a twenty-year-old with mental problems we gave an ID card to and then tell him he can go to any other base but this one. Go be a problem elsewhere but not here please … He has no friends, no girlfriend, and there's only one reason he would still be in town. I believe he's waiting out his five-day mandatory waiting period for a gun purchase, and guess what. You're about number four on his list."

The next day, Mellberg entered the Sunwest Bank in Clovis, carrying a large brown paper bag that appeared to be stuffed full of clothing. He walked out, turned, and reentered the bank three times before finally making contact with an alarmed employee. Mellberg whispered haltingly, eventually communicating that he wanted to withdraw his savings and close his account. He appeared so disoriented, the teller thought he might have been drunk or on drugs. The bank employees took extra precautions before closing his account and even contacted Mellberg's first sergeant. After determining everything was in order, they processed the transaction.

Mellberg had sent several thousand dollars home for his mother to invest but he still had well over $6,000 in the bank. The teller tried to convince him to take at least part of his savings in traveler's checks, but he insisted on cash, preferably fifties and hundreds. The teller counted the bills out onto the counter, and Mellberg scooped up the cash. He slid a hundred-dollar bill to the teller and said, "This is for you, since you were friendly and really helpful." The teller told him she could not accept the money. Mellberg laid a second and then a third hundred on the counter, and when the teller continued to reject the gratuity he tucked all of the cash in the cloth bank bag the teller provided him and left.

Later that day, Mellberg entered the Hat Barn western clothing store. He bought a pair of Roper boots, Wrangler jeans, a Brush-Popper shirt, an Australian Outback hat, and a black duster coat. After paying for the new outfit, he asked an employee to call him a limousine.

The dispatcher at White Castle Limousine service was unable to locate her driver, and by the time she called the Hat Barn the store was closed. She drove by the store in her personal car and saw Mellberg sitting on a nearby fence. After determining he had called for a limo, she asked Mellberg where he wanted to be driven. He replied, "I don't know. I want to go to Amarillo or Albuquerque. I don't care." She informed him she could not provide him with a limousine today and asked him to call and schedule one tomorrow.

Mellberg asked the woman where she was going. She said she was taking her family to Lubbock, a two-hour drive. Mellberg asked, "How much would you charge me to go with you?"

When she told him she could not take him with her, he abruptly replied, "At least take me to the base!"

An acquaintance of the woman, a civilian contractor on the base, drove up to see if she needed assistance. He agreed to give Mellberg a ride. As they drove to the base, the man attempted to carry on a conversation with Mellberg, but he made it clear he did not want to talk. Not knowing that Mellberg had been barred from base, the man drove to the main gate, and was waved on to the base by the guard.

Mellberg went to the CRS dorm and tried to find someone to go into town with him. The dorm residents almost didn't recognize him in his western attire, so unlike his usual hand-me-down clothes. The SPs were called, but Mellberg was gone upon their arrival. One SP eventually tracked him down outside Amici's, a restaurant on base. When the SP handcuffed and searched Mellberg he noted his new clothes still had the price tags attached. He transported Mellberg off base and released him. About an hour and a half later, Mellberg called the law enforcement desk and told them he had left a bag in the CRS dormitory. The SPs found a plastic garbage bag in the day room containing $6392 and some clothing. They met Mellberg at the main gate and reunited him with his property.

On Saturday, 28 May 1994, Mellberg arranged for a White Castle Limousine to take him to Lubbock, Texas. According to the driver, when he picked Mellberg up at the Clovis Holiday Inn, he was wearing his western outfit and carrying a plastic garbage bag full of clothing. Before leaving town, the driver asked Mellberg if he "wanted to get some booze." Mellberg told the driver he was not twenty-one and was against drinking and smoking. The driver bought Mellberg a Coke from McDonald's instead. Over the course of the two-hour trip, Mellberg didn't talk other than to ask how to raise the privacy partition. He did make four calls from the limousine's car phone, three to the Cannon AFB operator and one to the second floor of the CRS dormitory.

When the limo arrived in Lubbock, Mellberg told the driver he wanted to go to a club. The driver headed to Cowpokes, an eighteen-and-over western club. As they arrived, Mellberg saw some women getting out of a car and yelled at them from the window of his limousine. When the women waved back, Mellberg jumped out of the limo and trotted into the club after them. The driver waited in the parking lot and checked on Mellberg several times. Each time, he observed Mellberg sitting by himself, not interacting with anyone. An hour and a half later, Mellberg came out, and the driver took him to another nightclub and a topless bar, but he was turned away from each for being underage, which caused him to pout in the back seat of the limo. The driver took Mellberg to The Tunnel, an alternative rock club. Mellberg went into the club and returned for his bag so he could change into a T-shirt and jeans. He stayed until closing and then stood up through the sunroof of the limo, grunting at the women who walked out of the club into the parking lot. After Mellberg told the driver he wanted to stay in Lubbock, he dropped him off at the Sheridan Hotel. Mellberg paid the round-trip fare of $360 plus a $17 tip.

The following day Mellberg flew from Lubbock to San Antonio and made his way to Lackland Air Force Base.

Return to San Antonio

Around midnight on Sunday, 29 May 1994, Dean Mellberg appeared at Faith's dorm room door. She was shocked to see him and refused to let him inside. Instead, she put on a robe and walked him to the day room, where the two could talk. Mellberg told her he had been discharged from the Air Force and he was headed to Alaska. He said he hoped the move would allow him to make a fresh start. Faith wondered what Mellberg would do for work in Alaska and asked him how he was going to survive. Mellberg pulled a large knife out of his bag saying, "This is how." He said that he and his brother had hunted before, when they were younger. He begged Faith to accompany him to Alaska, but she declined, telling him she had a boyfriend. Mellberg looked surprised and saddened by the news. He told Faith, "I thought we would get back together." Faith told him they were never together in the first place.

Over the next few days, Mellberg tagged along with Faith and her boyfriend. On one occasion as they wandered around downtown San Antonio, Mellberg skipped down the sidewalk ahead of them, laughing to himself. When Faith showed interest in a statue across the street, Mellberg darted through heavy traffic to read the inscription. When he dodged back through traffic to tell Faith what he had learned, she told him, "That was a really stupid and dangerous thing to do!" Mellberg laughed and continued skipping down the sidewalk.

When Mellberg was alone with Faith, he continued to press her to marry him. When he began making sexual advances, Faith told her boyfriend, who confronted Mellberg and told him if he continued, things would get "ugly." The boyfriend's threat didn't seem to upset Mellberg, but afterward Faith said he looked at her as if she had betrayed him.

Shortly before Mellberg was scheduled to fly to Alaska, he met Faith in the foyer of her dormitory to say goodbye. He again tried to convince her to come with him to Alaska, but she refused. Mellberg hugged her tightly and then groped and kissed her before she shoved him away saying, "Never do that again."

On Friday, 3 June 1994, at 1500, Dr. Campbell was working on the Wilford Hall Medical Center psychiatric ward when Dean Mellberg suddenly appeared carrying a large gym bag. He asked Dr. Campbell if they could talk, and the doctor suggested they go to his office so they could speak in private. As they walked down an isolated hallway, Dr. Campbell regretted his decision. In a break from his usual routine, he left his office door open during the meeting.

Mellberg appeared sad as he asked Dr. Campbell several questions regarding his commitment to the psychiatric ward. He asked about autism and if Dr. Campbell thought he had a psychiatric condition. Campbell told him he did think he had a psychiatric condition and was frustrated that since he had not reached a definitive diagnosis he could not recommend a specific treatment. Mellberg asked who had ordered his commitment, and Dr. Campbell told him it had been command directed. Mellberg disagreed and grew agitated, asking, "What about Public Law 102-484?" intimating that he had been committed against his will. Mellberg asked if Wilford Hall had released any of his information. Dr. Campbell told him he was unaware of any outside requests for his medical records. Mellberg appeared to accept this.

Mellberg told Dr. Campbell he had been diagnosed with paranoid personality disorder and discharged from the Air Force. Dr. Campbell empathized with Mellberg over the loss of his career and told him the diagnosis should not interfere with his ability to gain civilian employment. He even offered to speak to prospective employers on his behalf. The two shook hands, and ended the meeting. Dr. Campbell said, "At no time did Dean appear menacing or make threatening statements, yet I felt relieved with his departure."

On 4 June 1994, Mellberg flew out of San Antonio on his way to Alaska.

Lt Col Mark McGeehan

*"When we think of those who went before us, we should do so
with humility, respecting their great personal sacrifice. When
we honor our heritage and those with whom we share a
common bond and purpose, we are all enriched, and our lives
are made a little more worth living."*

—Lt Col Mark McGeehan, June 1994
(From an article in the FAFB newspaper)

Mark McGeehan grew up in Chester, West Virginia. He came from a
large Catholic family and he was a devout member of the Catholic Church.
His family wasn't well off but they were rich in values. In 1978 McGeehan
graduated from the Air Force Academy where those values had been rein-
forced. He lived by the academy's honor code: "We will not lie, steal, or
cheat, nor tolerate among us anyone who does." McGeehan's peers said he
was the "consummate professional officer. … Top-notch in every respect."
He was a born leader with a bright future in the Air Force, but as much
as he was dedicated to his career, McGeehan was an equally strong family
man. Early in his Air Force career, he married his high school sweetheart,
Jodie McIntosh. Jodie followed her husband through several assignments,
taking care of their home and caring for their three sons, Patrick, Brendan,
and Collin. McGeehan was an attentive father, active in Little League and
the Boy Scouts.

Not long after taking command of Fairchild's 325th Bomb Squadron,
Jodie said her husband came home one evening and she could tell something
was weighing heavy on his mind. After the kids were asleep, he confided in
her that he and his crews were concerned about a dangerous pilot. According
to Jodie, "He said that he would never be able to live with himself if something like this was to continue and one of his crew members was killed."
Lieutenant Colonel McGeehan intended to take the issue up with Colonel
Pellerin. It was a courageous decision. He had only been at Fairchild for a

year and had only been in command of the 325th Bomb Squadron for a couple of weeks. Asking the operations group commander to ground his chief of Stan/Eval would amount to questioning his judgment and could halt McGeehan's career progress. There was only about three months before the bomb squadron deactivated and Holland would likely retire. But McGeehan had made up his mind. Grounding Holland couldn't wait.

McGeehan was also aware that some of the junior pilots in the Stan/Eval office were emulating Holland's dangerous maneuvers. In the summer of 1993, a young captain piloted one of Fairchild's B-52s in a Canadian air show. He performed Holland's high-pitch-angle climb. The plane went near vertical and buffeted as its speed dropped to a dangerous level before the pilot could push the nose over. Reportedly, the crowd loved it, and Canada's aerobatic team, the Snow Birds, were impressed. But the young pilot was shaken after getting himself and his crew into an almost unrecoverable position.

McGeehan set up a meeting with Holland's boss, the 92nd Operations Group commander. He wrote in his scheduling book, "17 March—Meeting with Colonel Pellerin. Ground Bud Holland!" After the meeting, one of McGeehan's ops officers, Major Thompson, asked him how it went. McGeehan said, "Colonel Pellerin agrees with us. … We are going to remove Bud from flying." McGeehan showed up for a second meeting to further discuss the issue with Pellerin and was surprised to see Holland was also in the office. According to McGeehan's ops officers, "He thought it seemed like two kids that were having a fight were being brought together to shake hands." Capt Peter Donnelly said McGeehan told them that Bud Holland was upset, like he had been stabbed in the back. He said the meeting became a personality conflict at that point.

During the meeting, Pellerin told McGeehan that he had reprimanded Holland but he would continue to fly. Pellerin later defended his inaction. "I felt that a verbal reprimand in front of the guy who charged him with violations of air discipline and regulations was enough of an embarrassment to a professional twenty-four-year lieutenant colonel with five thousand hours in a B-52. … And since I was able to elicit from him his word of honor that there would not be any further breaches of air discipline, whether they involved clearance plane or anything else, I thought that was a sufficient embarrassment to warrant appropriate punishment."

McGeehan made his case to ground the rogue pilot. When he was unable to convince Pellerin, he told his boss "that he would not allow his crews to fly with Bud again." Pellerin said, "I told Mark that I'd make those decisions … and that Bud would fly a normal schedule." As McGeehan left the office, he looked at Pellerin and told him that he just wanted to make sure that he completely understood him, that he did not think that Lieutenant Colonel Holland should be able to fly anymore, and then he shut the door.

Two days after the meeting, Captain Jones ran into Holland on the flight line and got a little insight into how hostile the meeting had been. Jones said Holland pointed to McGeehan and said, "That little fucker tried to get me grounded." According to Jones, Holland told him that during the meeting, McGeehan had accused him of being dangerous and Holland called him a "weak dick" and said he didn't respect him as a man, as a commander, or as a pilot.

Mark McGeehan didn't share many details of the meeting with his wife, other than to say that "Colonel Pellerin had changed his mind and that Bud would continue to be able to fly." Jodie could tell her husband was troubled. She said, "I know that he was emotionally upset, not just angry, but hurt."

The personality conflict extended to the aircrew's families. Jodie McGeehan attended an officers' wives' luncheon where she encountered Sarah Ann Holland. Jodie said, when the air show came up in conversation, "Sarah Ann turned to me and said, 'You know that there was not anybody that could do anything to stop my husband from flying the way that he wants to fly.' … I think she was upset because I think she knew what Mark had done."

When McGeehan saw no other option to protect his men, he told them, "Nobody else flies with Lieutenant Colonel Holland until this squadron is deactivated. I'll do it, I'll be his copilot." He kept track of Holland's flying schedule and advised the schedulers "that whatever flight Colonel Holland was going to be on that he wanted to be on as well."

As summer approached, the base began preparation for the 1994 air show, scheduled for Sunday, 26 June. Colonel Pellerin selected Bud Holland as the B-52 exhibition pilot, saying, "The issue of who the aircraft commander was going to be was virtually a non-issue."

Several aircrew members were concerned that Holland might try something crazy at his final air show. Captain Fleming said, "A lot of us weapons officers would sit around training flight and talk about Lieutenant Colonel Holland, and we predicted the worst air show disaster in history when we found out that he was gonna fly." Fleming heard that even Holland couldn't believe they were going to let him fly. "He was really excited about that. Prior to this, Lieutenant Colonel Holland had openly boasted about wanting to roll a BUFF before he finishes flying." Fleming said, "My personal feeling is that he was going to try to roll the B-52 at the air show."

McGeehan's oldest son, fourteen-year-old Patrick, was upset by comments made by a female schoolmate. Throughout the year she repeatedly bragged that Bud Holland was the best pilot in the squadron. The girl boasted that if anybody is going to do an aileron roll in a B-52, Bud Holland is going to be the one to do it. What truly bothered Patrick was that he believed the girl was parroting the beliefs of her father, the deputy commander of the operations group, Lt Col Stephen Harper.

Capt Alexander Brown recalled a conversation he had with Holland at a going-away picnic. "Colonel Holland implied he was going to roll the aircraft, that he had a month to retirement and nothing to lose. And I remember the phrase that he used, 'What are they going to do, ground me?'"

Col William Brooks took command of the 92nd Bomb Wing on 30 August 1993. As the base commander, he was responsible for all actions performed by the groups and squadrons that made up the wing. Brooks had never seen any of Fairchild's previous air shows, but he was familiar with Bud Holland. Holland had been assigned to qualify Brooks as a staff flier, since his previous assignment had kept him out of the cockpit for over a year. Brooks said, "Bud flew the airplane very precisely." He was "probably the most knowledgeable guy I've flown with in the B-52 … very proficient, very capable in the airplane, very knowledgeable and aggressive in the aspect of precision."

On 15 June 1994, Colonel Brooks held a meeting to review the air-show plans. The meeting was attended by several commanders, as well as representatives from the base security police, fire, and medical services. Also in attendance were Colonel Pellerin, and Colonel Wolff, the vice wing commander who had flown the two-ship low-level mission in the Black Rock Desert with Holland.

During the meeting, Brooks sat at one end of a conference table and Holland sat to one side on the opposite end. Holland briefed his flight profile using the same slides that he had used for previous air show planning meetings. The B-52 and a KC-135 would fly identical maneuvers at intervals. As one aircraft passed the viewing area the other would be approaching.

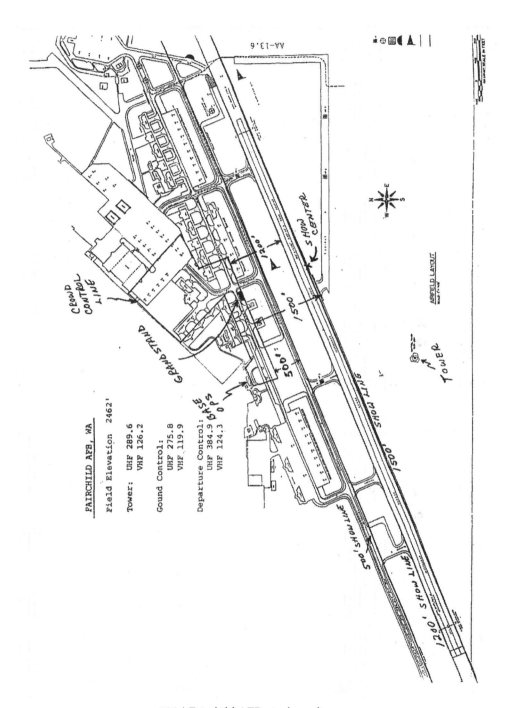

1994 Fairchild AFB air show diagram

B - 52 FLIGHT PROFILE

- **Maximum Performance Takeoff and Climbout to 5000' AGL - (Unstick + 10 Kts)**
- **Wingover**
- **High Speed Pass with Climbout to 12000' MSL**
- **Overhead Pattern (Landing Attitude Demo)**
- **Formation Approach with Pitchout to Landing**

AA-13.9

B - 52 FLIGHT PROFILE

- **Taxi to Parking - Sign Autographs and Take Pictures with Fans**

AA-13.10

Briefing slides used by Holland during air show planning meeting

As Holland ran through his maneuvers, the chief of security police, Lt Col Dennis Hunsinger, was struck by his laid-back demeanor. "He never got up … and addressed the slides from a standing position. … He sat most of the time facing the slide with his hand over the chair and kind of looking back at the wing commander." Hunsinger said Brooks questioned the safety of some of Holland's planned maneuvers. "There were a couple of times that he and the wing commander had an exchange, and Lieutenant Colonel Holland just kind of said well, okay, whatever, we'll do it that way. And it just struck me as being cavalier and to the point of almost being insubordinate."

Holland proposed one change to the routine he had flown in previous years. Upon takeoff, he would perform a 360-degree turn around the air traffic control tower. Brooks said, "Tell me how you are going to do this."

Holland said, "Well, we're going to roll into sixty degrees of bank and do a climbing closed—"

Brooks objected. Wolff spoke up for Holland, saying "it could be done." Holland bragged that he could crank it pretty tight and pop up to sixty-five degrees starting at two hundred feet.

Brooks was adamant. "No, absolutely not." He limited Holland to forty-five degrees as a maximum bank angle for turns. Holland didn't like it.

Brooks' pilot experience was with the FB-111. He wasn't as familiar with the B-52, so he relied on his vice commander, Col Robert Wolff. Brooks said, "I respected Bob's aviation experience, and when anything came up that would be of question whatsoever, in a meeting or stuff like that, I'd kind of look over at Bob to kind of do a sanity check. He had a lot of time in a B-52; he had a lot of combat time in a B-52." Brooks may have believed his order to limit the bank angle to forty-five-degrees was conservative. It still exceeded the thirty-degree bank recommendation in the flight manual, but no one at the meeting openly objected.

No one recalls any discussion of the wingover maneuver depicted on Holland's slide, but when he briefed the B-52 and KC-135 formation approach, Brooks said, "There will be no formation in any way, shape, form, or fashion. There won't even be a perception that there's any formation." Worried that the planes might get caught in each other's turbulence, Brooks ordered a mile of separation at all times. Next, he asked Holland, "Now in this climb to twelve thousand feet … are you talking about an accelerated climb going to twelve thousand? What are we talking about?"

Holland said, "Well, I'm raising the nose to about fifty to sixty degrees."

Brooks said, "No, I'm not going along with that either. … The max I think you should probably raise the nose is about twenty-five degrees, because that is about an airliner departure." Brooks said he didn't want any maneuvers that might give the impression that the aircraft was not fully under control. He was concerned about the safety of the crew and the people on the ground. He directed Holland to fly conservatively and cautioned him not to fly over the spectators.

Maj Teresa Cochran attended the meeting. She was the 92nd Medical Group nurse manager and the spearhead of the air show disaster preparedness committee. Major Cochran sat next to Fairchild's assistant fire chief Robert Mirasole. They were both concerned about a potential air show disaster, and Bud Holland's briefing didn't allay their concerns. As he briefed the bank, pitch angles, and altitudes he intended to fly, Cochran said, "Bob and I looked at each other, and Bob is going, 'he's fucked,' and I said I just hope he crashes on Friday, not Sunday, so I will not have so many bodies to pick up." Cochran later said, "Those words did return to haunt me."

Colonel Brooks closed the meeting with a five-minute safety lecture. He referenced an August 1988 air show disaster at a US air base in Ramstein, Germany, where at least seventy people were killed and more than five hundred injured when three jets from an Italian stunt team collided near the crowd. One of the planes tumbled into the spectators, engulfing them in a fireball of jet fuel and debris. Brooks said, "My concern is over where the crowd is going to be, how we keep the crowd safe, because that's my civilian populace that is coming out to view the professionalism of the base. … We are not going to do anything that would even be perceived as being out of the ordinary, out of control, out of compliance."

Assistant Fire Chief Mirasole was on edge during the briefing. He remembered the KC-135 that crashed during the Thunderhawk practice flight in 1987. "I had a very bad feeling we were being set up for another accident. … I was still at edge until Colonel Brooks directed these individuals not to violate any of the rules, make sure that they meet all the tech orders, and stuff like that—I don't know specifically what he said, but I knew that it took the edge off of my concern." But Chief Mirasole was not completely relieved. He said, "Colonel Brooks was very direct on what he wanted. … It's just that for some reason, I still had that uneasy feeling that they were going to do something that wasn't appropriate."

Brooks was similarly concerned. After the meeting he asked Pellerin to fly the practice profile with Holland to "make sure that we're not violating any regulations."

17 June Air Show Practice

In preparation for the bomb squadron deactivation on 1 July 1994, most of the bomber crews had relocated, and all but one of the B-52s had left the base. A B-52H model, serial number 61-0026, stayed behind to maintain pilot proficiency and weapons load training. It was also slated to be the last Fairchild B-52 to perform in an air show.

McGeehan made good on his promise to keep Holland from flying with his crews. He also volunteered to fly as Holland's copilot in the 26 June 1994 air show and the two practice flights that preceded it. McGeehan's ops officer, forty-one-year-old Lt Col Kenneth Huston, would ride on the lower deck as the radar navigator. Huston was described as a very meticulous professional and an extremely competent radar nav.

Maintenance crews worked over Fairchild's last remaining B-52, ensuring it was safe to fly the air show practice flight. B-52 crew chief, SrA Antonio Garcia Jr., oversaw the hours of preflight inspections and maintenance. He recalls the process was fairly routine. "To me, the only difference was that everything was taken out. The oven was taken out, the sextant, all the loose articles." Senior Airman Garcia explained, "I was told they didn't want stuff flying around when they were doing all the turns and stuff."

The first practice flight occurred on Friday, 17 June 1994. Holland's boss, Colonel Pellerin, was on board as a safety observer, sitting in the instructor pilot seat behind and between the two pilots. Holland didn't like having a senior officer looking over his shoulder, but it didn't seem to intimidate him. Before the flight, Major Thompson overheard Holland saying, "I'm going to fly the air show, and yeah, I may have someone senior in rank flying with me. He may be the boss on the ground, but I'm the boss in the air, and I'll do what I want to do."

As Holland flew the air show profile, he exceeded the bank and pitch angles laid out by Brooks in the planning meeting. B-52 test pilots Col Paul Deehan, Maj Richard Ingalsbe and Capt David Zehr, described the maneuvers they saw. "We thought the profile was unbelievably aggressive, and that he's flying it aggressively at really slow speeds. … The plane cannot maintain that kind of bank angle … without exceeding the g limitations on the aircraft. At low altitudes your nose is going to drop or you over-g the plane. You cannot maintain—no matter what—you cannot maintain that attitude in a bank angle."

Colonel Brooks and several other officers witnessed portions of the practice flight during a retirement ceremony rehearsal for Col Lynn Gunther, the support group commander. From the reviewing platform, the B-52 was observed flying east making a low pass along the runway, then banking hard to the left, flying over the parade grounds. Lt Col Dennis Ballog, civil engineering squadron commander, was on the reviewing stand and saw the plane flying overhead, "fairly low and thoroughly well into a bank." He estimated the elevation was between two and three hundred feet. Then the aircraft flew west down the runway and pulled up hard into a high-pitch-angle climb, "to where you can basically see the whole back of the aircraft from nose to tail. As they started getting to the top, fuel was starting to come from the wing tips."

The B-52 test pilots described the climb. "To us it looks like he got as high as seventy degrees of pitch, and we see fuel coming out of both the surge tank areas on the wing and also out of the fuselage areas as he pushes over at what looks to be a negative g. … I think we all thought that that was kind of a questionable maneuver, just because of boost pumps becoming uncovered … so that whole maneuver is unbelievably aggressive."

In the reviewing stand, Colonel Brooks made comments indicating he was not happy with what he saw. He later claimed his only concern was that Holland's turns might have been over the air show spectator area.

McGeehan's family was worried about him flying in the air show. Patrick watched the practice flight, anxiously waiting for his dad to land. Jodie McGeehan said, "He was extremely agitated. He just kept walking back and forth, and when Mark got down he just said, 'Dad, I just really don't want you to have to fly in the air show.'" Jodie said her husband assured Patrick that "everything would be perfectly fine."

The practice flight was Pellerin's last flight before leaving Fairchild for another assignment. As he stepped off the airplane, he was surprised by a *fini* flight celebration, a traditional celebration of an aviator's last flight where family and friends greet them on the flight line and wet them down with hoses and Champagne. In the midst of the celebration, Brooks congratulated Colonel Pellerin and asked him, "How did it go?"

Despite his own concerns with the routine he just witnessed, Brooks said Pellerin told him, "I didn't have any problem with it, looks good to me, looks very safe, well within parameters."

Flight Surgeons

Lt Col Robert Grant was a flight surgeon at Fairchild. He was fairly new to the Air Force, and although he had flown the B-52 a few times, he wasn't fully sure of its capabilities. Dr. Grant had seen Holland fly in the 1993 air show and thought his maneuvers were unsafe, especially the high-pitch-angle climb. He became concerned when he heard that Holland was going to fly in the 1994 air show. Dr. Grant saw the 17 June 1994 practice flight. "I was standing outside … watching him do the maneuver, and he banked very sharply, came around, across the base and then did this very high straight-up maneuver … to the point of near stall and then pulling the nose over." Dr. Grant spoke to his colleague Dr. Earl, who had flown with Holland on a 1993 air show practice flight. Dr. Earl told Dr. Grant the climb had "to be perfectly timed, otherwise the plane would literally fall backwards on itself."

Dr. Grant said, "Pushing anything to that limit bothers me, obviously. I like a little more cushion underneath me." His colleague seemed to agree. Dr. Grant said, "Dr. Earl didn't want to fly on it again. I know that."

When members of the bomb squadron came to Dr. Grant for routine medical appointments, he probed them for information about Holland and his maneuvers. At least one of the fliers told Dr. Grant that he refused to fly with Bud Holland.

When the 92nd Bomb Wing's chief of safety, Lt Col Michael McCullough, showed up for an appointment, Dr. Grant expressed his concern about Holland's dangerous maneuvers. Dr. Grant said the chief of safety assured him that Holland was a good pilot who had done the maneuvers before, so they must be within the limits of the airplane. He recalls, "At the time, it seemed to allay my concerns somewhat, not totally … because I was not comfortable with the whole concept of the air show." Dr. Grant was not the only flight surgeon with concerns about the safety of Holland's flying. Dr. Isaak, the chief of flight medicine, began making inquiries into the safety of Holland's maneuvers but stopped pursuing the issue when he heard that it had been brought to the attention of Fairchild's chief of safety.

When the chief of safety, Lieutenant Colonel McCullough, was asked about the conversation, he could not recall the specifics. But he later said, "I probably mentioned the fact that I flew in the practice ... in the [1993] air show and had seen everything he had done and had no problems with it."

Preparation

I joined to serve my country
I was so proud
Although I would not
Follow the crowd
Hassle me they did
I was a helpless kid
To fight the Gov't my friend
Is a losing battle to the end
Sent me away an forgot about me
All I could do is get on my knees
Released by their demand
I felt less of a man
Went to see the country side
All the while hurting so bad inside
Hostility was not like me
All I wanted was to stay in the military
They hurt me so bad
The lies they told made me so sad
One day I broke inside
All my emotions I couldn't subside
I went back to those who took away my career
Now left to questions are those too near
They killed me psychologically, then physically in a fight
Know one will ever know my plight
                —poem found among Dean Mellberg's papers

On 5 June 1994, at 1024, Mellberg checked into the North Star Inn on Elmendorf Air Force Base, Alaska. He was put in a room with another service member, a common practice for military billeting. Mellberg's roommate, Kirk Langer, was assigned to a Coast Guard cutter off the coast of Alaska and had checked into billeting while he recovered from illness.

Mellberg told Langer he was in Alaska visiting family, but Langer said he never saw any evidence to support this claim. When Langer attempted to talk with Mellberg further, he just stared silently at the floor.

Mellberg slept fully clothed and didn't change his clothes during his stay in Alaska. He usually slept until 1100 and stayed out as late as 0300. He acquired a bicycle from the base rental center, but no one knows what he did to occupy his time at Elmendorf. He may have traveled to Alaska in search of Dr. London. The doctor had recently received orders to the 3rd Medical Operations Squadron at Elmendorf AFB, but he had not yet finished his assignment at Fairchild. Around 13 June 1994, the receptionist at Fairchild's mental health center took a phone call from someone asking if Dr. London was still on staff, and at 2200 that evening, Mellberg left Elmendorf headed for Spokane. On the afternoon of 14 June 1994, Mellberg checked into Room 16 of the Liberty Motel on North Division Street and took a cab to Fairchild the following morning.

A former co-worker was driving past the base theater at 0830 and saw Mellberg, dressed in jeans and a T-shirt, walking in the direction of the base hospital. A half hour later he spotted him again at the corner of Medical Lake and Graham, headed toward the hospital annex. When he honked and waved, Mellberg waved back. When the former co-worker returned to the lab, he told his co-workers that he had seen Mellberg on the base. Some of them joked that Mellberg had returned to get them. Others assumed their co-worker was mistaken.

Later that day, Mellberg wandered into a dormitory and saw a sign posted on a bulletin board listing a MAK-90 rifle for sale. The dorm manager, who had posted the sign, said that when Mellberg walked into his office and inquired about the rifle, "He smelled like he hadn't taken a bath in days." The dorm manager put Mellberg in touch with his friend, Mike Carroll, a federaly licensed firearms dealer who sold guns out of his home in Spokane. Mellberg spoke with Carroll on the telephone and took down his address.

Mellberg took a cab back to Spokane and checked out of his motel room. At about 1300 he took a cab to Carroll's North Spokane home to purchase the Chinese-made Norinco MAK-90.

The MAK-90 (pronounced "mack ninety") is an AK-47 variant. The *M* stands for modified and the *AK* for automatic Kalashnikov. The 90 indicates the year of design. The rifle was designed to fire 7.62×39mm ammunition and this particular rifle had a stock with a thumbhole as opposed to a pistol grip, and it had no flash suppressor. These modifications brought the rifle into compliance with a 1989 gun control law banning the importation of certain firearms.

Mike Carroll was a gun enthusiast with a love of hunting and the outdoors. Carroll applied for and received a federal firearms license, thinking it might be a good way to add to his collection at a discount and maybe make a little extra income. He placed ads in the paper and had been selling firearms out of his home for a couple of years—a completely legal practice.

Carroll said Mellberg was casually dressed and well mannered. Nothing in their conversation led him to believe he was mentally unstable. Mellberg looked over the semi-automatic rifle and worked its action before asking Carroll if he had any thirty-round magazines. Carroll told him he only had the five-round magazine that came with the rifle and suggested he check the Army Surplus store for additional magazines. Mellberg filled out an ATF Form 4473, which asked a series of questions regarding a purchaser's citizenship, illegal drug use, criminal convictions, whether they had been dishonorably discharged from the military and so on. Mellberg initialed appropriately in the yes or no box after each question until he reached the question, "Have you ever been adjudicated mentally defective or have you ever been committed to a mental institution?" He failed to disclose that he had just spent ninety-three days in the psychiatric inpatient ward of Wilford Hall Medical Center.

There was no way for Carroll—or the ATF, for that matter—to verify his answers. Even today, few states make disqualifying mental health information available to the National Instant Criminal Background Check System database. Carroll followed the letter of the law. There was no waiting period for rifle purchases and no requirement to conduct a background check. Mellberg paid $450 cash for the rifle and asked Carroll to call him a taxi. He put the rifle back in its styrofoam packing box and stuffed it inside his gym bag. The long white box protruded from the bag as he walked outside to wait for his ride.

When the taxi arrived, Mellberg picked up his gym bag and crawled into the back seat. As the cab drove toward the Liberty Motel, Mellberg peeked nervously out the rear window as if he thought someone was following him. The cab drove through the 6000 block of N. Division and as they passed Arnold's Motel, Mellberg told the driver to stop. He checked into Room 102, paying $34 a night. At some point, Mellberg went to a local retailer and purchased eighty rounds of 7.62 ammunition and an AK-47 drum magazine, with a capacity of seventy-five rounds.

On the afternoon of 16 June 1994, the day after Mellberg purchased the rifle, Dr. George Estes entered the men's bathroom on the first floor of Fairchild's hospital annex. In the last toilet stall on the right, he found a small empty cardboard box with the words "magazine" and "Made in China" printed on it. Next to the box he found a chunk of white styrofoam. The doctor assumed the items had been left behind by members of the Combat Arms Training and Maintenance section (CATM) who had recently been in the annex for their annual physicals.

Operating the seventy-five round magazine, that Mellberg had purchased, was not intuitive. Loading the magazine required the removal of a back cover in order to place the cartridges inside the spokes of a large spindle. Once the magazine was loaded, a butterfly key on the front of the magazine had to be wound to apply tension to a clockwork spring that fed the rounds into the rifle. The process was too complicated for Mellberg to figure out on his own.

On Saturday afternoon, 18 June 1994, Mellberg walked one block from his motel room to the Sportsman's Surplus store on North Division. He took the rifle and loaded magazine out of his gym bag, placed them on the counter, and told the clerk the magazine wasn't feeding correctly. The clerk said Mellberg was pleasant but "strange." He acted nervous and seemed to be in a hurry. The clerk determined Mellberg had wound the magazine too tight. He fixed the problem, and Mellberg left, walking in the direction from where he had come.

Mellberg was ready to execute his plan but would have to wait until Monday. At around 0300 Sunday morning, he took a cab down Sprague Avenue and arrived at the Déjà Vu Gentlemen's Club just before closing time. He still had a considerable amount of cash and took a liking to a particular dancer. Mellberg talked to her extensively, telling her his life story. He spent about a thousand dollars—paying her to entertain him in the privacy of the fantasy booth.

The housekeeper at Arnold's Motel, twenty-year-old Cecily Pearson, said Mellberg was unusual. "When I would go into his room early in the mornings and I'd open the door, most people jump up and get startled, but he didn't. He'd just lay there and just look at me. … The lights were always dark. He'd just be laying there. Every time I'd walk in. … It was weird. It was crazy." On Sunday afternoon, Mellberg wasn't in his room. Cecily made his bed and found a large double-edged knife under his pillow. The blade had prominent serrations that grew progressively larger from the tip of the blade to the handle. Cecily said it was shaped like a Christmas tree.

Sunday afternoon Mellberg returned to Déjà Vu. He talked to the dancers about UFOs and aliens invading Earth to impregnate women. He spent another thousand dollars in the club, most of it on one particular dancer. As he was leaving, one of the women asked if he would be back on Monday. He replied, "No, I don't know where I will be." The women were happy to have his money, but Mellberg made them uneasy. They were concerned enough to ask the bartender to walk them to their cars at the end of their shifts. Their fears were warranted. Mellberg hired a cab and followed one of the dancers as she drove out of the club parking lot. The woman made it safely to her room at the Best Western on North Division. Mellberg sat on her van and loitered in the hotel parking lot until he was chased away by security.

Mellberg eventually returned to his room at Arnold's Motel. At 0300, Faith's telephone rang in her dorm room at Lackland AFB. No one replied when she answered, but she could hear breathing on the other end of the line. The caller eventually hung up without speaking.

Mellberg was scheduled to check out of Arnold's on Monday 20 June but slept past the checkout time of 1100. Sometime after 1300, Cecily went to clean Room 102 and found Mellberg asleep in the bed. She cleaned all of the vacant rooms, and before leaving for the day, told the manager that Room 102 was still occupied. The manager, Marlene Anderson, went to Mellberg's room and knocked repeatedly before he finally opened the door. She angrily asked him if he planned on staying another night. When Mellberg replied, "Oh no, I'm checking out," she told him she would have to charge him for another night since he overstayed. Mellberg agreed and apologized. Marlene returned to her office and Mellberg stuffed most of his belongings into the motel dresser drawers. These included his hat; boots; a silver belt buckle with a gold D on the front; a Sun West Bank bag containing a shaving kit; two unopened bottles of vitamins and a bottle of Stress Tabs; *Playboy*, *Popular Science*, and *Anchorage* magazines; and a billfold insert containing his Selective Service card and voter registration card. He wouldn't need them anymore.

Mellberg paid Marlene for an additional night but checked out of the motel, leaving his room key on the counter. He sat on a planter in front of the motel, and at about 1410 his taxi arrived.

Mellberg entered the cab carrying his oversized gym bag with the white styrofoam case protruding out the top. The driver realized the case probably contained a gun but didn't question it. Mellberg was barely audible from the back seat as he told the driver he wanted to go to Fairchild. The driver attempted to make conversation, but Mellberg mumbled and spoke so quietly, he thought he was on drugs. They sat in silence for the forty-minute ride. As they drove down Highway 2 and approached the base, Mellberg said he wanted to go to the base hospital. He instructed the driver to go past the main gate and turn left onto Graham Road. The taxi drove down Graham and pulled into the circular driveway, stopping in front of the hospital's main entrance. The meter read $35.88. Mellberg spent several minutes counting the money to pay his fare.

20 June 1994

Aerial view of Fairchild Air Force Base hospital campus, 20 June 1994.
Crime scene photo

The taxi idled in the circular driveway outside the Fairchild Air Force Base hospital. In the back seat, the would-be gunman took four minutes to count the twenty-dollar bill and sixteen ones to pay his fare. He tipped the driver twelve cents and stuffed his wallet containing $106 into the pocket of his dirty black jeans. He emerged from the cab with his gym bag and stood in the summer heat at the hospital main entrance waiting for the automated door. With a clunk and a mechanical hum, the door slowly swung open to a small vestibule. The clunk and hum repeated, and a second door opened to the hospital's main lobby, which doubled as the pharmacy waiting area. To the left, a hallway led to the family practice wing.

Mellberg turned right, walking past the pharmacy dispensing windows, headed for the north doors at the opposite end of the lobby. The lobby was uncomfortably warm and filled with a myriad of people. Several waited for prescriptions, sitting in neatly arranged rows of chairs. The lobby was a literal hub of activity as people walked into and out of the three wings of the hospital.

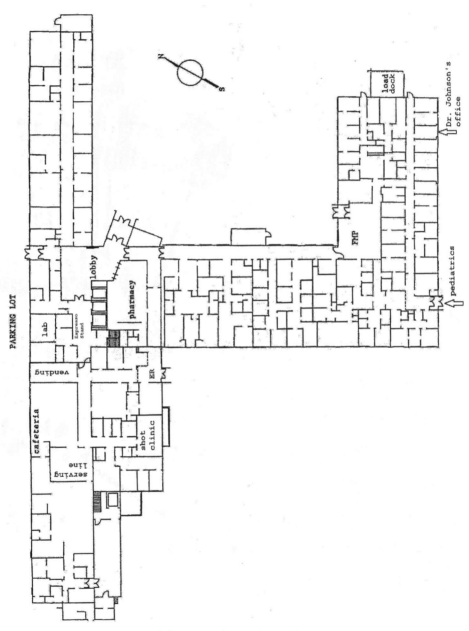

Schematic of main hospital.

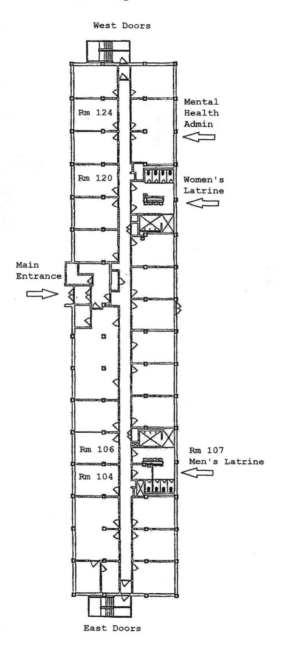

Schematic of hospital annex.

Forty-one-year-old MSgt Dennis Moe and his wife, forty-year-old Marlene, sat in the pharmacy lobby with their daughters, fifteen-year-old Melissa and thirteen-year-old Kelly. Dennis had left early from his job in Fairchild's weapons storage area to be with his girls for their dermatology appointments.

Both of the teenagers were babysitting for family friends during the summer break from school. Melissa Moe was taking care of four-year-old Anthony and five-year-old Janessa Zucchetto. That morning she had helped the kids get ready for the day. Janessa wore a blue plaid dress with white sandals, Anthony a T-shirt and shorts. Kelly Moe was taking care of four-year-old Ryan and eight-year-old Christin McCarron. She had spent the night at the McCarron home, and that morning Christin told Kelly she loved her and thanked her for being her babysitter. After the Moe girls finished with their appointments, they sat with their parents in the crowded pharmacy lobby, entertaining the four kids while they waited for their prescriptions.

Twenty-one-year-old Brandy Pentecost sat nearby. She had grown up in Spokane and recently married an airman who worked at Fairchild's supply squadron. Brandy worked as a lifeguard to help pay for her criminal justice studies at Eastern Washington University. She wore an EWU sweatshirt and a pair of shorts.

Orbin "Hap" Joplin, sixty-three, a retired airman who worked as a civilian supply clerk on base, sat in the pharmacy lobby talking with his friend, TSgt Patrick Deaton. Deaton worked in the civil engineering squadron and was waiting to pick up a prescription for an ear infection.

Sixty-nine-year-old Omer Karns stood in the pharmacy lobby. Karns tried to enlist in the military after the 1941 attack on Pearl Harbor. He was passing the entrance exams until someone behind him tried to start a conversation. Although Karns was an excellent lip reader, a childhood bout with the mumps had left him deaf. In 1991 Karns found another way to serve his country, driving veterans to medical appointments as a volunteer for the Kootenai County Disabled American Veterans (DAV). He waited for a veteran in the pharmacy lobby, proudly wearing his dark blue DAV cap with gold oak leaves embroidered on the bill.

Eva Walch was a fifty-seven-year-old mother of two grown daughters and the widow of a military retiree. She had worked as a waitress for thirty-four years at a Spokane department store. Having been raised by a single mother, who struggled to provide for her, Eva was a compassionate woman, especially when it came to children. She often bought coats for needy children she saw downtown. Eva sat in the pharmacy lobby waiting for a prescription.

Michelle Sigman, twenty-five, was married to an airman. She had brought their five-year-old son, James, in for a 1400 pediatrics appointment with Dr. Tappel. Afterward, she dropped James's prescription off at the pharmacy. Michelle, who was five months pregnant, stopped by the lab for some tests before returning to the pharmacy to find that the prescription wasn't ready. She and James sat down in the lobby to wait. James sat across from Eva, and he bragged to her about getting his blood taken. He wore a sticker that read "I've been shot."

Deena Kelley, thirty-seven, had been on the second floor of the hospital with her six-month-old daughter, Becky. Becky had been hospitalized for several days due to an infection, but was scheduled to be released after a final ultrasound. When a nurse took Becky in for the test, Deena took the elevator down to the pharmacy lobby and gave a prescription to the pharmacy technician behind the counter. When her name was called, she got in line at the pharmacy window behind Hazel "Joy" Roberts and the two women struck up a conversation. Joy Roberts, sixty-one, was married to a retired airman and had been to see her cardiologist.

Seventy-one-year-old Ruth Gerken wore a floral print dress to her dermatology appointment. Afterward, at 1400, she walked with her cane to the ER to have her blood pressure checked before making her way to the pharmacy lobby to wait for the 1500 bus to take her home. She sat across from Dennis and Marlene Moe and the six children as she waited impatiently, anxiously checking the clock on the wall. At precisely 1450, she took her blood pressure pill.

The would-be gunman walked through the lobby and stood at the north doors, waiting for them to open. Once outside, he crossed the parking lot and made his way to the east end of the hospital annex, near Graham Road. He entered the annex through the east door and stepped into the dimly lit corridor.

On the opposite end of the annex, in Room 120, Dr. Alan London sat with twenty-three-year-old Brittany Gray*. Brittany was a former airman and her husband was stationed at Fairchild. She was seeking Dr. London's counsel to guide her through a difficult time in her life.

Dr. Thomas Brigham was two doors down, in Room 124, waiting for his 1500 appointment with Mark Hess. Hess, thirty-five, had taken early retirement from the Air Force. When he arrived at the annex that afternoon for his appointment with Dr. Brigham, receptionist Cathy Shea told him she hadn't received his medical records. She asked him to retrieve them from the records section in the main hospital. As Hess walked down the hall, he saw Dr. Brigham standing in his office with his back to the doorway.

The would-be gunman walked to the men's latrine, Room 107. A med tech held the door for him as he struggled to get inside with his large gym bag. The med tech stood at the urinal, and the man went into the last toilet stall on the right, locked the door, dropped the bag to the floor and sat down. When the man was alone in the bathroom, he affixed a large double-edged knife and sheath to his belt, removed the MAK-90 rifle from its case, and inserted the seventy-five-round drum magazine. He left the bag and its contents, including a loaded five-round magazine, in the stall as he stepped into the hallway with the rifle.

Dr. Doyle Isaak and CMSgt Michael Pinault stood talking in the hall outside the flight surgeon's waiting room, near the center of the annex. Pinault looked down the hall and saw a man walking briskly toward them "carrying what appeared to be an AK-47 … with the muzzle level to the floor." Pinault said the man had "a blank stare on his face" and was "concentrating on something down the hall." As the man walked past the two men, the barrel of his rifle brushed across Pinault's stomach. Pinault backed into the waiting room. He said the man briefly stared at him before continuing silently down the hall, "looking at the names on the doors of the doctors' offices."

Dr. Isaak warned the people in the waiting room, "There is a man walking down the hall with a gun." Isaak said he looked down the hall as the man "pushed open Dr. London's door" and "fired a shot." Isaak yelled, "Call security police" and yelled for people to "Get out."

Inside Dr. London's office, Brittany Gray sat in disbelief as the man "busted the door open and shot Dr. London." The gunman turned and pointed the rifle at her, said something unintelligible, and walked out of the office.

Med tech Almon Foster had been walking down the gloomy annex hall when he heard the first gunshot come from the mental health center. The sunlight from the windows of the west exit doors revealed the silhouette of a man with a rifle coming out of Dr. London's office. The gunman walked down the hall, pushed through Dr. Brigham's office door and fired another shot. Almon turned and ran to Room 104. He grabbed his office phone and dialed the ER before ducking under his desk. "I told the ER to call the SPs, that there was a guy in the mental health clinic shooting at people." Almon then fled out the east door to Graham Road, where he warned people away from the area.

From down the hall, Dr. Isaak watched the gunman move two doors down, where he "opened up Dr. Brigham's door and fired a shot." SSgt Karl Anderson and receptionist Cathy Shea were in the mental health administrative office across the hall. Anderson, "heard two loud bangs in the hallway" and got up to investigate. "As I approached the [reception counter] a white male with dark hair pointed what appeared to be an AK-47 rifle in my direction. The secretary took cover under her desk. I took cover behind a file cabinet." When the man disappeared from the reception counter and headed for the office's second entrance, Anderson said he "ran to the other door" and locked it about "one second before the suspect attempted to open the door."

Medical technicians SSgt Jennifer Werder, SrA Kevin Seeley, and Airman First Class Raynes were in the audio room, Room 106, administering physicals to two young patients. They had just put the two youths inside the steel soundproof audiometric booths when they heard a gunshot from down the hall. They reasoned the sound was a door slammed closed by a summer breeze. When the sound repeated, one of them joked that it was gunfire. Then a woman's scream echoed down the painted cinderblock hallway, "Oh my God, help, he's bleeding!" The scream was followed by a third shot. The med techs heard people running down the hall, yelling, "Get out! Get out! Someone is shooting!" They dropped to the floor, grabbed the patients out of the booths and locked the office door.

Thirty-six-year-old LeDeane Stewart was a civilian data specialist. LeDeane said, "I heard the first shot. … I thought a door had slammed. The annex got warm during the summer, and we had no air conditioning on the first floor. So it was not unusual for a door to be open. Approximately five seconds later, I heard the noise again. Then I heard screaming. … I will never forget the screams. After the second shot, I stepped out of my office and looked to my left and saw people running. … I asked, 'What's going on?'"

The gunman stood near the west door. He fired down the hall, narrowly missing LeDeane and the people fleeing out the east door. He then turned and left the annex.

Twenty-five-year-old SSgt Laura Rogers was a billing specialist in the annex resource management office. She sat on the steps of the fire escape outside the west annex door, the first to arrive for the 1500 smoke break. When the door opened, Rogers looked up and screamed when she saw the gunman run out of the building. She said the gunman was calm and non-chalant as he walked by and shot her.

Caroline Goodman was working at a computer terminal in the upper level of the annex when the shooting started. Caroline said, "I joked with my co-worker that it sounded like someone was shooting, so I said I better lock the door." Instead, Caroline opened the door. "People were running wild. An employee yelled for us to run."

Maj George Estes was a thirty-nine-year-old flight surgeon working internal medicine on the first floor, east end of the hospital annex. Dr. Estes was in his office with a patient when he heard noises he associated with the wind slamming doors closed. When a group of people fled past his office, shouting, Dr. Estes looked down the hall and saw someone run out of the door with a chart. He ran with the crowd, thinking someone had stolen a medical chart. Once outside the east door of the annex, Dr. Estes realized that someone was in the area shooting. Dr. Estes ran to the window of his office and pounded on the glass yelling for his patient to get out. He then went back to the east end of the annex and saw people coming out of the second- and third-floor doors, walking slowly down the metal fire escape stairway, as if they thought it was a drill. Dr. Estes yelled at them to hurry up, that someone was shooting and they needed to get to cover. He directed some people to move north down Graham Road to block traffic from entering the area.

John Urick, sixty-nine, was retired from a career in the Navy. He and his wife, Doris, stood outside the north doors of the hospital getting some fresh air as they waited for John's appointment following a laser eye treatment. John and Doris heard the gunfire coming from inside the annex and men on the third-floor landing shouting, "He's got a gun!" The Uricks saw the gunman coming toward them. They ran inside the hospital but apparently didn't warn anyone inside of the approaching danger. John turned right and sat down in a row of chairs facing the pharmacy windows. Doris turned left and ran down the east wing toward the records section, searching for an unlocked door.

The gunman fired randomly as he trotted across the parking lot to a sidewalk that ran the length of the hospital. He moved quickly toward the north doors. As he approached a clump of pine trees outside the entrance, he fired more deliberately.

Joneil Delrosario, a fifteen-year-old visiting his military brother, was in a Ford Bronco parked near the hospital's north entrance. He waited in the back seat while his sister-in-law ran into the pharmacy for a prescription. Joneil's four-month-old niece lay in a car seat up front. Joneil said, "I was sleeping in the car when I woke up and heard a boom. I thought it was a firecracker." Joneil closed his eyes again. He heard another gunshot and looked to see a gunman running toward the car. "He was right behind me. He passed us up. I guess he didn't see us." Joneil ducked. "I looked up again and saw him chase a guy and shoot him by the door. ... I grabbed the baby and I took her out of the car. Then I saw a man that was [shot] in the leg running, so I grabbed my niece and ran." Joneil ran to the annex and hid in a third-floor office with a group of men and women. They barricaded the door, and the women fed the baby Sprite from their fingertips to help keep her quiet.

Tyrone Hoard Jr. was in the hospital outpatient records section, the windows of which looked out into the parking lot between the hospital and the annex. Tyrone said, "I heard two gunshots in the parking lot and a lady screaming. Then I saw a white man with brownish, dirty blond hair, in a black T-shirt, run by the window I was looking out of."

Orson Lee was a sixty-four-year-old retired Army staff sergeant who had served in the Vietnam and Korean Wars. Lee and his wife had traveled from Boise, Idaho, along with their golden retriever, for a post-cataract surgery exam. Lee's wife, Marlene, waited in the car with the dog as her husband walked toward the north doors. As Lee neared the entrance, the gunman approached from the opposite direction and spotted him through the pine trees.

Tyrone described the gunman's encounter with Orson Lee. "He saw an elderly man coming up the walkway into the hospital, and he fired at him with what looked like an AK-47. The first shot missed, but then he fired another shot, and I saw the man go down. Then he fired another shot at the fallen man."

The gunman continued to the north doors.

Marlene Lee said, "I was sitting in my car when I heard noise that at first I thought was Fourth of July crackers. As I looked at my husband going to the north door of the hospital, the noise came closer and closer. I then saw my husband holding his chest and then falling down. He tried to get up, and he fell again. … He came toward the car. I went toward him, and after I hid behind cars in the parking lot, the noise stopped."

Mark Hess had retrieved his file from the outpatient records section of the main hospital and was headed back to the annex for his doctor's appointment. As he waited for the first exit door to open, he glanced to his left and saw an acquaintance, Dennis Moe, sitting in the pharmacy lobby. He considered stopping to talk but noticed he was busy with his family. When the first door opened, Hess stepped into the vestibule, triggering the second door to begin opening. Through the tinted glass door, he saw a man running from the direction of the annex with a rifle and Orson Lee approaching from the opposite direction. Hess heard a gunshot and saw Lee double over.

Hess stood in the vestibule with nowhere to run. The door behind him was closing as the door in front opened to the approaching gunman. He turned and dove for the floor. He heard a gunshot and felt a thump as a bullet passed through his right leg. The gunman ran past Hess and into the hospital lobby. The gunfire continued in the lobby as Hess jumped up and ran to the annex, leaving a trail of blood through the parking lot. Hess made his way down the annex hallway and saw Dr. Brigham facedown on the floor of his office. He ducked into an office across the hall and attempted to call security police, but the line was busy. Hess's leg was bleeding profusely. Initially, the adrenaline kept him from feeling the pain. Hess said, "I was more pissed than anything." He tugged his belt from the loops of his blue jeans and strapped it tight around his upper thigh to stem the loss of blood. He then used the office phone to call his new employer, telling his boss, "I won't be at work tomorrow. I just got shot."

* * *

Ruth Gerken checked the clock on the pharmacy lobby wall and peered outside looking for her 1500 bus. It was 1458. Within minutes she would hear the sound of gunfire and Dennis Moe shouting.

Dennis Moe walked toward the north doors to investigate the sound of gunfire outside. He thought it might be an exercise until he saw the gunman trying to come in through the "out" door. Dennis yelled, "Oh my God, he's got a gun, everybody run!"

A bullet shattered the glass door, square jewels of tempered glass shot into the lobby and scattered on the carpet, quickly followed by the man with the gun. Dennis Moe stood between the gunman and his family as they fled the lobby. The Moes grabbed the younger children and joined a crowd of people who were funneling through a set of fire doors into the west wing hallway.

The gunman fired from the hip and moved continuously. His first shots flew toward Hap Joplin and Patrick Deaton. Deaton initially thought he heard a car backfiring until a bullet tore into him. Joplin saw the gunman but assumed it was an exercise. A bullet ripped through a computer kiosk Joplin was seated next to, splattering his face with fragments of particleboard. Joplin realized the danger was real and ran for cover down a hall behind the pharmacy. When he saw that Deaton hadn't followed him, Joplin looked around the corner and saw his friend lying wounded on the floor. He ran out and pulled Deaton into the hall, where a medic helped him drag Deaton into a record's room. Once inside, they closed the door.

Omer Karns couldn't hear the gunfire. He saw people running and had begun to follow them, when he felt a vibration in his lower back as a bullet splintered his pelvis.

The gunman turned right and shot John Urick, seated nearby. The bullet hit Urick in the thigh, breaking his femur. The gunman turned left and fired down the hall as Doris Urick sought an unlocked door. Two bullets flew past her head as she slipped into a doctor's office. She found an airman inside holding his one-year-old child. Doris hid under a desk with the child as the airman dialed 911.

Michelle Sigman thought it might be an exercise until she smelled the acrid gun smoke and heard people yell, "He's got a gun!" Michelle grabbed James and moved toward the pharmacy island counter. She heard a loud boom and felt a tingly sensation as she was shot in the back. She threw James to the floor, shielding him with her body.

Deena Kelley heard shots and screams behind her as she stood in line for her prescription. Deena dove to the floor, lying on her stomach beside the island counter. When she realized the shooting was real, she pleaded with God—if He had to take one of them, let it be her and spare her infant daughter Becky.

Eva Walch heard the gunfire, which she described as "pop, pop, popping" like "early Fourth of July." She jumped from her chair, diving under the pharmacy island counter six feet away. She looked out from under the counter and saw the gunman firing continuously as he moved through the lobby toward the west wing hallway, pursuing the fleeing crowd.

Neal Cox, eighteen, was just inside the hallway, standing behind the counter of a small espresso stand. It was his first day on the job selling drinks to patients and staff. His boss, Gordon Fagras, an entrepreneur and a captain in the Air Force Reserve, had left Neal in charge while he went to announce drink specials over the hospital's loudspeaker. As soon as Fagras left, Neal heard gunfire and screams coming from the lobby. Neal said, "I recognized it as gunfire immediately."

Neal reasoned that this was a military hospital and that this must be a drill. He reacted immediately. "I decided not to wait and see but instead threw a garbage can out from under the cart and hid underneath in its place. Then a crowd of screaming people, running in a pack, rushed past me as I sat underneath the cart. I watched them run down the hallway as the sound of [gunfire] was going off close behind me. I was frozen in fear underneath the cart, watching and hearing what was happening, when I heard a voice say, 'Go. Go now.'"

Neal stood up and noticed a door to his right. "I went toward it, and it was unlocked." He pushed through the door and fell inside, landing on the floor of the hospital lab, Room 121. Neal burst through another door into the office of Capt James Singleterry, the lab's officer in charge, who was sitting at his desk. According to Neal, Singleterry asked, "What the hell is going on out there?"

Neal scrambled under Singleterry's desk as he responded, "Someone is shooting at people."

"Is someone playing around out there?"

"No, someone is shooting and killing people out there. People are dying."

Captain Singleterry left his office and stood at the door of Room 121. As the gunfire continued in the hallway he "listened and waited."

Before the first shot was fired in the lobby, Marlene Moe heard her husband yell, "He's got a gun, move it!" She grabbed four-year-old Anthony as she and her family fled with the crowd toward a set of propped-open fire doors. The group frantically funneled into the hallway of the west wing that led to the ER, cafeteria, and shot clinic. Their escape was slowed further when one of the double doors swung closed. Dennis was near the end of the group, ushering his family away from the gunman. He saw five-year-old Ryan running aimlessly. Just as he snatched him up and tossed him through the doorway, he felt the sledgehammer impact of a bullet penetrating his left hip. Dennis fell in the doorway, landing on his daughter Kelly, unable to move his legs. Kelly crawled out, grabbed Ryan, and continued down the hall. Someone grabbed Ryan, and Kelly ended up behind the espresso counter.

The gunman jumped over Dennis as he fired down the hall into the fleeing crowd. Marlene Moe searched for somewhere to hide. She looked back and saw the gunman approaching. She was hit and fell to the ground, laying on her back at the far end of the espresso stand. Anthony fell out of her arms and was lost in the crowd. Marlene was temporarily paralyzed from the waist down. She screamed, "Why are you doing this? Stop, you're hurting people!" Kelly Moe thought better of her hiding spot. She ran out from behind the espresso cart. A bullet flew past her face, another passed through her right thigh and into her mother's leg. Kelly fell to the floor beside her mother. She saw Ryan nearby and pulled him to her, holding him close.

College student Brandy Pentecost went to the floor beside Kelly. Anthony wandered toward her. She grabbed him and tucked him between the wall and Kelly's legs. She put her arm around Kelly's shoulder and lay beside them, telling them to be quiet, keep their heads down, it will be okay. Brandy watched the gunman move quickly away from them, down the hall, shooting from the hip.

Thirteen-year-old Sam Spencer and his father had been on the second floor visiting Sam's mother following her elbow surgery. Sam had gone down to the ER waiting room to get a soda from a vending machine. Sam heard popping sounds and looked out into the hallway. He saw several people running from a gunman who, he said, was jogging down the hall shooting "at everyone in his way." The gunman, ten feet away, fired into the small room. Sam was hit in the leg. He crawled into the corner and hid behind a chair.

Seconds earlier, fifteen-year-old Melissa Moe was sitting with her family in the pharmacy lobby with five-year-old Janessa Zucchetto on her lap. Melissa heard her father yell and saw a bullet blast into a wall. She picked up Janessa and ran down the hall with eight-year-old Christin McCarron. While the gunfire erupted behind them, the three ran past the ER and reached the end of the hall. As they pushed through a swinging door that led to the cafeteria serving line, Melissa was hit near her tailbone. A fragmented bullet struck her knee. She fell through the door, landing on the cold tile floor as the door swung closed behind them. Melissa cried out, "Oh my God, I've been shot!" She said it felt as if "someone poured gasoline" on her leg and "lit it on fire."

* * *

Seconds before the gunfire erupted in the hospital, the phone rang in the ER. It was Almon Foster calling from the annex, warning them of a gunman shooting at people in the mental health clinic. The person who answered the phone heard gunfire coming from the pharmacy lobby down the hall. Others saw people running and falling in the hallway. A med tech ran in from the hall yelling, "Hit the duress button." Not waiting for his co-workers to react, he jumped over the reception desk, pushed the silent alarm button and shouted, "Take cover. Someone's shooting!"

The ER staff and patients hid in offices and a record's room. Several med techs and nurses locked themselves in the cramped control room behind the reception desk. They tracked the path of the gunman by the changing sound of gunfire. In between the gunshots they heard screams and moans emanating from the corridor. The gunshots moved past the ER, down the hallway toward the dining hall. The gunman turned left at the swinging door of the dining hall and moved down a short hall that ended at the doorway of the shot clinic.

Karina Tutini, a twenty-two-year-old immunization technician, sat at her desk facing the entrance of the shot clinic, talking on the phone with a patient. The small clinic was filled with parents and children who were seated in short rows of chairs.

Margaret Lum, twenty-eight, was the wife of an airman who was attending SERE instructor training at Fairchild's Survival School. She had worked a half shift at a Spokane florist before heading out to the base hospital to get her allergy shot. Margaret had originally intended to pick up her son from the base childcare center to get his two-year-old shots but decided against it at the last minute.

Sgt Michael Lecker was a fitness specialist in the services squadron and a former security policeman. He sat in the shot clinic with his two-year-old daughter in a chair next to the propped-open clinic door.

Lt Col Joe Olenoski was a B-52 navigator who worked a staff position in Fairchild's Bomb Wing. Lieutenant Colonel Olenoski sat in the clinic with his sixteen-year-old daughter, Stacy, who had just received an allergy shot. Olenoski said, "While sitting in the clinic with Stacy, I heard a banging that initially sounded like locker doors being slammed." He quickly recognized the sound to be gunfire that was growing louder. "I assumed someone was coming in our direction. We had no place to go. I hollered to everyone, 'Get down!' No one seemed to know at that instant what was going on." But everyone responded, doing their best to hide behind the meager furnishings of the small office. Olenoski saw his daughter crouch in the corner behind a couch. The sound of gunfire approached. Olenoski said he saw the shadow of a person coming toward the clinic entrance. "I didn't see anything else that I could do. … I dove behind some chairs in the middle of the room. All I saw looking under the chairs was feet at the door." Then, Olenoski heard a commotion.

Margaret Lum had received her allergy shot and waited in the clinic to ensure she didn't have an adverse reaction. She said, "I heard a couple of popping sounds, then again and again. I remember looking at the man next to me, and I said 'that doesn't sound good' … and seconds later I knew it was not the backfire of a car. People were screaming, and the shots got louder. I could hear people running and screaming 'Oh my God.' I looked around the room for someplace to hide. There was nowhere to run and nowhere to hide."

Sergeant Lecker heard the shots in the hallway, and his first thought was the security police must be conducting an anti-robbery exercise at the pharmacy. That thought faded quickly as the shots and screams in the hallway intensified. Lecker tucked his daughter under his chair and then stood on it, crouched and waiting, his eyes fixed on the doorway. He said, "I wasn't going to let him get her." He heard the gunfire approaching and saw the muzzle of the rifle jut through the doorway. Lecker lunged and grabbed hold of the barrel. The repeated firing of the rifle had heated the steel, which burned his hands as he pushed the weapon toward the floor. As Lecker struggled for control of the rifle, he was struck in the head with the butt of the gun. Still he managed to shove the gunman out into the hall. Lecker slammed the clinic door closed. Through a small window, he saw the gunman retreat, running down the hall toward the dining facility. Lecker saw the door to the cafeteria serving line open and heard the gunfire resume. Lecker pushed a chair in front of the door, scooped up his two-year-old, and hid in a storage closet with Tutini and two boys aged four and nine.

Olenoski also heard the shots resume in the hallway, "very close but going away from us. I jumped up and grabbed Stacy's hand and tried to find an exit. There was a large window with a screen in it. I pushed the window up and kicked the screen out. I went through and pulled Stacy through. Fortunately, the ground was just a few feet down." Once outside, he ran with his daughter, as fast as her flip-flops would carry her. "I wanted to get her away from the gunshots as fast as possible. ... She just couldn't move fast enough. ... I had to slow down so she wouldn't trip. We were running through some grass when the gunshots started to get louder. ... We lay in a grass ditch for a short period of time until the shooting stopped. We got up and ran to the nearest house and banged on the door. A guy opened it with a rifle in his hand!"

Margaret had witnessed Lecker struggling with the gunman at the door. "The shooter and I made eye contact. All I could do was plead with my eyes, while his looked empty." After the gunman was repelled from the shot clinic, Margaret's thoughts turned to escape. She saw Olenoski kick out the window screen. "He and his teenage daughter climbed out. ... I followed. We ran to the field behind the hospital and fell down into the grass when we heard the shots outside."

A group of people hid in the field near Margaret. When there was a pause in the shooting, they ran to the nearby base housing neighborhood and sought shelter in the home of a stranger.

After his encounter with Lecker in the shot clinic, the gunman retreated down the hall and approached the swinging door of the cafeteria serving line. On the other side of the door, Melissa Moe and Janessa Zucchetto sat on the floor. Christin McCarron stood nearby screaming, concerned about her little brother, who was elsewhere in the hospital. Christin pulled the door open just wide enough to look into the hall.

SSgt Douglas McCray was a dietician aide. "I was working in the hospital kitchen when I heard three bangs, each bang louder than the first one." Staff Sergeant McCray walked to the serving line's pass-through window and saw fifteen-year-old Melissa, who he described as a blond lady, and Christin near the swinging door. "I ran to the kitchen entrance and looked down. The lady on the floor was holding her thigh and saying, 'Oh my God, he shot me.' ... The child was screaming. I took a step toward them. Then the little girl opened the door about twelve to eighteen inches. ... I heard a bang and saw a blast through the door." Christin "was thrown back. ... Her hands flew up in the air." McCray said, "The loud bang caused my ears to ring. I turned and ran back through the kitchen yelling to everyone to get out."

Sheri Lien was a hospital housekeeper. "I was in the basement and went to the back dock to have a cigarette. I heard someone screaming and two shots fired. ... Two people came out of the dining hall and said to call 911;

two people were shot. I ran downstairs and screamed for my boss, Dave Lish, to call."

Dave Lish said Sheri was hysterical. "I attempted to calm her at this time so as to determine if indeed shots had been fired." The housekeeping supervisor had followed Sheri down the stairs. When he corroborated her story, Dave called the base police.

"Crime Stop, are you reporting a crime or emergency?"

"Yeah, this is Dave Lish with housekeeping. I just got a report two people got shot in the dining hall in the hospital. One of my housekeepers just notified me."

The Security Police law enforcement desk had already received several calls reporting the gunfire. The first had come in less than a minute before Lish's call. Law enforcement patrols were already en route, and in less than another minute the gunfire would end.

The gunman turned right at the cafeteria door and retraced his steps toward the pharmacy lobby. Inside the cafeteria serving area, Melissa and Janessa crawled behind the stainless steel food service line and hid in a space under a sink. Melissa dragged a metal cart in front of them, hoping the trail of blood wouldn't give away their hiding spot.

Janessa asked, "Missy, are you ok?"

"No Janessa, I've been shot."

The five-year-old replied, "Missy, my neck itches."

Melissa looked at Janessa's neck and discovered she too had been wounded. She did her best to comfort the little girl and keep her safe. Melissa whispered, "Don't move, don't cry, just be real quiet. ... Pretend we're playing hide-and-seek, if you're really quiet we'll win." They were too overwhelmed to cry. In addition to Janessa's wound, her own injuries, and the violence she had just witnessed, Melissa was worried about her family and the other children. She wondered where they were.

Brandy Pentecost, the college student who fled with the Moe family from the pharmacy lobby, heard the approaching gunfire and saw the gunman returning down the hall. She warned the others who were on the floor with her near the espresso stand, "Be quiet, he is coming." Marlene saw the gunman's eyes. "It was like looking into a shark. There was no expression at all. ... When I looked at his face, it was just like looking at death, because there was no feeling, no emotion."

When Ruth Gerken fled from the pharmacy lobby, she ended up in an alcove that led to a stairwell door across from the espresso bar. She stood there with her cane, peeking around the corner down the hall. She saw the gunman returning and tried to open the stairwell door but couldn't. Unable to run, she shrank into the corner as the gunman moved past her. He stopped in the pharmacy lobby doorway. Standing over Dennis Moe, he turned toward Ruth and fired a series of shots. Ruth said she felt as if she flew into the air. She landed on her back with her head near Marlene Moe, who was in severe pain, "screaming about her six children and about her back."

Dennis Moe lay facedown not far from his wife and daughter. "I heard kids screaming back in a corner, but I couldn't see anything. I was paralyzed and couldn't move." Marlene was similarly immobilized by injuries to her lower spine.

The gunman moved into the pharmacy lobby and approached the island counter in front of the prescription windows, where four women were attempting to hide. Michelle Sigman was shot a second time as she lay on the floor shielding her son. James wriggled free and ran past Eva Walch, who instinctively pulled him under the island counter, shielding him from the shooter. The gunman stood over Eva and fired twice, hitting both of her feet. He moved to the other side of the counter so quickly that Eva thought there were two gunmen. She looked him in the eye as he fired again hitting her in the calf. The gunman fired again. Eva said she felt her femur shatter and saw tissue fly as her leg "exploded." James ran. Eva played dead, and the gunman turned and shot Deena Kelley in the lower back. The gunman moved toward Joy Roberts, who also lay nearby trying to hide. He shot her in the back and moved down the hall toward family practice. Deena said Joy asked her if she'd been shot. "I said yes, and then I heard Joy screaming."

Five-year-old James ran back to his mom and tried to perform CPR on her, something he had seen on the television program *Rescue 911*. James realized his mom needed professional attention and ran down the hall seeking help. He encountered a major and her daughter who had sought shelter in the record's room of the ER. She asked James where his mom was, and he told her she had been shot. The major grabbed James and ran out the ER doors, past the hospital steam plant, and into the field. They ended up in a stranger's home in base housing with several others, where they waited for hours.

Timothy Baldwin stood with his crutches in the family practice area, turning in his x-rays before getting a broken foot casted. He heard steady gunfire coming from the pharmacy lobby area and looked down the hall.

When he saw the gunman, Baldwin yelled that someone was "coming with a gun. Get out!"

Thirty-year-old medical technician SSgt Deborah Foster worked in the family practice clinic. Foster said, "I heard popping noises down the hallway toward pharmacy." She went to the edge of the waiting room and peered down the hall. A patient took off running. Foster heard him yell, "It's for real. He's got a gun. He's shooting people."

Foster said, "I proceeded to holler at everyone and told them to get out of the building. I stayed to see if I could help anyone." Foster saw the gunman shooting into the pharmacy waiting area. She said, "I saw a lady running down the hallway and I hollered at her to run. She fell, dropped her glasses, and went to get them. I told her to leave them and come on. At this point, I saw the gunman coming down the hallway. I grabbed her and ran outside with her to the loading dock. I ran into Staff Sergeant Joe Noone, who was helping a lady with a walker trying to get away from the building. I stopped to help and saw the gunman come out the door. I realized we were too close and couldn't help this lady, so I took off running toward the pediatric clinic door. Joe Noone dove into the bushes. I heard Joe get shot. Buddy Day was by the door and told me to run and dive in the bushes; he was coming. I felt I'd be trapped and kept running. Two shots went over my head and into the wall outside the door. I curled up and dove into the open door."

SSgt Joe Noone had stopped by the hospital to get a signature on his leave form. He planned to travel to Seattle with his pregnant wife, who was attending a midwifery course. Noone and SSgt William Gadbois were at the front desk of the internal medicine area. Foster ran into the waiting room, warned them of a man shooting in the hospital, and ran back out. The men heard gunfire, and Foster returned, yelling that the gunman was coming their way.

As Noone made his way toward the exit he saw a woman with a walker moving slowly. She thought the warnings of a gunman were a joke until Noone grabbed her arm, saying, "Let's go!" Noone guided the woman down the hall and out the loading dock door. As people fled out the door they scattered in all directions. Some jumped inside passing cars. Staff Sergeant Gadbois ran east with several others and hid behind a row of cars parked along Graham Road.

Noone brought the woman with the walker outside, where another med tech guided her to cover behind a green minivan parked nearby.

Noone heard the door slam open behind him. He turned and saw the gunman come out the loading dock door. Noone was caught in the open between the hospital and the parking lot. Something diverted the gunman's attention and when he turned and fired toward Graham Road, Noone ran and hid behind the shrubs that lined the side of the hospital.

* * *

Terri Melton, a technician in the physical therapy department, heard shouted warnings about someone having a gun and then heard a boom. She opened her door and immediately closed it when she saw a flash of gunfire.

Thirty-five-year-old, SSgt David Root grew up in nearby Spirit Lake, Idaho. He had been in the Air Force for ten years and had worked in the ER at two of his previous bases. Root, the non-commissioned officer in charge (NCOIC) of Fairchild's pediatric clinic, was a security-minded man, perhaps more so since the hospital was not within the perceived safety of the base perimeter fence. One pediatrician remembers, shortly after meeting Root, she saw him "dancing around our clinic, going room to room to look out the windows, trying to see someone in the parking lot." Root thought the person was suspicious. The pediatrician thought Root was paranoid. Today she thanks God "for Dave's vigilance and watchful eye over our clinic."

On the afternoon of 20 June 1994, Dave Root heard what he believed was the sound of exercise equipment being assembled down the hall. For the past few days the physical therapy techs had been working on a project. Root said, "They were just making a racket ... and I told them a couple times, 'Look fellas, why don't you do it after work or something? You're just raising hell and making a lot of noise and upsetting my docs and my patients.'" When Root heard the noise again, he said, "That's it, I've had it," and headed across the hall. Root stopped short in the hallway. He poked his head around a corner into family practice and saw the gunman. "I really didn't see *him* as much as his big-ass rifle. ... I pulled my head back, and as I did the corner just exploded."

The gunman was twenty feet away when he turned and fired at Root, who ran to a set of fire doors that separated his clinic from the family practice waiting room. Root swung the doors closed and leaned into them. He didn't think about it. He wasn't even sure how he got to the doors. But he knew he had to stop the man from entering his clinic. He shouted a warning to the pediatric clinic, "Get out!" The fire doors bumped and rattled. Root looked through the narrow glass windows and was face to face with the gunman who was attempting to push his way inside. Again Root turned and commanded, "Get out!" Some people stood bewildered. Others moved slowly, thinking it was a fire drill. Root saw their hesitation and reiterated, "Get out now! Take the kids and parents and run!"

Twenty-two-year-old medical technician, SrA Melissa Danley didn't see the shooter but she heard Root's initial warning. Senior Airman Danley said, "I was checking in a child in the pediatric clinic when I started to hear someone yelling. I couldn't understand, because there were screams in the background that I was hearing also. My supervisor, Staff Sergeant Root, yelled, 'Get out' and shut the fire doors to the entrance of the pediatric clinic."

About twenty parents and children streamed out of offices into the clinic hallway, some asking why they had to evacuate. Danley wasn't sure but said it might be a fire. "I quickly walked around and told people to go outside, and we all calmly walked out ... all of us confused."

On her way out, Danley met up with a pediatrician and a pediatric nurse practitioner, Maj Ann Barshney. The three walked outside with the others, still unaware of the shooting. Danley said, "I remember walking across the parking lot. ... Parents and their kids were scattering. ... I looked around the corner and saw people climbing out of the first-floor windows. ... At this point, I thought there was a fire in the building."

Root stood firm at the fire doors as the clinic emptied. The pushing stopped and Root heard the gunfire resume as the gunman headed through the family practice waiting room. He saw his chance to escape. He checked to ensure the clinic was empty as he ran out the exit. Root made it to the parking lot and stood behind his wife's white four-door Toyota as the gunman emerged from the family practice emergency exit.

Melissa Danley and the group from pediatrics had just started across the parking lot. Danley said, "We heard shouting, gun shots, and someone yelling that someone had a gun. We started running toward the tree line beyond the parking lot. We got into the ditch and instructed a family to go to the housing area for safety." Danley and many of the hospital personnel felt like easy targets. Their brilliant white uniforms glowed through the shrubbery as they lay in the green grass.

Root stood behind his wife's car, feeling especially vulnerable in his hospital whites, as he watched the gunman pursue his co-workers. Staff

Sergeant Noone, wearing a white tank top and white shorts, sprinted toward Root and dove under the hedge that lined the exterior wall of the pediatric clinic. Noone curled up and tried to hide, but the lower branches had been trimmed, leaving him exposed. An airman said Noone told him that as he crouched in the bushes, he yelled at Mellberg, telling him not to shoot, that he had a wife and kids.

Root saw the gunman shoot toward Noone. Three shots hit the dirt, growing progressively closer. A fourth shot passed through Noone's arm, grazing his leg. Root said, "Joe yelled at the shooter, 'You fucker, you shot me.'"

The gunman canted his head and looked quizzically at Noone before he swung the rifle toward Root, who crouched behind the trunk of the car. Root said, "I was making myself as small as I could." He heard a barrage of gunfire. Several bullets struck the car and were absorbed by the engine compartment. Then Root heard "a loud, very audible click," followed by the sound of the rifle's action being worked and more clicking. Root recognized the sound. He had recently bought the same drum magazine for an SKS rifle that he customized for his son. The gunman's drum magazine had run out of spring tension and was no longer feeding rounds into the chamber.

When the gunman paused to wind the spring, Root saw an opportunity to put distance between himself and the gunman. He ran through the parking lot toward the ER. Root said, "He got his gun loaded and cleared to fire in a blink. I didn't get but thirty or so yards from my hiding place when he opened up on me running across the back hospital parking lot behind the ER." As Root ran for his life, the gunman's attention was diverted again.

Deland Romine was outside the hospital near the pediatric clinic. "I saw a man with a rifle shooting at two persons alongside the hospital building. ... He ran as he fired. At first he ran westward to near the pediatrics entrance, then turned as persons hid or ran away, and ran back eastward alongside the hospital and continued across a parking lot to the main street, firing repeatedly at anyone in his path."

* * *

Lorraine Murray, the sixty-two-year-old wife of a retired military member, was in the family practice clinic of the hospital for an appointment with forty-two-year-old father of two, Dr. Delwyn Baker. Dr. Baker was talking with Lorraine when a female technician ran from the front desk into his office yelling for them to get out of the building immediately. Dr. Baker initially thought it was a fire drill. As he and Lorraine made their way to the exit, Dr. Baker heard what he thought were firecrackers. They ran out the emergency exit and moved toward Graham Road with several other people.

Twenty-year-old Preston Kershner was in the cardiopulmonary lab. Kershner said, "I was in the treadmill room and heard three to four shots fired. I was hooking up a patient for a treadmill. Then I heard a scream from a woman. I looked out the door of the room I was in and heard and saw people running, saying, 'Get the fuck out of here, there's a guy with a gun.' I ran out the back entrance and halfway to the parking lot, then realized I left the patient, ran back in, and grabbed him. Then we started running toward the annex. At this time, I heard more shots. I turned around and saw a man with a gun shooting."

Preston said the man had dark hair but other than that, "all I saw was the gun. It was an AK-47." Preston and his patient ran to the annex seeking shelter.

John Tappel, a pediatrician in his late thirties, had just wrapped up an appointment with five-year-old James Sigman. Dr. Tappel was tired. He had been on call the night before and was summoned to the hospital to treat a sick newborn. He hadn't had a chance to go home before his duty day began. Dr. Tappel retrieved his next patient from the waiting room, a little girl in a wheelchair accompanied by her mom. He had just closed the door of his small, cinder block-walled office, when he heard and felt the percussion of a gunshot.

When he heard more shots and yelling, he shouted, "Get down." The wheelchair fell over as the mother brought her daughter to the floor and shielded her with her body. As the clinic chief, Dr. Tappel felt it was his duty to evacuate the clinic and the crowded waiting room he had just left. He stepped out into the hallway. He looked to his right and saw the waiting area was empty. He looked left toward the family practice clinic and saw two people exiting the door at the far end of the hall, silhouetted by the incoming sunlight.

Dr. Tappel saw the dark silhouette of a rifle barrel emerge from a side hallway in front of him, followed by a dark figure with a flattop haircut. The figure turned with the rifle, and Dr. Tappel jumped into his office just before the rifle fired. A bullet struck the frame of an open fire door and sank deep into the cinder block wall. Dr. Tappel closed the door of his office, which had no windows or outside exit. Thinking the gunman was pursuing him, he stayed low and held the door closed with one hand. "So this is how it ends," he thought, as he pulled the phone off his desk and dialed 911. The operator answered, "If this is about the Fairchild shooting, we are already aware."

Sixty-one-year-old Pauline Brown had a 1420 appointment with Dr. Joe Johnson. The doctor was running late, and Pauline had just gotten in to see him at 1500. She sat near the office door. Dr. Johnson heard the sound of screaming and running in the hallway. He excused himself and stepped into the hall, leaving the door open. Dr. Johnson said, "Everybody was running out the fire escape door, and I followed them, assuming there was a code blue outside." Once outside, Dr. Johnson realized the crowd wasn't responding to a medical emergency but was fleeing a gunman who was still inside the hospital. The emergency exit door had locked automatically behind him. "I turned around and pounded on the door, hoping to help my patient in my office." The door burst open as someone fled. Gunfire could be heard coming down the hallway. "I yelled in, saying 'Get out, Get out.' ... The gunfire was getting very close now, and at that point I ran to a blue Ford minivan."

From her chair in Dr. Johnson's office, Pauline saw the gunman come down the hall with a rifle. She thought he was an "Air Policeman" until he poked the rifle through the doorway and shot her in the left shoulder. Pauline kicked the door closed and got under Dr. Johnson's desk as the gunman continued down the hall to the loading dock exit.

Dr. Johnson hid behind the minivan. "I saw the gunman exit the same door I did. ... He had his weapon in the semi-ready position and no emotion on his face [as] he headed for the van I was hiding behind. I was crouched in front of the van, and he paused near the passenger side rear wheel. I believe he reloaded his weapon. I was watching his feet, and he went around the back of the van. I went around the opposite side of him. He went into a slow jog away from the cars onto the grass. At that point I ran back into the hospital and started seeing patients."

Richard Martinez Jr. recalled, "I was checking my mailbox in base housing and heard shots. I knew they were gunshots. ... I saw the man with the rifle and stopped and turned around. ... I really couldn't describe the gunman, because once I saw the rifle, I headed for cover."

Once outside, Lorraine Murray and Dr. Baker realized the evacuation of the hospital was not due to a fire drill and the firecracker sounds they were hearing was actually rifle fire. Dr. Baker ran toward a row of cars parked along Graham Road. He hid behind his blue Dodge Caravan with Anita Lindner, a thirty-nine-year-old mother of four who had come to the hospital to pick up a prescription.

Dr. Baker's patient, Lorraine, ran across an open grass area toward Graham Road, heading for the housing area. A witness hiding behind the hedge of trees that separated the hospital from the houses recalled, "I saw a woman, followed by a man on crutches, running through the parking lot. The woman stumbled, caught herself, got back up, and continued to run away from the hospital to the east. Suddenly she grabbed her leg, went down, and laid still. She fell just below the Emergency Room sign."

Despite having to use crutches, Timothy Baldwin made it out the loading dock exit and headed for the road. Baldwin looked back and yelled, "Here he comes." He made it past the tree line and dove behind an above-ground horizontal steam pipe. Baldwin lay there watching the gunman approach. Then a car drove down Graham from the housing area, changing the gunman's focus and direction. He fired at the car as it drove by, then turned and headed down Graham Road toward the annex.

People scrambled down both sides of Graham Road and through the hospital parking lot. They moved down a ditch and circled around cars, attempting to keep distance and cover between them and the gunman. Others stayed put, peering under vehicles and peeking out the windows of annex offices. Several watched helplessly as the gunman approached Anita Lindner. One witness said, "The suspect was moving at a fast jog in a northerly direction toward the hospital annex when he saw people running and ducking behind cars. He turned sharply toward the parking lot and slowed his pace a little. I saw a person squat behind a car in the parking lot so that they did not see the suspect. I yelled for the person behind the car to run, but they did not. I watched the suspect walk almost behind the person hiding and raise the gun to his shoulder and shoot the person in the head. The suspect fired again at this person after they fell." The impact of the bullets showered asphalt onto the rooftops of nearby vehicles.

The gunman also fired at Dr. Baker, who hid behind a vehicle. The bullet traveled under the vehicle and struck him in the forearm and chest. A witness described Baker's reaction: "Another man who had also been behind the vehicles moved into the grass near a little red car and dropped facedown in the grass and didn't move, like he had been shot." The gunman continued down Graham Road toward the annex, firing to his left toward the hospital and to his right toward the perimeter fence of the base.

Beyond the perimeter fence, deep within the base, came the sound of emergency sirens. Police vehicles navigated the maze of winding roads and intersections as they sped toward Offutt gate on their way to the hospital. Melissa Danley and her pediatrics co-workers lay behind the trees bordering the hospital's southern perimeter. Danley said, "I could hear shots and the sirens very far away. I thought they would never get here before he found us. I was worried that he would be able to see our white uniforms through the green trees even though we were lying on the ground."

SSgt Daniel Elliott and several others had fled from the annex building and sought cover across the street. Elliott said, "As people were leaving [building] 9010 and [building] 9000, we were huddling behind cars in the ditch running along Graham Road. In that short span of time, maybe two minutes, the gunman was in the main parking lot off Graham Road. The gunman appeared to be shooting at people in the parking lot."

Elliott saw the gunman heading toward them and yelled for people to move up the road. He saw a civil engineering dump truck stop to allow people to climb aboard. "Shooting was going on during this time. ... I don't know how many people made it on to it. ... I then saw the bike patrolman." Elliott yelled, pointing out the gunman, "He's right there, he has a rifle." The patrolman didn't see Elliott or hear his warning. He was focused on the gunman. Elliott said, "In one motion, or so it seemed, he dismounted the bike and took a few steps to a kneeling stance, positioned just outside the 9010 entrance door," with his pistol trained on the gunman.

Two hundred yards behind the gunman, Melissa Danley lay behind the tree line listening desperately to the gunfire. During a pause between gunshots she heard what she described as "the sweetest sound," a commanding voice: "Police! Drop your weapon!"

East end of hospital annex. Crime scene photo

Hospital annex, latrine stall showing gunman's gym bag and styrofoam rifle case.
Crime scene photo

Hospital annex hallway facing east. Bullet hole in door frame above evidence marker. Crime scene photo

Dr. London's office sign. Crime scene photo

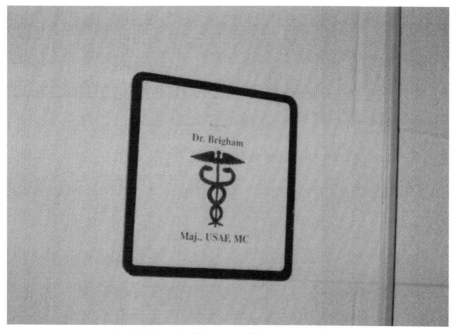

Dr. Brigham's office sign. Crime scene photo

West end hospital annex. Crime scene photo

FAFB main hospital north entrance. Crime scene photo

Hospital lobby upon entering north entrance. Crime scene photo

Hospital lobby showing west wing hallway entrance. Some chairs have been removed from the area. Crime scene photo

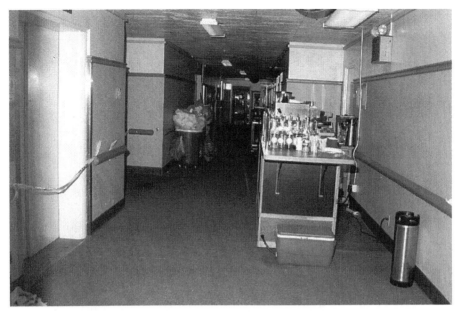

Hospital west wing hallway showing cafeteria serving line doorway (background),
espresso cart (right), elevator door and alcove leading to stairwell door (left).
Crime scene photo

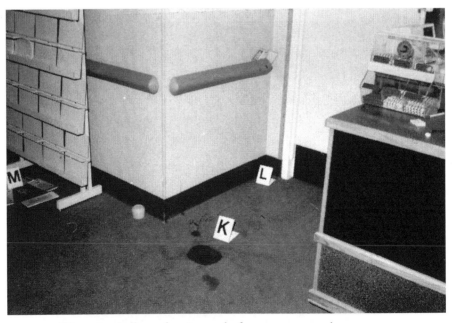

West wing hallway showing end of espresso cart and entrance to
the lab (Room 121). Crime scene photo

West wing vending/waiting room across from ER. Crime scene photo

West wing hallway facing cafeteria serving area entrance. Crime scene photo

Family Practice waiting room. Crime scene photo

Exterior of hospital showing Family Practice emergency exit door and
loading dock area. Crime scene photo

Graham Road, east of hospital, facing annex. Crime scene photo

Police Response

*Blessed be the LORD my strength, who teaches my hands to
war, and my fingers to fight.*
                                            —Psalms 144:1

The sound of gunfire resonated through the halls and up the stairways of the three-story hospital annex. Several people dismissed the noise as doors slamming, construction, or a backfiring car. When shouts echoed down the halls, "Someone has a gun. Get out," people locked themselves in rooms, jumped out windows, or fled down the fire escape stairs. Some of them were still in disbelief, hoping it was a training exercise.

One man in a third-floor corner office above the mental health center paused at his desk. He thought he had heard a car backfire. When he heard the sound again, he got up to investigate, "suspecting gun shots, but not believing it." His bosses met him in the hallway asking if there was an exercise going on. The man stepped out the west fire escape door and stood on the metal grate landing. A gunman moved though the parking lot below, headed toward the hospital, firing a rifle as people scattered for cover. The man ran back inside, pulled the door closed and ran to his office yelling, "This is not an exercise … There's a man running through the parking lot shooting people." He telephoned the base Crime Stop line, and although he misidentified the weapon as a shotgun, he was the first person to alert the base police.

An office worker on the second floor, directly above the mental health center, also heard the gunfire and called the base Crime Stop line, Spokane 911, and the base operator. All three phone lines were busy. The calls for help were already overwhelming the emergency systems. A patient in a nearby doctor's office managed to make it through to Spokane's 911 call center. The operator answered the phone, asking if the call was in reference to shots being fired at Fairchild. When the caller didn't know the current location of the shooter, she moved to the next call in line.

A1C Kent Overton was an hour into his first day working alone as the desk sergeant. All of his telephones rang simultaneously, and the piercing tone of the ER duress alarm sounded, indicating the gunman was already inside the main hospital. Overton snatched one of the telephone handsets. "Airman Overton, law enforcement desk." There was silence on the line. "Airman Overton, law enforcement desk?" He moved to the Crime Stop line.

"Crime Stop, are you reporting a crime or emergency?"

"Uh, emergency crime, there's a guy in the hospital running around with a shotgun."

"Copy, all right, we'll send somebody over."

As Overton reached to key the radio microphone, he yelled at two patrols in the room, "There's a guy in the hospital running around with a shotgun!" before immediately broadcasting, "Fairchild Police to all posts and patrols, we have an alarm at the ER. Informational, we have an individual in the hospital running around with a shotgun."

Stacy Morrison and her officemates on the second floor of the annex immediately recognized the sound of gunfire. Stacy stepped onto the fire escape and saw the gunman exit below. In the days before cellular phones were widely available to the public, Stacy used a nearby office phone to dial 5555, the Crime Stop hotline.

The phones continued ringing on the desk. As soon as Overton hung up the Crime Stop line, it rang again. "Crime Stop, are you reporting a crime or emergency?"

Stacy Morrison replied, "Emergency, crime, I don't know. There's a guy bolting out of building 9010 right across the street from the hospital with a gun, *firing!*"

"Running out of building 9010?"

"Yes, right across the street from the hospital."

Overton broadcast, "Fairchild Police to all responding patrols, the individual just ran out of building 9010 across from the hospital, firing off rounds out of his shotgun."

I didn't take the time to acknowledge the radio call. I didn't advise that I was en route. I rode away from the gate, headed down Graham Road to the hospital about three-tenths of a mile away. I knew someone was at the hospital with a gun and visualized myself reacting to what I might encounter. I felt strangely calm. Vehicles slowed as they approached me. The occupants tried to tell me what they had witnessed, but I couldn't hear them. A slow-rolling military dump truck approached. I saw people standing in the dump bed; others clung to the cab alongside the passenger door. It seemed like a macabre parade: people leaned over the tall sides of the dump bed, waving and yelling down at me as I rode by. I didn't hear my supervisor on the radio coordinating the response of the motorized patrols as they sped toward the hospital. My sole focus was on getting to the scene.

Our counterparts in the security control center took a call from the hospital and relayed the message over the law enforcement radio channel. It occurred at some point during my response, but I don't remember hearing it.

"Fairchild Police, Fairchild Security, just received a notification from the hospital, you have individuals down. Repeat. You have individuals down."

As I neared the annex, a crowd of people fled toward me, moving rapidly down Graham Road. I didn't have a description of the gunman; I scanned the crowd for weapons as I coasted toward them. Riding through the crowd, I shouted, "Where is he?" The group collectively pointed behind them, down Graham Road, saying, "There's a man with a gun. He's shooting people. He's over there."

I rode further, searching the area ahead. As I approached the annex, the deep boom of gunfire reverberated off the surrounding buildings. Standing on the bike's pedals, I coasted and scanned the area ahead of me. A man wearing dark clothes appeared in the middle of the road. He walked toward me, holding a long gun at his waist. As he walked, he fired toward the housing area to his right, then swung the weapon to his left and fired toward the hospital.

My field of view shrank. I had tunnel vision, focused solely on the man on the road. I veered right, gliding the bike up onto the sidewalk in front of the annex. I leapt from the bicycle; momentum carried me forward as I grasped my pistol, unsnapped the holster strap with my thumb, and drew my Beretta. I knelt on the sidewalk, sat back on my right foot and braced my left elbow on my left knee. I was in the open, unaware of the fire hydrant, telephone pole and large metal electrical transformer box nearby, that would have afforded me protection from gunfire. Instinctively, I thumbed the safety lever of my pistol upward, ensuring it was in the fire position, as I gripped the pistol with both hands and steadied it in line with my target. My eyes never left the gunman, but I was aware of movement around and behind him, people scurrying and crouching behind cars and what looked like a person lying exposed behind a vehicle about 125 yards down the road.

I yelled, "Police! Drop your weapon, put it down!" He continued moving toward me and fired again to his side. I didn't see anyone in his line of fire, though I knew I needed to stop him. I also knew shooting at him would endanger others in the area. I yelled again, "Police! Drop it! Put it down now!" He picked up speed, almost running at an angle toward me and toward the annex. He slowed and took more deliberate aim, firing in my direction. I felt a sense of relief: the threat he posed outweighed the danger of me shooting in the vicinity of innocents.

Without conscious thought, my index finger slid inside the Beretta's trigger guard. My finger pressed the trigger as I tracked the threat.

I wasn't immediately aware of how far away the man was. I had no doubt I could hit him, but I struggled to find him in my sights. His body was nearly obscured behind the narrow steel post that served as the front sight of my Beretta. I finally aligned the front sight with his upper torso and the notches of my rear sight as I continued to press the trigger.

I focused on the sights, unable to clearly see the gunman; but several people witnessed him firing at me. A man on the second floor of the annex, watched from his office window and said the gunman "started walking toward building 9010, firing as he went. He seemed to be firing at one point over and over."

Another witness who lay on his stomach looking out from underneath a car said, "The gunman was shooting down the street with the gun aimed in the SP's direction ... steadily firing it."

The hammer of my Beretta crept rearward, then dropped sharply, sending a 124-grain ball of copper-jacketed lead down the barrel and toward the gunman. The witness under the car said, "The gunman acted as if something happened to his left shoulder."

I didn't see him react. He was still standing and still moving toward me as I lined up the sights for a second shot. The pistol was in single-action mode now, requiring only a few pounds of pressure on the trigger to drop the hammer.

I fired again. He was still moving toward me.

He was now on the grass that separated the annex parking lot from the street. I tracked him and lined up the sights and fired a third time. I saw no reaction. My shots had been controlled and reflexive, as rhythmic as a heartbeat. I was singularly focused on working my handgun and didn't hesitate in lining up the next shot, but a thought flashed in my head—"Nothing's happening. I am shooting him, and nothing's happening!"

It was the occupational nightmare of law enforcement officers. I had dreamed it many times, and now I was living it. I followed through with the trigger press, the hammer dropped, sending a fourth projectile toward the gunman. From behind my recoiling pistol I saw the man leap into the air midstride, his legs kicking as he spun around, landing flat on his back in the grass. His legs, arms, and rifle were all motionless and pointing away from me. I exhaled, feeling relieved and in control again.

It was later determined, based on the location of my spent 9mm brass and the location of the downed gunman, that my final shot was made from a distance of 68 to 71 yards.

Keeping my eyes and handgun trained on the man in the grass, I stood and moved down the sidewalk, headed for a silver pickup truck parked adjacent to Graham Road, the last position of cover between me and the downed gunman. Halfway to the truck, I realized I hadn't radioed the desk. I knelt down and keyed the mike that was clipped to the collar of my shirt. In a calm and professional manner, I relayed my call sign, what I had observed, and what action I had taken. At least that's how it sounded to me at the time. In reality my words spewed forth in an adrenaline-induced, unpunctuated burst.

"Fairchild—Six, shots fired I took him down he's down this is Police Six he's down!"

I continued moving to cover, jogging toward the truck. Back at the desk, Overton dutifully relayed seconds-old witness reports over the radio, "Fairchild, Police One, Police Two, this individual is still in the hospital. He's firing off rounds. Copy. Two people are down."

I assumed the desk hadn't heard my transmission. I knelt down again and radioed in a calm but frustrated tone, "Fairchild, Police Six, I shot him. He's down."

An unexpected yet familiar voice acknowledged, "Roger that, Six."

The voice belonged to TSgt Tony Rizzo. He had been in his office down the hall from the desk, working on the Security Police duty roster for Fairchild's upcoming air show, when he heard about the shooting. Tech Sergeant Rizzo said, "The door to the LE desk flew open and two patrolmen came running down the hallway." When the patrolmen said there were shots fired at the hospital, Rizzo ran up to the desk. He said, "I started helping out with the calls and the radio. Initially we were getting lots of calls from the hospital—people were locked in rooms and offices saying they could hear gunshots and people running. I wanted to stay on the phone with some of them as long as possible, but there were so many calls we just started trying to get to them all."

In between phone calls and radio transmissions, Rizzo contacted the Spokane County Sheriff's Office. "I told the dispatcher what was happening and requested any assistance they could provide. They put the call out to all agencies, and every cop with a radio in Eastern Washington knew what was going on." Spokane County sheriff's deputies, Washington State Patrol and police officers from Medical Lake and Airway Heights responded to the hospital. They would help seal off the perimeter and search the area for additional threats.

As TSgt Gloria Robinson sped to the scene in her patrol car, she heard me radio that I had shot the subject. She radioed back, "Be there in a second."

Rizzo radioed, "Six, what's your location? Where is the individual?"

I responded, "Out in front of the ER."

I wasn't "out in front of the ER." I was focused on the gunman and making my way to the truck and the cover it would provide me. I relayed the most prominent landmark I could see, a red and white sign, 170 yards in front of me that read, "ER Entrance." I reached the truck and leaned over the hood, my Beretta trained on the upper torso of the supine man. I shouted, "Don't move!" The rifle was in his left hand, which, like him, was still motionless.

As I waited for backup, I realized I hadn't checked my surroundings for additional threats. I quickly scanned left, right, and behind me. I saw small groups of personnel standing on the metal exterior stairs of the annex. Frustrated, I yelled, "Get out of the area! If you are not a medic, get back!" I didn't know how long they had been there and was confounded that anyone would be standing where bullets had just been flying. I was still the only cop on the scene and quickly returned my attention to the gunman. It seemed like minutes but was mere seconds before my supervisor, Police 2, ran up to the truck beside me. Tech Sergeant Robinson was a strong, wiry woman with inner city confidence, and I was glad to see her.

Other patrols arrived as Robinson left cover and moved toward the gunman. When she did, I raised the muzzle of my pistol and thumbed the safety lever down to de-cock the hammer, putting the pistol back into double action mode. The hammer fell safely against the firing pin block with a loud click. I flicked the lever back to the fire position and covered Robinson as she approached the gunman.

With her own pistol at the ready, Robinson lifted the gunman's rifle with her foot and kicked it aside. She yelled for a medic, but it wasn't necessary. Sgt Steven Walker was already sprinting toward the man he had seen fall. Walker rushed in and assessed his patient's injuries.

The phones continued to ring at the law enforcement desk. An airman in the ER called the Crime Stop line to relay information he received from someone on the second floor of the annex. "I just got done talking to the orderly room ... They say that they have a sniper up on top of the annex."

Overton relayed the information. "Fairchild Police to all responding patrols—the sniper is on top of the annex."

I hadn't seen any evidence of a sniper, but I was too close to the annex to see the rooftop. If someone was up there, they had a clear shot at Robinson and the medics tending to the gunman. I ran from the truck and knelt near the gunman, tracking my pistol along the annex rooftop. The roof appeared to be clear.

I glanced behind me at the man I had shot. A large knife with a blade shaped like a Christmas tree had fallen partially out of a sheath attached to his belt. Dried streaks of blood trailed down his left arm, coming from under the sleeve of his black T-shirt. I returned to scanning the area. At the time I didn't notice the bullet-sized hole on the bridge of his nose. I also wasn't aware that one of my shots had passed through his shoulder. I didn't know the extent of his injuries, but I knew he was no longer a threat. I must have noticed the other injured people in the area, the medics assisting them, and the stream of law enforcement officers arriving on the scene.

Rizzo came up on the radio. "Six, this is Fairchild."

"Six, go."

"Roger, Six, what's your status?"

"Secure, one individual down. There are several wounded down."

"Roger. Do you have assistance yet?"

"Affirmative, we have a lot of patrols on scene."

"That's a good copy. Be advised. ... County has been notified. They should be arriving soon. ... We'll be contacting OSI [Air Force Office of Special Investigations]."

Robinson directed me to set up a perimeter near the annex. I ran across Graham Road, slid down the bank of a deep ditch, and made my way back toward the annex. As I came up out of the ditch I saw some law enforcement officers talking to a woman on the side of the road. Her description of a "second gunman" sounded familiar. I approached the woman from behind asking, "Did he have a large knife on his belt?" The startled woman screamed and jumped away from me. I apologetically explained to her and the officers that the man she described was likely the same man I had just shot.

I took cover behind a security truck parked broadside at the corner of Medical Lake and Graham Road. I acknowledged the driver, an NCO crouched behind the front fender with his firearm at the ready. I smoked the cigarette he offered and sat back against the rear wheel. I dropped the magazine from my Beretta and confirmed that I had fired four rounds. There was a full magazine in a pouch on my belt, but it didn't occur to me to do a tactical reload. I reinserted the magazine and holstered my weapon.

Graham Road was choked with emergency vehicles that had responded from Spokane and the surrounding area. I wasn't needed for traffic control. Occasionally, a resident of the homes across the street inside the base perimeter fence would poke their head out of a door or window. If their curiosity outweighed their sense of self-preservation and they lingered too long, I yelled at them to get back inside. I didn't know what else I could do to help, but I wasn't feeling particularly useful on the perimeter.

The base fire department responded immediately and staged outside the perimeter, waiting for police to secure the scene. They were soon joined by numerous civilian fire, rescue, and ambulance personnel, all waiting for the police to make the scene safe. Only moments after the gunman was neutralized, security police waved some of the rescue crews into the scene, where they went to work assisting hospital medics with the wounded.

Calls reporting a gunman continued pouring into the desk. Tech Sergeant Rizzo said, "We were still getting calls from the hospital from people trapped inside the building, and we were getting different descriptions of the shooter. Some were saying he was dressed in black and carrying a rifle and others were saying he was wearing shorts and a T-shirt, armed with a shotgun."

The scene was chaotic. Several witnesses reported gunmen to on-scene security police. Our flight chief, MSgt John Shenk, call sign Police 1, moved to the annex and radioed his patrols. "We have a possible in the annex. We don't know if he's on the roof or on the floors."

Robinson radioed, "Copy. You think there's somebody in the annex?"

"Roger, I got a report that they don't know if he's armed or not. He's second or third floor or maybe even the roof."

Rizzo radioed Shenk, "Fairchild, Police One, status?"

"Roger, about ready to take the annex."

"Roger that, have you confirmed any reports of personnel up there?"

"Roger. We have a witness—believes the man is up on the third floor. Description is a white male wearing black clothes and red hair."

"Roger that. Is this individual armed?"

"Yes he's armed—rifle."

"Roger that. All units, be advised information is there's an individual in the hospital annex possibly third floor with a rifle adjacent to one of the windows."

In addition to the exterior fire escape stairs on either end of the building, the patrols needed to cover the central stairwell of the annex to prevent anyone from entering or exiting the building during the search. Police 1 positioned his patrols. "Roger. I'm gonna need someone to block the Graham Road side. We have an access there." He radioed to another patrol, "I need you to cover that stairwell, and don't let no one come down."

Fifty-two on- and off-duty security police personnel responded to the scene. Teams worked to evacuate the housing areas on either side of the hospital grounds. Others searched the area for additional threats and wounded. The Security Police Emergency Services Team (EST) was re-called. They posted a sniper team equipped with a .308 caliber rifle on the roof of a nearby home. The team had a view of the third floor and roof of the annex, providing long-range cover for their colleagues.

Fairchild's security police and fire department had no way of communicating with the civilian law enforcement and fire agencies on the scene. Communications were also impeded by the near-constant radio traffic as security and law enforcement specialists broadcast their observations and the numerous reports they received from witnesses on the scene.

Some of the radios weren't picking up direct messages, receiving only the ones relayed through the more powerful transmitter of the law enforcement desk. Shift commander 1st Lt Scott Kolar, call sign Defender 4, did his best to maintain control of the scene and squash any erroneous reports. In one situation, a report relayed by an anonymous first responder started an undisciplined radio exchange that could have wasted precious resources if not for Lieutenant Kolar.

"We got a report of shots fired in housing."

"Which housing?"

"Copy. What housing?"

"Police One, Security One."

"Go."

"You copy we have a report of shots fired in housing?"

"Which housing? Can you give a location?"

"Directly behind the annex."

Kolar stepped in. "Fairchild, Defender Four."

"Transmit, Four."

"Roger. Be advised that's probably spillover calls from previous, copy? I'm out here on scene, haven't heard anything."

As security police worked to clear the annex, Rizzo radioed from the desk.

"Defender Four, this is Fairchild."

"Go ahead."

"Roger, Defender Four. Two things—been notified of a child possibly left inside a gold Bronco. Apparently the parent departed and left the child there when all the trouble began."

"Copy. I'll take care of it."

"Also, if possible, I need to try and get a list of injuries of all personnel involved and names if I can."

A team of security police searched the parking lot for the gold Bronco. They found several vehicles matching the description, but none of them contained children. Another team of security policemen swept the hospital parking lot in a small armored vehicle known as a Peacekeeper. They happened upon several airmen tending to Orson Lee. The driver radioed the desk, "Roger. Be advised I have one individual wounded. He's in stable condition, and I'm transporting same to the hospital. Copy."

Master Sergeant Shenk and K9 handler, Sgt Kevin Schindler cleared the first and second floor of the annex. As Shenk moved to the third floor, he contacted Lieutenant Kolar on the radio. "I believe suspect is on the third floor. I've got one group in the middle and a civilian patrol at the end of Graham Road."

At my post on the inner perimeter in front of the annex, I couldn't help thinking there was something more productive I could be doing. I wasn't picking up the majority of the radio traffic and was unaware of the room-to-room search taking place in the annex. I jumped at the sound of breaking glass. I reached for my gun and spun to face the top floor of the annex, where I saw Lieutenant Kolar and a small team of law enforcement officers outside the third-floor door. I relaxed when I realized they had used a baton to smash the door's window in order to gain access.

Kolar and his team of civilian and military law enforcement officers searched the third floor of the annex. No one could locate a master key. The lieutenant announced himself before kicking in locked doors where he found groups of people huddled in rooms.

Rizzo juggled the radio traffic of the security police on scene and the unrelenting telephone calls coming into the law enforcement desk. He said, "On top of all the people at the hospital calling, we were getting calls from the command post wanting information. All I could tell them is units were responding and we would tell them more later." The calls from the command post were persistent, forcing Rizzo to press for information even while the search for additional gunmen continued. At 1545, Rizzo radioed Lieutenant Kolar.

"Defender Four, this is Fairchild."

"Go."

"Roger, Defender Four. I need as soon as possible to obtain information on injured and names. Copy?"

"I copy. It's a little hectic over here, and I can't make my way to the first-floor. Copy?"

"Yeah, I understand Defender Four. I have personnel that are really interested in that."

"Roger. We'll get it when we clear."

"Roger that."

Fairchild's Security Police law enforcement desk also fielded calls from command posts and security police squadrons of other Air Force bases. They called during the height of the response, concerned about the possibility of a terrorist incident. The desk received numerous calls from local and national media. They also continued to receive routine calls from unknowing military members wanting copies of police reports or help getting the keys out of their locked cars. Still others called asking when the base lockdown would end and the gates would be reopened.

Master Sergeant Shenk and Sergeant Schindler searched the third floor of the annex, moving from room to room. Schindler prepared to enter a training room and spotted a man standing by the chalkboard, dressed in a full chemical resistant suit and gas mask, holding an M16 rifle. Schindler shouted, "Put your hands up!" but the man didn't respond. Schindler said,

"I cut my dog loose to do his job. I immediately noticed the dog did not show any interest whatsoever." The man was motionless and unresponsive. Schindler approached the man with his gun drawn only to discover the rifle was a replica, held by a mannequin used as a chemical warfare training aid.

Police finished clearing the third floor of the annex at 1555. They had discovered several groups of people in offices, some had barricaded the doors with desks and other furniture, but there was no sign of additional gunmen. The access door leading to the roof was padlocked from the inside; but just to be sure, EST responded with bolt cutters and cleared the rooftop. EST posted a man on the roof to watch over search teams as they worked in the parking lots below.

*   *   *

OSI Special Agent, Jim Carroll, moved up to my position, and I asked him if there was anything I could do to help. He said they needed security at the ER and offered me a ride. I slid into the front passenger seat of his unmarked government sedan, and we drove slowly down Graham Road. I stared out the window at the gunman, who now lay unattended in the grass. As we approached the ER driveway, we rolled past a person lying behind a vehicle parked adjacent to the road. I recalled the image of people moving in the background as I confronted the gunman. I remembered seeing a person lying exposed behind a vehicle. As we drove by I could see it was a woman, her upper body now covered with a white sheet. The fabric near her head was soaked with blood.

I stood guard outside the ER doors, scanning the surrounding area and watching the hands of everyone who approached the building. Medics scrambled in and out of the ER doors pushing gurneys, holding IVs, loading patients into ambulances. I stopped a medic as he rushed past and said, "There's a woman out there on the road. I'm sure my background was clear, but I'm worried one of my bullets might have—"

The medic interrupted. "I can assure you, she was dead before you arrived. The only bullets that hit her came from him." Despite the tragedy of his words, I was relieved to hear them, though I wondered what he had experienced that day to be able to speak with such certainty.

Reports of a second gunman continued to come over the radio. Several other security policemen and I moved through the hospital, searching and clearing every room. I began on a section of the first floor, throwing open office and bathroom doors before entering with my gun at the ready. Inside a doctor's office, sitting against a wall spattered with blood and tissue, was a chair with a bullet hole in the backrest. I cleared the office and moved on without taking the time to process what had happened there.

Down a hallway I kicked open the door of a small office and found a frightened mother huddled under a desk with her children. I told her, "You're safe. Stay here until someone comes for you."

I had cleared most of my section of the hospital when I came to a room at the end of a hallway. I stood beside the swinging door and peeked through the window. The interior was dark, so I pulled the heavy Maglite from my belt and held it in one hand, with my pistol in the other. I shouldered through the door into the cafeteria serving area. The metallic smell of death hung in the thick, humid air. I stepped to look behind a stainless steel steam table, and my feet slid on the white tile floor. When I had cleared the room, I flipped on a light switch and saw I was standing in a pool of blood. It felt like I had walked over someone's grave.

* * *

Our chief of security police was away on personal business. Capt Ben Martin was the acting chief and kept in telephone contact with the desk as the situation progressed. When he called to ask about the status of the search for the second gunman, Rizzo relayed what he knew. "They confirm they got the one shooter down and dead."

Martin asked, "What's the rumor on this second one? ... Where did we get that all started from?"

Rizzo said, "I think that's bogus. In fact, we're pretty sure it's bogus. ... They had no sightings of the second individual. ... They've searched the entire building. ... In here, we're comfortable there was only one shooter. He's dead. ... They got him outside. ... Police Six shot him."

Captain Martin responded, "We're gonna need to set him up, because he's gonna be in a world of hurt when he gets through with all of this."

Intersection of Medical Lake and Graham Road. Sidewalk at east end of annex where SrA Brown knelt and confronted gunman. Crime scene photo

Staff Sgt Sue Conard points out where Mellberg fell after he was shot. Credit: Sandra Bancroft-Billings, *The Spokesman-Review*

Aerial view of Fairchild Hospital Campus showing distance between where the gunman fell and Brown's firing position. Crime scene photo

SrA Brown takes cover behind a security vehicle shortly after stopping the gunman. Courtesy of FAFB Historian

Scott Dearduff (left) and two other Fairchild security policemen on the perimeter of the hospital, 20 June 1994. Courtesy of FAFB Historian

On-scene command post, security police First Sergeant Joe Markin (BDU's) and Wing Commander, Col William Brooks (on a cell phone), 20 June 1994. Courtesy of FAFB Historian

On-scene command post, annex in background, 20 June 1994.
Courtesy of FAFB Historian

Graham Road facing south. Mazda Miata with 9mm bullet hole in right rear fender
shown in foreground, 20 June 1994. Crime scene photo

Graham Road choked with emergency vehicles on 20 June 1994.
Courtesy of FAFB Historian

Base Housing

SSgt Scott Orth was a SERE instructor at Fairchild's Survival School. He taught aircrews, and other at-risk military personnel, the skills of survival, evasion, resistance and escape. Staff Sergeant Orth was off duty at his home in the Air Force housing neighborhood that bordered the hospital on the south. His small, single-story home on First Street, in the back corner of the neighborhood, butted up against the same wheat field that ran along the west perimeter of the hospital campus.

Orth and his wife, Danette, were outside enjoying the warm weather, washing cars in the driveway with their four-year-old daughter, Tara, and their twenty-three-year-old nephew, Trey, who was visiting from out of town. They heard the sound of gunfire coming from the direction of the hospital. Orth thought it might be a drill until a panicked woman came running down First Street screaming, "There is a man with a gun and he is shooting people!"

Orth said, "I could tell it was not an act or a joke or anything like that. It was just genuine horror she was expressing." He instructed his nephew to get Tara into the house. Trey scooped Tara up and headed to a bedroom where the Orths' four-month-old daughter was sleeping. Orth sprinted to his gun cabinet inside the hallway closet, where he grabbed his loaded Taurus .357 revolver, a 30-06 rifle, and a box of shells. As he moved to the kitchen counter to load the rifle, he heard Danette yelling outside.

Danette was running for the safety of her home when she noticed something behind the hospital that caused her to stop. Several people were attempting to hide in a field, but the sparse vegetation did little to conceal them. Danette ran behind a storage shed and signaled the group. "When I saw all those people in the field crawling around, I knew I had to do something. I was behind the shed, jumping up and down, waving my arms and yelling for them to come this way." The group was over a hundred yards away and were not immediately aware of her attempt to help.

Scott Orth threw open a side door of the house. He spotted his wife and asked her what she was doing. Danette told him, "There are people out in the field."

From his position he couldn't see the field, but he knew it well. He told his wife, "They are sitting ducks out there. There is no cover."

Danette said, "I know, but I can't get them to come in."

As he stood at the door, Orth saw his wife disappear around the corner of the shed, running toward the field. Knowing the police would be responding, he resisted the urge to follow her. "I had stayed inside the doorway, as I didn't want to bring my guns outside and get shot. When I saw her leave, I turned around and put my guns on the counter and went to find out where she went. As I ran out, all these people ran past me and into the house."

The crowd had responded to Danette's call. They emerged from the weeds and ran toward her house. "I could not believe how many people there were." She noticed that not all of them were able to run. "A man on crutches stood up and started toward me, and I ran out into the field and helped him." With the assistance of a man who stopped to help, Danette brought the man to the safety of her home. Once inside, they locked the doors and closed the window blinds and curtains.

Orth secured his revolver in a shoulder holster, loaded his rifle, and took a position at the kitchen window, which afforded him a clear view of his neighborhood. Danette said the back of the house was also well guarded. "Our dog was in the back yard, which made me nervous for him. But I knew that he would alert us if anyone was back there."

People continued to come to the house seeking shelter. Orth said there were "a few timid looks from a few folks as they entered our home, but the majority had a look of relief." When they saw the armed homeowner, they greeted him with "Thank God" and "Thank you" as they slipped inside. As the afternoon progressed, Orth said the house guests "came over several times to thank us for protecting them, saying how comforting it was knowing they had an armed person at the door to defend them."

The refugees in the Orth home were both civilian and military, officers and enlisted. Most of the officers congregated in a bedroom. Most of the enlisted gathered in the living room at the rear of the house, intently watching the television for news of what was happening at the hospital, only two hundred yards away. A few were on guard, watching for suspicious persons outside. Orth said, "I asked them not to peek out the blinds, fearing that might alert someone outside if they were near the home."

Security police moved through the neighborhoods that surrounded the hospital searching for additional gunmen. They evacuated the homes nearest the hospital as a precaution against a rumored sniper in the area. When the SPs reached the Orth home, they decided to use it to consolidate the evacuees, including a neighbor's home daycare. The SPs used a Peacekeeper armored vehicle to shield the kids and caretakers as they moved to the safe house. Danette volunteered to help. "I followed alongside the armored truck with quite a few policemen, and we each carried a child across the yard."

When the transfer was complete, Orth said, they "stationed an SP under the big pine tree in our front yard in a prone position to secure the house. They suggested I put my rifle away, obviously fearing I might shoot one of them. ... I am well trained in weapon use and truly was never concerned about mistakenly shooting one of our own." Several people in the house worried that Orth would lock up his guns. He said, "I reassured them I would not and would remain on guard just in case the worst happened. That seemed to calm them back down again."

The Orths' girls and about ten other children were sequestered in a back bedroom, where Trey read them stories and there were plenty of toys to keep them entertained. The room was the safest in the house, as it was the farthest from the hospital. It also protected the children from hearing the television news or stories the guests recounted of the horrors they had witnessed. Staff Sergeant Orth said, "One of our temporary guests was in the lobby when the gunman came in. ... He tripped on her leg but did not shoot her, she thinks because she smiled at him."

Scott and Danette Orth estimate there were about fifty people in their home. Every room was filled, and a single window-mounted air conditioner did little to cool the small house. Danette made her rounds checking on her kids and her guests, offering cold drinks and snacks. "A lot of them asked if they could use my phone to notify families. I later hunted down the phone to call my mother and father to notify them of what was going on, that we were fine, and I would call them later because others needed to make calls."

The security police eventually ruled out the rumors of the sniper and the second gunman and declared the scene secure. The SPs worked their way through the neighborhoods, looking for witnesses to the shooting. The Orth home slowly emptied as the SPs shuttled witnesses in armored vehicles and buses to the base community center.

Hospital Aid

Aerial photo of FAFB hospital campus showing southern perimeter tree line and steam pipe, 20 June 1994. Courtesy of FAFB Historian

Dr. Victor Barton crouched behind a red car along with a sergeant and a lab technician. Seconds earlier, the doctor had been writing letters to patients at his office desk in family practice. Gunfire and shouted warnings had brought him outside and across a parking lot to Graham Road, where he watched as the gunman emerged from the hospital firing a rifle.

Dr. Barton hid behind the car, listening to the shouts and gunfire. He helped the sergeant hold the lab technician down, shielding her from the gunfire that she believed was part of a hospital exercise. The shots grew louder. Bullets struck nearby vehicles, ricocheting into the ground, propelling dirt and gravel into the air. Dr. Barton heard footsteps on the other side of the vehicle, followed by "numerous loud shots." He looked under the vehicle and saw Dr. Baker and Anita Lindner lying on the other side of Graham Road. When the gunman ran north, toward the hospital annex,

Dr. Baker yelled that he had been hit. Dr. Barton ran to help him. Like countless others at the hospital that day, the transition from a target of violence to caregiver was immediate.

Medical technician SSgt William Gadbois was the first to reach Dr. Baker. He saw the doctor was bleeding from his chest and forearm. Gadbois removed his shirt and used it to apply pressure to the wounds. Gadbois and several others who worked in internal medicine had fled the building when they saw and heard the gunman inside the hospital. Some in the group jumped into vehicles that happened to be leaving the area. Gadbois ran for the road and hid amongst a row of parked cars. Gadbois said, "There were four or five of us hiding behind cars on the main street of the hospital when shots started again."

Gadbois saw the gunman approaching and thought for sure he had been spotted. Instead, the gunman slowed and fired several shots at people near a minivan. The gunman moved quickly down the road, passing Gadbois, headed toward the annex. Gadbois heard several more gunshots. A 9mm bullet struck the rear fender, on the opposite side of the red Mazda Miata he was hiding behind. When the gunfire ceased, Gadbois ran to the minivan, where he assessed the injured and rendered aid. In the initial response, several medics, doctors, and law enforcement officers stopped to assesses the injuries of Anita Lindner. Some were preempted by shouts to "leave her be, there's nothing you can do." Anita had been struck by gunfire at least five times. The location and severity of her wounds removed all doubt: she was gone.

Thirty-three-year-old physician assistant (PA) 2nd Lt Timothy Street and Sgt Steven Walker had been in a minor surgery room in the family practice hallway, prepping a young woman for a mole removal. They heard gunfire, which Lieutenant Street, a former pararescue team leader, recognized as the distinct report of an AK-47. Street and Walker stepped into the hall and were met by the smell of gun smoke. A spent shell casing lay on the carpet, and to their left, the emergency exit door swung closed with a bang. Walker hid their patient in Street's office. He looked out the window and "noticed people lying on the ground by the cars in the parking lot." Street yelled for Walker to bring some roller gauze to Dr. Johnson's office, where he had found Pauline Brown under the desk, suffering from a gunshot wound.

As Street applied a pressure dressing to Pauline's arm, Walker described what he had seen. "I told him there were people hurt outside, and he told me to get some supplies and follow him."

Walker went to a supply closet and filled his arms with bandages and dressings. He and Street ran out the emergency exit; the bullets were still flying. Walker said, "As we ran across the parking lot toward the cars, it sounded like bees flying around my head, but I was focused on Staff Sergeant Bill Gadbois … and the fact he had his shirt off, holding pressure on Dr. Baker's chest. … Bill was yelling at me, but I couldn't understand him, either due to me running, the buzzing sound, or because I was focused." When Walker got within reach, Gadbois pulled him down, spilling some of the supplies he was carrying. "He said 'Get down. He is shooting at you,' and like an idiot I look up over the car and said 'who?' That is when I saw someone fly up in the air a few feet and fall to the ground."

Walker and Street helped bring Dr. Baker's bleeding under control, then Walker ran to the man he had seen fall. He focused on the patient, initially unaware of the rifle lying a few feet away in the grass. Walker said, "I noticed he was all in black and had a large knife strapped to his leg, one bullet hole near his nose exiting the back of his head. … He had a great pulse but wasn't breathing." The 9mm bullet had passed through the gunman's brain. Walker summed up the injury. "As we say, he was gone; his body just didn't realize it yet."

For more than thirty minutes Walker worked instinctively to save the patient. As others arrived to assist, he sent them to retrieve equipment and supplies from an ambulance parked near the annex. He performed artificial respiration, applied suction, and administered oxygen. After an exhaustive effort, Walker used a pen to write on the gunman's chest, "Code canceled 1540 hours."

* * *

As soon as the gunfire stopped, SrA Melissa Danley got up to help the wounded. Maj Ann Barshney, the pediatric nurse practitioner who had hidden with Danley, said, "Melissa was on her feet despite my saying 'stay down.' She was running to the corner of the parking lot, saying a woman was down and looked hurt."

Danley headed toward Lorraine Murray, the sixty-two-year-old who had fled Dr. Baker's office. Danley said, "I ran down the tree line and found a group of people helping a woman with a wound to her leg. I asked if the shooter was down. … They said yes, so I ran across the parking lot to the ER and grabbed a wheelchair."

As Danley ran back from the ER she reported that more people had been hurt inside the hospital. One pediatrician had fled into the field. Major Barshney considered following her and returning safely home to her three children. Ultimately, she followed Danley's lead and ran into the hospital to assist the wounded.

Danley reached Lorraine with the wheelchair. "I … put her in it and took her to radiology, where there was some form of triage starting. I did a quick bandage and left for the record's room, because I was told there were wounded in there. Pat Deaton was lying on the ground with a gunshot wound to his right arm. He told me to go help someone else and that he was fine. He was stable, so I ran to the pharmacy and saw that people were being worked on there. I then went to the ER."

Medical personnel scurried about the emergency room, shouting for supplies and equipment as they tended to the steadily rising stream of wounded. To an outsider the ER looked like a panicked frenzy of activity. But if you asked the staff, they would tell you it was organized chaos.

Dale Bates assisted doctors and medics in the ER by providing them with supplies and working the phones at the reception desk. He wasn't a member of the ER staff—only moments before he had been a patient at the hospital. Dale worked for the US Public Health Service, and his position gave him access to medical services at the base. He had been scheduled for a cardiac stress test and was about to step on a treadmill when he and a medical technician heard gunfire and screaming outside the cardiopulmonary lab. People ran past the room yelling, "Get out! Get out!" but Dale was tethered to a monitor, unable to comply. The technician yanked the leads off his chest and the two fled down the hall toward a fire exit, the sound of gunfire at their heels.

Once outside, Dale and the med tech zig-zagged across the lawn, through the parking lot and into the hospital annex. Dale's EMT training from twelve years earlier came back to him as he assisted medics inside and out of the annex eventually finding himself in the ER where he was asked to man the phones.

He took calls ranging from hysterical spouses to people seeking routine care. Calls came from the security police and the sheriff's office. He took calls from military medical staff and civilian hospitals who had lost radio contact with their personnel on scene. Dale wanted to call his wife and let her know he was alive, but by the time he figured out how to dial an outside line he discovered all the outgoing circuits were busy.

Throughout the campus, rooms, and hallways of the hospital, patients were stabilized and brought to the emergency room, which became the casualty collection point. As patients arrived, swarms of medical personnel cared for them. According to Danley, "The first aid ranged from a simple bandage to full-out blood transfusion." Dr. Baker had been wheeled in from the parking lot; the medics parked his gurney near the reception desk. Danley described the care he received. "One of our doctors had several gunshot wounds … I started one or two IVs on him. Another doctor asked me to start a blood transfusion. I was not trained for that, so I found an RN and asked her to start the transfusion."

Dale Bates' reception desk had become a repository of medical supplies. He assisted the medics who were treating Dr. Baker who, Dale said, was bleeding heavily from his shoulder and chest. Dale tore open bandages and IV wrappers for the medics. He said, "At one point I handled the phone with my right hand and with my left I held an IV bag up in the air."

Danley looked to see where else she could help. She said, "I then went back to the record's room and saw that Deaton was being worked on. … We cut his jacket and shirt off so we could see the wound." The bullet had fractured Deaton's humerus and torn away much of his bicep. He was bleeding heavily and was ashen white. Danley said, "I bandaged it, and one of the PAs came in to help start the IV."

* * *

Forty-one-year-old TSgt Mark Wellsandt was in the dental clinic, a single-story square building in the northwest corner of the hospital compound across from the annex. Tech Sergeant Wellsandt, a SERE instructor at Fairchild's Survivor School, had been scheduled for a routine dental appointment that afternoon. He stood at the reception counter scheduling a follow-up appointment with Master Sergeant McBride. Wellsandt said, "While at the counter, I heard the first bang and noticed a truck on the road next to the clinic, and my initial thought was it had backfired."

McBride looked out through the tinted glass front of the building and said, "That was a gunshot."

Wellsandt said, "I wasn't sure at first, but as soon as we saw people running, it was clear that something bad had happened."

The gunman ran in front of the dental clinic—headed toward the main hospital. McBride yelled, "Get away from the door!" He ran to the entrance, reached up and deactivated the automatic sliding glass door and yelled for everyone to move to the rear of the clinic. Wellsandt saw people outside running toward the dental clinic seeking shelter. He stayed up front near the door, switching it on and off as people approached, allowing them to slip inside. McBride yelled from the back of the clinic to keep the door closed, fearing the gunman would enter the building. Wellsandt was similarly concerned but could not bring himself to abandon people outside, exposed. Wellsandt looked toward the hospital and saw Orson Lee lying wounded in the parking lot, his wife at his side. Wellsandt said, "I pointed out that there were wounded in the parking lot that needed assistance. Some felt we should stay inside and wait for help." Wellsandt disagreed. "Something about SERE instructors and their need to help or take charge, I guess."

Col Donald Sprague, a dentist, stepped forward. Gauze, oxygen, towels, and other medical supplies were brought to the front, where a small group stood in the doorway, readying themselves to run to Lee's aid. They again heard gunfire, and at first, couldn't tell where it was coming from. Wellsandt looked toward Graham Road. "I saw the gunman running with a weapon from south to north at the east end of the hospital parking lot." Dr. Sprague saw him too, and when they determined the gunman wasn't shooting in their direction, they all ran toward Orson Lee. The men moved Lee in between two rows of parked cars and assessed his injuries. One of the bullets fired at Lee struck a pine branch, nearly severing it. The bullet fragmented, peppering Lee's right arm, chest, and face with splinters and shrapnel. Wellsandt said, "My impression was he had been hit by shotgun pellets because of the spread of the wounds." The medics covered Lee's wounds and administered oxygen. Security police driving an armored Peacekeeper arrived sometime later and transported Lee to the ER. Wellsandt stayed in the parking lot with Mrs. Lee and the couple's golden retriever. He said, "We still did not know if there was a threat of additional gunfire. I told Mrs. Lee that we would work our way to the west end of the parking lot, and once there we would make a dash for the back doors of the dental clinic." Wellsandt carried the squirming dog as he guided Mrs. Lee to the rear entrance of the dental clinic where they were allowed inside to safety.

* * *

Dr. London sat in his small recliner, holding his arm tight against the wound in his side. After the gunman left, the psychologist managed to speak. "Call 911." Brittany called the base fire department and reported the shooting. Unable to find anything in the office suitable to hold against the doctor's wound to stop the bleeding, Brittany ran to the bathroom across the hall and grabbed handfuls of paper towels. Brittany said, as she ran back she saw Laura Rogers in the hall holding her wounded arm, screaming, "Oh my God, I've been shot." Brittany closed the office door and knelt beside Dr. London, pressing the towels against the wound in his side.

From his office twenty feet down the hall, Dr. David Earl had heard two gunshots but attributed the noise to doors slamming. The third gunshot was unmistakable. Dr. Earl was in with a patient, who he told to hide as he closed his partially open office door. He heard Laura Rogers screaming in the hall and pulled her inside, where he bandaged her wound.

* * *

The med techs in the annex audio room, Werder, Seeley, and Raynes, had just heard a warning over the intercom. "Get out of the hospital!" Seeley cranked the office window open and pushed out the screen. Airman First Class Raynes hopped out and stood ready to help their two young patients through the window. Seeley said, "Seconds after Raynes went out the window, I viewed about thirty to forty people running in pandemonium away from the main hospital toward the annex up Graham Road." Then Seeley saw the gunman. "I realized he was heading back toward the 9010 annex building. The window was still open, so I yelled twice to Raynes to lie down against the building, and she did. I saw her head go down out of my view. I initially thought to try to grab her and get her back into the office, but there was no time."

Seeley crouched behind the audiometric booth. Someone ran down the hallway yelling, "He's coming." Seeley heard a shout coming from outside the east end of the annex, "Drop your weapon!" He looked out the window and saw the gunman fire in the direction of the command, followed by the distinct sound of pistol fire. Seeley saw a "mist of red" burst from the gunman's head right before he fell to the ground.

Word quickly spread that the gunman had been incapacitated. Those who had fled the annex and hidden nearby now made their way back inside to help the wounded. An airman heard that Dr. Brigham had been shot and went to his office. The airman said, "He was lying facedown in his office in the southwest corner. I turned him over. There was blood, a bullet wound in the left chest. I gave him two breaths, checked for a pulse, there was none." The airman began CPR.

Dr. Estes, the internal medicine flight surgeon, had jumped a fence and taken cover under a tree in the housing area just north of the annex. When he heard that the shooter was incapacitated, he ran back into the annex. He and Dan Elliott entered Dr. London's office and sent Brittany into the hall. They eased the doctor out of his chair and began CPR. Dr. Estes noted the bullet had entered the doctor's right anterior lateral chest and exited the left lateral chest traveling across the chest and heart.

Brittany ran across the parking lot to the hospital in search of additional medical supplies. She ran through the hall, maneuvering around and hurdling over the wounded and their caregivers. She encountered a pediatrician and told her that Dr. London had been shot. Shouts warned of a second gunman and that no one was to leave the building. The pediatrician stuffed rolls of gauze in Brittany's hands then turned her attention back to treating the wounds of a four-year-old boy. Brittany ignored the warning to stay put and ran back to the annex where she delivered the supplies to the medics who were aiding Dr. London.

Despite loudspeaker announcements warning of a second gunman in the area, hospital personnel and patrons continued to seek out the many wounded. One doctor said, "There was no sense of heroism, just the sense of duty. We were careful not to become additional casualties, but no one seemed afraid to risk personal safety to help others."

The threat didn't prevent the wounded from receiving care, but it did temporarily delay efforts to transport the survivors to four downtown hospitals.

Maj Ann Barshney assisted in stabilizing the wounded and transporting them to the ER. "Someone came through and told us to lie low and avoid doors and windows, as they didn't know if there was one shooter or two and until the area was clear, to not move around more than necessary." As she crawled around on the lobby floor, she was reminded of the military hospital's training days where the staff wore fatigues, flak vests, and helmets. During one such exercise, a nurse told her, "You know, Ann, when something really happens we'll all be in nylons and skirts or class A blues, crawling around on the floor, not this battle dress."

* * *

Seeley and Werder left the audio room and sped down the hall with a crash cart. They pulled the cart to a stop outside Dr. London's office. Inside, Dr. Estes, Staff Sergeant Elliott, and other medics were on the floor working to save the psychologist. The medics already had a jump bag filled with emergency medical supplies. They sent Seeley and Werder down the hall to Dr. Brigham's office, where the crash cart and its life-saving contents might be of more use. For several minutes, the medics worked on Dr. London. The projectile had damaged his heart, piercing a vein and artery. The bullet severely damaged his liver before exiting his lower left back. When it became clear that nothing could be done to save Dr. London, Dr. Estes moved down to Dr. Brigham's office to see if he could help.

Inside the psychiatrist's office, Seeley had grabbed an Ambu bag off the crash cart, handing it to a medic who knelt near the doctor's head. Seeley knelt beside Dr. Brigham and started chest compressions. The medic used the Ambu bag to force air into the doctor's lungs. Air gurgled from the hole in the doctor's side. Another nurse and med tech arrived. Seeley asked the nurse to seal the doctor's wounds. He continued with the compressions, but the doctor still had no pulse. A medic began prepping defibrillator pads and epinephrine. A PA reassessed Dr. Brigham as the resuscitation effort continued. The projectile had passed laterally through the doctor's chest "causing extensive cavitary disruption" to his heart and lungs. The decision was made to call the code. By 1531, Dr. Brigham and Dr. London were both declared dead. Seeley leaned over and gently closed Dr. Brigham's eyelids. The doctor's office phone rang and SrA Lance Peak answered. When he realized he was speaking with Susan Brigham, he handed the receiver to a doctor. Susan had learned of the shooting on the news and knew in her heart her husband was dead. When the doctor confirmed her fears, Susan's scream could be heard from across the room.

* * *

Ruth Gerken lay on the floor across from the espresso stand, listening to loudspeaker announcements reporting the gunman's whereabouts. She looked down the hall and saw Dennis Moe lying in the doorway leading to the pharmacy lobby. At her head lay Marlene Moe. Marlene was in severe pain. She said, "I just kept screaming, 'We're shot, somebody help us.' … I was cussing and swearing and everything."

Inside the hospital lab, Room 121, Captain Singleterry "listened and waited" at the door. Singleterry said, "At the moment the sounds of gunfire moved off, I opened the door and looked out to see several … kids and adults on the floor in front of me." Brandy Pentecost was uninjured and helped the captain pull Anthony, Ryan, and Kelly Moe into Room 121. Singleterry held four-year-old Anthony at arm's length, pulled his shirt up, and looked him over, relieved to find no obvious injuries. He noted Kelly Moe, "was wounded in the right thigh … a clean wound." He told Brandy to apply pressure to Kelly's leg as he re-entered the hallway to check on Ruth Gerken. Singleterry said, "I went to the lady lying just outside the stairwell entrance and quickly examined her. She was wounded just above the left knee and had a large hole in her thigh." Singleterry retrieved supplies from the lab and bandaged Ruth's legs before moving to Marlene Moe, who he said "was in a great deal of pain." Singleterry assessed Marlene's injuries to her lower back and upper thigh. "I saw she was shot twice … with a frank amount of blood." Singleterry ducked back into the lab for additional supplies.

Tami Jessee, the assistant NCOIC of the laboratory, had witnessed the shooting in the pharmacy and quickly secreted herself and several hospital patrons behind the lab refrigerators. When the shooting stopped, Tami emerged. She saw the wounded in the hall and ran to the ER to summon help; at the time the ER appeared empty. As Tami headed back to the lab, she spotted twelve-year-old Sam Spencer in the ER waiting room, banging on a window and yelling for help. She went to him and held pressure on his leg to stop the bleeding.

Nineteen-year-old Heather Ford had been waiting for a prescription in the pharmacy lobby. When the shooting started she had escaped down the hall and into the lab. Heather worked at Sacred Heart Hospital as an EMT and was a nursing student at Eastern Washington University. She was the first to reach Dennis Moe as he lay immobilized in the hall. Heather checked Moe for injuries. "I found one entrance wound just below his left buttock. There was little bleeding from the wound. [His] color was poor and he was diaphoretic" (perspiring heavily). Heather could find no other obvious injuries, although the bullet had exited his abdomen, causing severe internal damage. She said, "He did complain of some back and right leg pain." As supplies were dispersed through the hospital,

Heather dressed Moe's wound and found his systolic blood pressure was about 90. A team of medics started two IVs, which eventually brought Moe's blood pressure to 130. Heather said, "This appeared to help, but he still complained of a great deal of pain." A passing doctor ordered 50 mg of Demerol by IV. Heather said the narcotic pain medicine didn't seem to help.

*   *   *

Inside the storage closet of the immunization clinic, Sgt Michael Lecker and immunization technician Karina Tutini heard a broadcast on the loudspeaker announcing that the gunman had exited the building. Lecker left his daughter in the care of a nine-year-old boy, telling them to stay in the closet until he returned. Lecker and Tutini left the shot clinic to help the injured. Tutini ran down the hall. She "saw many people lying on the floor, blood everywhere, and people screaming." Tutini went to Marlene Moe, who was "screaming for help," lying partially in the doorway leading to the hospital lab. Tutini helped cut away Marlene's white shirt and black jeans and applied pressure to the wound on her left upper thigh. Marlene was also suffering from damage to her spine, kidney and sciatic nerve. Tutini noted her "greatest pain appeared to be focused in the right leg."

Marlene identified her husband down the hall by his blue shirt. They yelled to each other and to passing medics, trying to locate the six children they had at the hospital. Marlene said, "I was telling people to get paper, write our names down, we had kids who weren't ours. Call their parents." She was desperate to find her own daughter as well. "Find Missy!"

Doctors, medics, and hospital patrons emerged from all directions, tending to the wounded. Singleterry and Tutini pulled Marlene out of the hall and into the lab, making room for crash carts that were being wheeled to the wounded throughout the hospital. Tutini and other medics continued to apply pressure to Marlene's wounds and started IVs before she was moved to the ER. Singleterry described the scene. "Everyone is crawling around on the floor ... Supplies are being kicked and everyone's screaming for a pair of scissors." A medical technician walked the hallway with an armful of supplies, shouting, "Who needs gauze?"

*   *   *

Neal Cox, the teenaged espresso stand worker, left Singleterry's office to assist the medics in the hallway. As more qualified people arrived, he felt he was in the way and returned to the lab where he noticed Ryan McCarron and Anthony Zucchetto. "I saw two small boys in the corner. One of the boys, who was around four, was not hit, and sitting quietly next to the second boy who was on his back and crying. I started talking to him to calm him down. At that point I noticed that his underwear was blood-soaked." Brandy Pentecost saw it too and directed Singleterry's attention to Anthony. Singleterry said, "I examined him and found he had been shot … and was the most critically injured. I had the girl apply direct pressure and I got up to find help." A pediatrician who happened to be in the hall examined Anthony. She found a small entrance wound on his buttock, but the exiting projectile had caused severe injuries. The pediatrician ran to the ER for gloves and dressings. While she was there she was approached by Brittany Gray who she said, "was begging for dressings for Dr. London. I provided her with two boxes of dressings but did not go with her to the annex, as I did not think it was safe." The pediatrician moved Anthony to a table in the cafeteria down the hall. She dressed his wounds and started an IV with a saline drip. Someone taped a rolled up magazine over Anthony's arm to help keep his IV in place. Once stabilized, Anthony was taken to the second floor, where a team of doctors watched over him and the other pediatric patients while they waited for medevac.

* * *

TSgt Delbert Collins had been inside the pharmacy, working at the prescription dispensing window, when he heard a gunshot followed by screaming. He reached instinctively for his sidearm, but it wasn't there. The thirty-one-year-old tech sergeant had recently cross-trained from the security police career field to become a pharmacy technician, and since only on-duty law enforcement personnel were authorized to carry firearms on base, he was unarmed.

Collins looked out into the lobby but his view was obstructed by a support column. He saw the front portion of a rifle, he saw it fire, and he heard more screaming. "I began screaming at the people in the pharmacy to get down and get away from the windows." Collins made his way to the back of the pharmacy, yelling, "He's shooting! Get down!" He continued to hear gunshots and screams outside as he grabbed a telephone. Collins said, "The shots sounded spaced and deliberate, like if someone was taking time to aim."

There were about ten people inside Fairchild's pharmacy that afternoon. Some had been in the back, preparing medications or working on administrative duties. Others had been up front serving customers at the prescription drop-off and pick-up windows.

A shout came from the rear of the pharmacy to close the rolling metal window shutters. A technician crouched below the drop-off window. When the sound of gunfire moved down the west wing, she jumped up and pulled the shutter closed. Another airman crouched and ran from the back of the pharmacy to the pick-up window. As he reached up, the sound of approaching gunfire dropped him to his hands and knees. The gunman re-entered the lobby and fired upon four women lying on the floor just outside the windows. The airman listened helplessly to the gunfire and screaming as gun smoke billowed through the opening above him. When the gunfire moved toward family practice, he pulled the shutter down, securing the pharmacy.

Tech Sergeant Collins couldn't reach the base law enforcement desk, and his call to the base operator resulted in a recorded message. Just before the second round of gunfire in the lobby, Collins connected with a Spokane 911 operator. Clearly, he was not the first to report the shooting.

"911, is this reference to shots being fired on Fairchild base?"

Collins spoke rapidly in his Texan drawl. "Yes it is, the hospital. There's a crazy guy out here shootin' with an automatic weapon."

"What hospital!?"

Collins struggled to hear over the gunfire. "Huh? ... Ma'am?"

The operator was flustered. "Okay ... all right."

Collins anticipated the information the operator would need. "It's one individual, all I got to see was the weapon, looks like an AK-47."

Collins then broadcast a warning on the hospital's public address system: "Gunfire in the pharmacy lobby, everyone take cover. There is a gunman in the hospital—take cover!"

Lt Col Milton J. Petrin was the officer in charge of the pharmacy. He went by the first name Joe, but his crew, who regarded him highly, simply addressed him as Colonel. Lieutenant Colonel Petrin directed his staff to the back of the room. The pharmacy dealt with controlled substances, which required it to be located in a secure room. It may have been secure, but it was not bulletproof. As Petrin gathered his crew in the rear of the pharmacy, he was prepared to lock them all inside the walk-in drug safe. It would have been a tight squeeze but would protect them from gunfire if the gunman attempted to breach the pharmacy.

The pharmacy staff tracked the sound of gunfire as it trailed down the hallway past radiology, past the OB/GYN clinic, and into family practice. As the gunshots faded, they were replaced by the sounds of the wounded. Petrin addressed his troops. "I told the pharmacy staff that there were seriously wounded folks in the pharmacy lobby and throughout the hospital and that we needed to provide medical care to those folks. I asked for volunteers to go with me but did not order them to, as some of them were already in a state of shock."

Although they didn't know where the gunman was or when he would return, the majority of the pharmacy personnel readied themselves to assist the wounded. They donned gloves and gathered towels and medical supplies. Collins called the law enforcement desk and spoke to an unidentified female SP.

"Law enforcement."

"Hey listen, is the gunman outside? Is he down?"

"We're not sure, we're still trying to find out."

Collins yelled to his co-workers, "Hey, they're not sure yet! They're not sure that he's down!"

The SP said, "Everybody needs to stay inside the facility until we can determine what's going on. Okay?"

"Okay, well, we need to know, 'cause we're in the hospital, and if he's down we'll start taking care of patients immediately."

In the background, the SP conferred with Tech Sergeant Rizzo. "Okay, does anybody know if he's down yet or not? Is it confirmed?"

Rizzo said, "He's down right now. I don't know his status."

The SP told Collins, "Okay, he's down, but we don't know his status yet."

Collins translated to the pharmacy staff, "He's down, but they don't know if he's dead or not."

The sounds of urgent discussion could be heard in the background of the pharmacy. Collins told the SP, "Okay, we're gonna get out and try to help people. There's a lot of people hurt. We're gonna need ambulances, and all we can get. Okay?"

The pharmacy staff stepped into the gun smoke-filled lobby. Petrin stationed people at the lobby entrances to watch for danger. He sent another airman to the emergency room to gather as much gauze, bandages, and tape he could find. Yet another airman was dispatched to the war readiness material room in the basement to get as many World War II–era olive drab stretchers as he could carry. Petrin and the rest of his staff began triaging the wounded.

*   *   *

Pediatrician John Tappel had just dodged a bullet outside his office. When the gunfire subsided, Dr. Tappel told his patients to stay down as he opened his office door and checked the hallway. It was empty. He ran through the halls toward the pharmacy lobby. As he got closer, the smell of gun smoke intensified, hovering thick near the ceiling. Dr. Tappel said, "I could hear yelling and groaning as I approached the pharmacy waiting area, and could now smell blood as well as the gunpowder." Dr. Tappel's mass casualty training took over as he triaged the wounded. "I checked one woman who had been shot in the lower back—she could talk and she seemed stable at the moment. The second person I came to was Eva Walch. She had multiple wounds in her legs but was stable for the moment, and I moved on."

Dr. Tappel moved to a third woman, who was lying facedown on the carpeted floor. He knelt to assess her injuries. "I could see the bullet wound in her back." When the doctor identified himself, Michelle Sigman looked up and replied, "I know." The doctor recognized her. "She was pale, and I stopped to treat her, as I knew her wound was the most serious of the people I had triaged. I also knew she was pregnant. At that time, other medics with a crash cart arrived. We dressed the wound and gave oxygen and asked for someone to notify the obstetrician if possible."

*   *   *

SSgt Daniel Lasich crouched behind a car in the parking lot near the family practice section of the hospital. He had just watched SSgt Joe Noone take a bullet in the arm and leg. Lasich signaled for Noone to stay under the hedge as the gunman moved away. As soon as the gunman walked by, Lasich sprinted to the hedge, grabbed Noone and helped him run around the corner of the hospital. SSgt Dave Root joined them as they headed toward the ER. The ER appeared empty. Some staff were hiding. Many had evacuated to the steam plant across the parking lot. The ER staff motioned for Noone to be brought to the steam plant where they began treating him.

Root went into the ER and met up with physician assistant Tim Street. The two grabbed IV supplies, bandages, tape, and scissors and headed down the hall. As they moved from patient to patient, Root started IVs and Street checked the patients over from head to toe. The pair of medics gave instructions to other first responders before moving on to the next patient. Root was impressed with Lieutenant Street and the skills he learned in pararescue. He said, "If it wasn't for him, I don't think quite a few of those people would have made it that day. His talents were amazing. It was like being a high school football player and getting to work with a Super Bowl quarterback." Root and Street made frequent trips back to the ER for supplies.

In the ER, a medic was attempting to start an IV on Joe Noone who was lying on a stretcher. Root said, "The medic was shaking pretty bad. I asked if I could step in. ... As I am working on Joe he looks at me and asks, 'You having fun yet?' ... He caught me by surprise. ... and I laughed with him. I think we were both just happy to be alive."

SrA Lance Peak was a medical administrative specialist assigned to the pharmacy. When Peak left the pharmacy to assist the wounded, the first person he came to was Omer Karns, the DAV driver. Peak couldn't see any obvious wounds and when he asked Omer if he was okay, the deaf man answered, "Yes."

Peak headed down the hall searching for additional wounded. At the end of the hall he opened the door to the cafeteria serving line and saw a young pharmacy tech sitting on the floor cradling eight-year-old Christin McCarron. Peak said, "At the time it looked like nothing was wrong, and he was just comforting a scared little girl." The tech looked up, his expression begging for help and direction. Peak said, "I knelt beside him and he leaned her away from his body, which was when I saw the entry wound in her chest. It was just a little hole, not too much damage visible around it." Peak noted Christin was conscious and crying, then he noticed a growing pool of blood on the white tile beneath them. The swinging door slammed open, and SSgt Dave Root blasted into the room with an IV bag and medical supplies. Root's previous experience as an ER technician took over. He shouted, "Move!" as he slid in beside Christin. He taped a piece of plastic over the hole in her chest to allow her lungs to inflate, then he scooped her up and ran to the ER.

* * *

After evading the gunman in the parking lot, Dr. Johnson had reentered the hospital to check on his patient, Pauline Brown. From there he moved to the pharmacy lobby and then to the cafeteria, assessing patients along the way. Dr. Johnson returned to the pharmacy lobby and took over Michelle Sigman's care, asking Dr. Tappel to check on an injured child in the cafeteria serving area. Dr. Tappel ran down the hall and pushed through the swinging door. He said, "I went from carpeting to tile, and slipped on the blood on the floor." Dr. Tappel found five-year-old Janessa Zucchetto. "She was lying on her back near the serving line in the cafeteria. As I got to her, a medic was getting an IV started. We did not have an IV pole, so we taped the bag of saline to the wall. As I bent down to do my ABC assessment, I noted she had what appeared to be an exit wound in her neck. I had seen some of the other wounds by this time and knew it was a high-powered rifle. I reasoned that there was no way that a small child shot in the neck could survive—there are too many vital structures in the neck—spinal cord, trachea, major blood vessels. And yet I rapidly found out she could talk, she was breathing through her mouth, and her cardiac status was stable. We stopped the bleeding from her neck, dressed her wounds, and finished establishing IV access."

Dr. Tappel was tracked down again and told he was needed in the ER. When he reached the ER, he found Lt Col Jim DeSantis and SSgt Dave Root working to save an eight-year-old girl. Dr. Tappel said Dr. DeSantis "was the first physician responder for Christin McCarron, but he asked me to take over to allow him to coordinate rescue efforts at a higher level."

Root told Dr. Tappel that Christin was talking when he brought her to the ER, but she had since lost consciousness. The doctor said, "She was intubated but no longer responding. We were doing chest compressions as well as breathing for her. ... We had pressure dressings on her wounds. She had an entrance wound in her right chest and an exit wound in her right lower back. ... She was not responding to any of our efforts. One of the surgeons arrived, and we discussed what else we could do. We were able to establish IV access, and at some time blood for a transfusion became available."

Every effort was made to save the life of the little girl. But her liver, lung and spine had all been damaged. There was nothing more Dr. Tappel could do. He said, "I made the hardest medical decision I have ever made.

I called the code off, ending the resuscitation, and directed the blood be used for another patient."

Dr. Tappel said, "I did not know who my patient was. She did not have any ID, and the family that brought her was nowhere to be found. I found Captain Doug McCormick, an administrator in the hospital, and asked him to help ... Somehow, he found out that there was a boy in the hospital who had not been injured, who had a missing sister; and we started to figure they were probably siblings. I remember sitting in a room, around a table, with Christin's brother, Ryan, and we gave him a soft drink. He was asking about his sister, and we had to distract him ... because we did not want to answer him directly. ... I kept thinking that I had this terrible secret—knowing someone's daughter and sister was dead ... I don't know how ... but someone made contact with the mom, who came to the ER. I met Mrs. McCarron outside the room where Christin was and introduced myself. A chaplain was with her. We explained to her that we needed to see if the girl in the room was her daughter; I already knew that she knew. The chaplain and I escorted her in, holding each arm. As we entered, she saw Christin's body, with a white sheet draped loosely over her. Mrs. McCarron's words were, "That's her shape!" and she went limp in our arms. We had to finish the process by bringing Mrs. McCarron over to Christin so she could see her and positively identify her. This might be the second hardest thing I have had to do in my medical career. We had to leave all of our resuscitation equipment in place on Christin's body, including the endotracheal tube and the IV lines, so the visual image Mrs. McCarron had was, I am sure, very hard to handle."

* * *

In the annex, Seeley stepped out of Dr. Brigham's office into the hallway where he was asked to help Mark Hess, who had been shot in the leg on his way out of the hospital. According to Seeley, Hess told him, "Don't let me bleed to death." Senior Airman Seeley and A1C Brandon Ford left Hess's makeshift tourniquet in place. They cut through his pant leg, applied a field dressing to his thigh, and started an IV. They placed him on a stretcher and carried him across the parking lot toward the main hospital, headed for the ER. Seeley said, "At this point we had no idea that anyone else had been shot, let alone did we know that the ER was overwhelmed with patients already." They carried Hess through the pharmacy lobby. Seeley said, "It seemed there were a hundred people kneeling over victims in the main lobby, all working frantically to save the lives of those that had been shot there." They carried Hess to the ER, stepping over and between the wounded and medics. The ER was full, and they were directed to take Hess to the second floor, where they found an empty bed. The two medics administered morphine and monitored Hess's vital signs. Seeley watched out the second floor window as multiple medevac helicopters landed in the field across from the Offutt gate. Ambulances from Spokane as well as Wellpinit, Deer Park, and Post Falls—communities as far as an hour away lined up to retrieve patients from the ER.

Fairchild fire department rescue squads arrived on scene outside the perimeter about six minutes after the first call for help. Approximately two minutes later, at least one rescue truck was waved into the scene by security police. Some civilian ambulance crews also entered the perimeter to treat wounded prior to the scene being secured.

Civilian medevac helicopters had been dispatched to the scene and began arriving at 1526. A member of Fairchild's fire department and a civilian ambulance officer were stationed in the ER as transportation coordinators. About thirty minutes after the first call for help, ambulances began entering the scene, two at a time. They shuttled critical patients to helicopters outside the perimeter and transported less critical patients via ground. The military stretchers did not fit into the civilian ambulances, and many of the wounded had to be transferred onto more modern gurneys and backboards before being transported.

SSgt Dave Root rode in one of the ambulances and helped transfer patients into the helicopters. When he attempted to re-enter the perimeter on foot, he was stopped by law enforcement. Root ran to his nearby home where he discovered his answering machine was full of messages from concerned family and friends. He recorded a quick outgoing message to let everyone know he was okay. Root took a quick shower and changed into a fresh uniform before returning to the medevac area where he joined a group of his co-workers.

As Root was talking with his friends, his hands began to tremble uncontrollably. He wasn't a smoker but bummed a cigarette in an attempt to calm his nerves. By the time he got the cigarette to his mouth, he was trembling so much someone had to help him light it.

Root said the shooting was the best and worst day of his medical career. "It was the worst day as to what happened as far as misery and death and injury. … But in another way for me professionally, in hindsight it was the best day I ever spent in my career, because I got to do all the stuff I had been taught to do and the training worked. I didn't have to think about it. I was just able to do everything."

After SrA Kevin Seeley delivered Mark Hess to an ambulance, he returned to the hospital lobby. An investigator asked him to help secure the scene to prevent it from being disturbed further. Seeley said, "He asked me to locate and mark any shell casings or holes in the lobby area. … I did so for the next ten minutes or so in and around the lobby and coffee cart area. I peered into the ER, and the floor was covered with blood. I also walked down toward the cafeteria area, where I saw more blood spatters and holes. While I was doing this, the entire lobby area and hallway seemed to be eerily quiet; and for a few moments it seemed as if I was the only one in the lobby area. It was a surreal moment … forever ingrained into my life experience, as was the moment I closed Dr. Brigham's eyes."

After the patients' needs were met, law enforcement directed all hospital personnel to gather in the family practice waiting room. One caregiver said, "The television was on. I wanted to watch it, yet hated to look at it. Everyone in the room was a part of those news briefs." The group was eventually directed outside where buses waited to take them to the base community center.

Overall, about four hundred witnesses were transported to the community center, where they were interviewed by Spokane police, sheriff, state patrol, security police, and OSI personnel. The witnesses provided hundreds of written statements. The process lasted long into the evening. Many of the witnesses had to call friends or family for a ride home, as their cars in the hospital parking lot were now part of a massive crime scene.

Maj Ann Barshney was among a group of hospital personnel who were bussed to the base bowling alley to wait for a ride home. Once inside the bowling alley, Barshney said she saw some of the base populace laughing and having fun and after what she experienced at the hospital, it struck her as unreal. She wondered, "How could life go on so normally with all that shooting and bloodshed just blocks away?" She imagined what it must have felt like to be a veteran returning from war. "The juxtaposition of all they saw … and were involved in … just hit home—to see this normal world carrying on as if nothing horrific was going on."

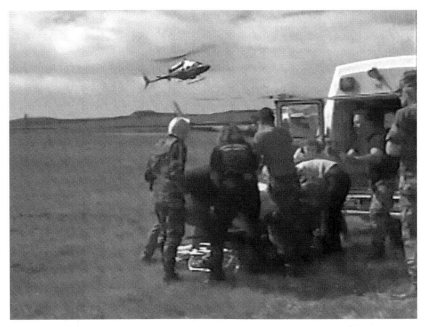

Medevac helicopter landing zone north of Fairchild's hospital, 20 June 1994.
Spokane KXLY channel 4 news screenshot

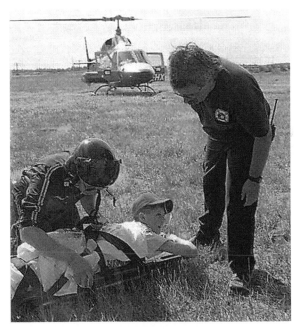

Medics prep Sam Spencer for helicopter medevac, 20 June 1994.
Dan Pelle, *The Spokesman-Review*

SrA Melissa Danley at medevac helicopter landing zone, 20 June 1994.
Spokane KXLY channel 4 news screenshot

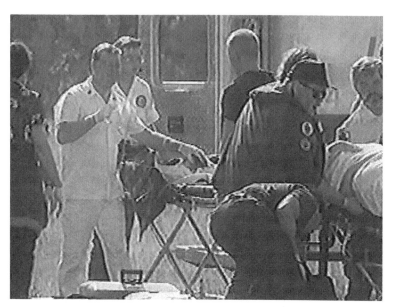

SSgt Dave Root assists in transport of patient to medevac helicopter,
20 June 1994. Spokane KHQ channel 6 news screenshot

Survivors

Lt Don Sanders telephoned the ER of Deaconess Hospital from inside a locked room in the basement of Fairchild's hospital, "We've got … seventeen wounded and two dead. They're all gunshot wounds."

Nurse Connie Pitts broadcast a message initiating the area's disaster plan. "This is Deaconess Medical Center calling all Spokane area hospitals. This is your hospital control center. This is a disaster call."

The Spokane hospitals had practiced the disaster plan before, but had never needed to implement it for real. The worst mass casualty incident the area had experienced up to that point had been a multi-car collision on an icy stretch of Interstate 90, and the injuries had been relatively minor. Another nurse thought the Fairchild lieutenant must have exaggerated the number of wounded, but Pitts telephoned three other Spokane hospitals to check the status of their operating rooms and determine the number of patients they could handle. Deaconess also dispatched their medevac helicopter to Fairchild. It was followed shortly by three other civilian medevac helicopters and two UH-1N Hueys from Fairchild. Twenty-two ground ambulances from Spokane and the surrounding communities also responded. The helicopters and ambulances staged at a makeshift landing zone in a field north of the hospital, waiting for the area to be cleared of a possible second gunman. Inside Fairchild's ER, the wounded were triaged, treated, and prepped for transport. By the time the ambulances began shuttling patients to the landing zone, television news crews were broadcasting live from the scene.

At Deaconess, medics anxiously watched the newsfeed and waited for the patients to arrive. As gurneys were wheeled from the rooftop helipad, down an elevator, and into the ER, it became evident that the military medics had worked under extreme conditions. Patients' names and vital signs were written on strips of tape affixed to their clothing. Some of the patients were receiving blood and most had IVs, but a few also had improvised bandages. The resourceful medics had sealed chest wounds with sheets of plastic and cigarette packages. One patient's leg had been splinted with a Wet Floor sign.

Dr. Delwyn Baker was the first patient to arrive. The medics examining his wounds were amazed that he was conscious and talking. He had a grazing wound on his forearm, an entrance wound in his upper right chest and an exit wound in his lower right chest. The medics feared the bullet had damaged internal organs but instead found it had tunneled just under the skin.

When thirteen-year-old Sam Spencer arrived, he lay on his stomach as doctors cleaned the wound that ran across his buttock and down his leg. Sam was scared, and asked if he was going to die. A nurse who saw that Sam could still wiggle his toes assured him he was going to be okay and told him to squeeze her hand if it hurt too much.

Doctors examined Deena Kelley and discovered a bullet had missed her spine by a fraction of an inch. She had sustained life-threatening blood loss and the swelling caused by the trauma put pressure on her spinal cord. She was temporarily paralyzed from the waist down and sustained injuries that would require multiple surgeries, but miraculously her major organs were undamaged.

Joy Roberts arrived, suffering wounds caused by a bullet that passed through her back and out her abdomen. As doctors were examining her, four-year-old Anthony Zucchetto arrived. He was pale and silent as the medics peeled back his bandages to assess his injuries. They rushed Anthony into surgery, fearing he wouldn't survive.

Anthony's father waited in the Deaconess cafeteria, periodically calling his wife, who was at Sacred Heart with their daughter, Janessa, who was undergoing surgery for her neck wound. Janessa and Anthony were survivors. Anthony required several additional surgeries and, although doctors were skeptical, he learned to walk again.

When Michelle Sigman arrived at Deaconess, she was screaming. Prompted not only by the pain she was experiencing, but the simultaneous concern she had for her unborn daughter and her son, whom she had lost track of during the chaos of the shooting. Michelle had severe internal bleeding and was rushed to the operating room, where doctors discovered, among other damage, a bullet had broken several ribs and pierced her lung. The doctors were hopeful that Michelle would not lose her baby. She required twenty-one pints of blood as doctors worked to locate and control the bleeding to bring her dangerously-low blood pressure back to normal. The Inland Northwest Blood Center delivered more than one hundred pints of blood to area hospitals as surgeons worked through the night to repair the traumatic injuries. The following day, Spokane residents and military members lined up to replenish the supply, donating 412 units.

In another Spokane hospital, doctors struggled to save Eva Walch's foot which had been severely damaged by a close range gunshot. She had been wounded in both feet and one bullet was still lodged in her calf. She eventually lost her leg, but Eva was forever optimistic. She liked to say, "When life gives you lemons, you make lemonade." When doctors finally removed the projectile from her calf they intended to turn it over to the sheriff's office. Eva insisted it was hers, and when the doctors succumbed to her charm, she had her bullet made into a pendant that she wore on a gold necklace.

Patients continued arriving at the four Spokane hospitals, their conditions ranging from stable to very critical. Dennis and Marlene Moe and their daughters, Melissa and Kelly, were all sent to separate hospitals. Initially, none of them knew where the others were or how they were doing. Kelly spent four days in the hospital. Melissa was hospitalized for twenty-five days and Marlene didn't get to go home for thirty-five days. Marlene lost a kidney and the damage to her spine and sciatic nerve would cause her to walk with a painful limp. Dennis Moe wasn't expected to survive his injuries. He defied the odds and was released after 117 days, but he required extensive physical therapy to learn to walk again. He was medically retired from the Air Force and had to find a new career at age forty-two.

All of the wounded who were transported to area hospitals survived, thanks in large part to the immediate care provided by the patrons and staff at the base hospital. Their actions helped save the lives of twenty-two men, women and children. Although four innocent lives were lost at Fairchild, the medics had done all they could to save them. According to doctors who read the autopsy reports, all of the fatalities had sustained unsurvivable wounds.

Victim Twenty-Three

Alton Spencer, a retired Navy petty officer first class, was on the second floor of Fairchild's hospital with his wife, Sharry, who was recovering from elbow surgery. His twelve-year-old son, Sam, had gone downstairs to the ER waiting room to get a soda from the vending machine. Not long after Sam left, Alton said he heard "firecrackers in the distance." Nurses ran into the room yelling that they needed to barricade the doors; there was gunfire downstairs.

Alton slipped out of the room and ran downstairs to find his son. He came out of the stairwell across from the espresso stand and scanned the hallway searching for Sam. "I didn't see anybody except for wounded people." He called out for Sam, and shouted, "Has anyone seen a twelve-year-old boy?" He delayed his search just long enough to find paper towels for a woman who was working to stop the bleeding on a young girl's leg wound. Alton resumed his search, running down the hall. The situation reminded him of his combat experience in Vietnam. "Everything was in slow motion—I thought that hallway was a mile long."

Alton found his son in the ER waiting room and helped carry him across the hall to the ER, which left his shirt and pants bloody. After Sam was treated, stabilized and transported to the medevac landing zone, a woman with a notepad approached Alton. She took down Sam's information and Alton gave his name as the father, assuming it was for medical record purposes. Alton said, "The next thing I know, my name was in the papers and on CNN." The news media listed Alton and his son among the wounded. They erroneously reported the number of wounded as twenty-three instead of twenty-two. Alton tried to fix the error. He told the Air Force officials who came to visit Sam in the hospital and even telephoned the base legal office. Alton said, "I told the chaplain at Fairchild. I told a public relations officer at the hospital." Despite his efforts to set the record straight, Alton continued to be listed among the wounded. He received phone calls and get well cards from friends as well as the base commander. Two months later he mentioned the mistake to *The Spokesman-Review* reporter Jeanette White. After she ran a short article about the mix-up, his name was removed from the list of wounded.

Czar 52

The Fairchild community was reeling from the shock of the hospital shooting. The air show was scheduled to occur later that week and most members of the 92nd Medical Group assumed it would be canceled. Fairchild's hospital personnel had not only been the targets of violence; they had also been the first responders. They were mentally and physically exhausted and the hospital itself was undergoing repairs.

Dr. Grant said the hospital staff discussed the air show and agreed that it should not continue as planned, "because the hospital was basically trashed and would not be able to respond to a mass casualty at the time, if it happened."

The decision rested with the wing commander, Colonel Brooks. He ultimately decided the air show should continue as scheduled, saying, "We need to get on an upbeat, and this keeps my people busy. It gets their mind off the shooting and … keeps them pressing forward. … It would be a great show for the people downtown and the fact that we will have gone from Air Combat Command to Air Mobility Command, and that the base is still alive and well and everything."

A final air show practice flight was scheduled for Friday morning, 24 June 1994. Brooks apparently still had some concerns about Holland's maneuvers; he intended to ask his vice wing commander, Colonel Wolff, to fly on the practice mission to ensure the profile was safe. Brooks and Wolff had a natural camaraderie, aside from working side by side as the commander and vice commander. Both of them were from Texas and had graduated from Texas Tech. Wolff was well liked by the people of Fairchild, who described him as a "competent and very professional" officer. He had been flying the BUFF since 1971. As a young pilot he flew 156 combat sorties in Vietnam and continued flying throughout his career, amassing 3,696 hours. Wolff was an effective proponent of the BUFF. If anyone called his plane ugly, he used his infectious smile and Texas drawl to convince them that the B-52 was the most beautiful thing in the sky.

At age forty-six, Wolff's flying career was coming to a close; he was slated for a desk job in Washington, D.C. and had already shipped his helmet to his new assignment. He had adamantly refused several offers of a fini flight celebration, concerned that he might break down emotionally. He said, "I don't believe in fini flights; and frankly, I don't think I could hold it together."

As the final practice flight approached, Brooks said he asked Wolff, "Why don't you just go fly in the jump seat, be a safety observer. Come back and tell me how everything is, if it looked okay." Brooks admitted he had a secondary motive. He wanted the practice mission to be a surprise fini flight for Wolff, "to say thank you for flying all these years in the B-52." Wolff reluctantly agreed. Brooks later said, "It's a decision I'm living with."

At 0700 on 24 June 1994, Holland, Huston, and McGeehan arrived at base operations to prepare for their practice flight, scheduled to take off at 1000. Wolff had a prior engagement and planned to arrive just before take-off. The crew received a weather briefing and filed a flight plan. Holland called Fairchild's control tower and briefed them on the flight profile. Their plane, Fairchild's last B-52, tail number 1026, was assigned the radio call sign Czar 52.

Capt Stephen Carlson was the pilot of the KC-135 tanker, call sign Earl 01, that would fly in the air show with Czar 52. Carlson had never flown in an air show, and although he and his crew had practiced the profile multiple times in a flight simulator, they had never flown it live with the B-52. Carlson and Holland had only informally talked about the flight profile, so on the morning of the practice flight, Carlson approached Holland at base operations and suggested they conduct a formal preflight briefing.

Holland replied, "Steve, we got to get one thing straight. This is an air show, and you're taking this a little too seriously." Carlson was shocked until Holland grinned, saying, "Okay, here's what were gonna do." The preflight briefing took place in the foyer of base ops and amounted to little more than Holland telling the captain that if they got into a position where the planes were nose to nose, they should both break right.

The Secretary of the Air Force, Sheila Widnall, and Congressman Tom Foley were scheduled to fly into Fairchild to receive a briefing on the shooting investigation and visit some of the survivors. Colonel Wolff informed Colonel Brooks that the visitors' arrival coincided with the air show practice flight and asked him if he wanted to delay the practice. Brooks said, "I don't want anything going on around the airdrome while they're here, so delay it." The practice mission was rescheduled for 1400, after the dignitaries were scheduled to depart the base.

Capt Brian Anderson, an aircraft commander with the 23rd Bomb Squadron at Minot Air Force Base, had flown into Fairchild earlier that week. Before he left Minot, some visiting crewmembers from Fairchild gave him a warning. Anderson said, "They were telling us before we went, to not even hang around during the air show and get as far away from there as you possibly can because the things they're doing are stupid and dangerous."

After their flight was postponed, the crew of Czar 52 returned to base ops. Lieutenant Colonel McGeehan ran into Captain Anderson, who was planning a sortie. McGeehan introduced himself and apologized for not meeting him when he and his crew flew in. Anderson said, "He meant to meet us there but was unable to because of the other situation that was going on at Fairchild as far as memorial services and those kind of events." Anderson said McGeehan told him, "they were supposed to be flying and that their takeoff was going to be delayed slightly because they didn't want them flying while the Secretary of the Air Force was going to be there. … He described some of the things they were going to do, and in his words, they were going to do some wild things." Later, while Anderson and his crew were preparing to launch their aircraft, his maintenance crew chief told them to try to get back and land ahead of time so they could watch the B-52 practice for the air show. "He said it was unbelievable, some of the things he had seen them do."

The crew of Czar 52 returned to their plane that afternoon and completed their preflight inspection. Holland failed to sign several forms indicating he had inspected various systems of the aircraft. Some forms that were required to be on board were left behind at base ops. The paperwork showed Czar 52 was ready for launch, weighing in at 274,500 pounds, including 86,400 pounds of fuel. The crew received clearance and started the engines at 1318. Holland sat in the left pilot seat, McGeehan sat in the right copilot seat, and Huston was at his radar navigator station on the lower deck. Wolff climbed aboard about twenty-five minutes later and sat in the instructor pilot seat. At 1345, Czar 52 taxied toward Runway 23 and took off at 1358, followed about two minutes later by Earl 01.

At takeoff, Czar 52 was put into maximum thrust and rose from the runway before it reached midfield. Holland immediately began a flaps-down 360-degree climbing turn around the tower. Fairchild's control tower was located in a field adjacent to the runway, on the sparsely populated south side of the base. Fairchild's Survival School sat about 450 yards south of the tower; about 450 yards to the east was the weapons storage area (WSA). Aside from these three facilities, the rest of the south side was relatively uninhabited flat land, providing a safe flight path to perform a wide 360-degree turn. Holland banked the wings at an aggressive sixty degrees, and made a tight 360-degree turn around the tower, flying over the top of the Survival School and the WSA. After circling the tower, Czar 52 turned right of Runway 23 and continued to climb. Earl 01 took off on a heading right of Runway 23 and followed in tandem with Czar 52. With the exception of the 360 around the tower, Earl 01 mirrored Holland's maneuvers, at a safe distance and in a more conservative fashion.

Holland circled left and descended, making a low-altitude medium-speed pass down Runway 05. The BUFF banked forty-five degrees and circled back again making a high-speed approach to Runway 23. Holland accelerated down Runway 23 and at about midfield, he pulled the aircraft up into a high-pitch-angle climb. In twenty-four seconds, the plane gained eight thousand feet of altitude. As every second passed in the steep climb, the plane lost air speed. At about 10,500 feet, Czar 52 pushed over. As its nose dipped below the horizon it began to regain air speed. Holland made a 90-degree descending left turn and made a 1,200-foot pass over Runway 05.

Circling left, Czar 52's landing gear came down. Holland lowered the flaps and made a low and slow pass down the runway to demonstrate landing attitude. At about midfield, Holland retracted the gear and banked the plane sixty degrees left into a climbing turn. Czar 52 circled back again and Holland executed a low-speed, low-altitude pass down Runway 23 at approximately 150 knots, less than two hundred feet above ground level. Holland reached the end of the runway and accelerated hard, banking eighty degrees into a climbing right turn. The plane entered a partial stall with a tail-first slide and lost a hundred feet of altitude before rolling out and continuing to climb to pattern altitude.

Holland turned right again and set up for a final approach to Runway 23. The exhibition profile was complete. On the day of the air show, Earl 01 and Czar 52 would land and let other performers take to the sky. Today they were scheduled to practice touch-and-goes for landing practice. Earl 01 was ahead of Czar 52 executing a touch-and-go on the runway.

Holland flew down the runway about thirty feet above the ground and lowered the landing gear. Earl 01 was still on the runway. Holland requested an unplanned 360-degree turn around the control tower to put some distance between the two planes. Holland radioed the tower, "How 'bout just a three sixty around you right now to get us some spacing?" The tower controller acknowledged the request. Czar 52 moved left, flying straight down the airfield between the runway and the tower.

The B-52's landing gear retracted as it rose to 250 feet above ground and maintained an airspeed of about 170–180 knots. Curling trails of black smoke streamed from the engines as Holland applied a small amount of additional thrust. The nose pitched up slightly as he began the level left-hand turn around the tower. The wings banked sixty-four degrees. Halfway around the tower, the left wing dropped to seventy-two degrees, and the slow-moving plane approached stall conditions. A tail-first slide cost the plane about a hundred feet of altitude. The left wing rolled up to about forty-five degrees of bank, breaking the stall and arresting the descent. The plane continued its turn and began to slowly reclaim some altitude. The aircraft had decelerated since it began the 360-degree turn, and no additional thrust was added. As Czar 52 rounded the tower, turning toward the runway, its left wing dipped and continued dropping until it was banked ninety degrees. Czar 52's nose began to fall. The pilot worked the controls, trying to lower the right wing and level the plane; but at this attitude and airspeed the controls had little effect. Czar 52 had stalled.

Numerous Fairchild airmen and civilians saw the practice flight. Pilots, aircrew members, and mechanics watched from the flight line. Firemen watched from inside their crash truck. A security police posting bus drove toward the WSA to relieve the day shift flight that guarded the nukes, stored in the hardened bunkers. At the nearby Survival School, several students took a break from exams and stood outside watching the flight, amazed by the maneuvers. Colonel Wolff's family watched from the edge of the flight line, waiting to celebrate his fini flight. Jodie McGeehan and her three sons watched the flight from their yard in base housing.

Captain Countess was in a building near the flight line and purposely stayed inside during most of the flight. He stepped outside just before Holland started the unplanned turn around the tower and he could see the plane was in trouble. "He was at ninety degrees of bank. The thing that concerned me was, he normally just went and touched ninety and rolled out. … I noticed too long of a delay, and I started yelling for them to get out of the airplane because I saw the nose coming down. … The plane was pointing directly at me. I could see the wing g was incredible. I have never seen the wings bow up like that. ... I know that fuselage does not have much of a lift capability, but it did have a positive angle of attack, and I knew as soon as he started heading toward a negative angle of attack on the fuselage that whatever lift it was providing was going to be gone. And as I saw the nose begin to track down and the plane not rolling out, that was the time I felt they needed to get out. I knew the plane was going to crash at that point."

The nose of Czar 52 continued to fall, as did its altitude. There was nothing the crew could do to save the airplane. Airmen on the ground heard the engines shut down to idle and saw the exhaust smoke trail off. The BUFF's wings stretched vertically from the ground to the sky. A lightning-white flash sent much of the base into darkness as the left wing severed an overhead power line. The wing crumpled as it touched the ground, followed by the nose. In an instant, a two-acre patch of dry grass alongside the WSA fence line was swallowed by a black and orange inferno. Intrusion alarms triggered in the weapon storage area. Sections of wing tumbled and sailed out of the flames as one hundred thirty tons of aircraft and fuel thundered to the ground.

Earl 01 was still climbing away from the airfield when Captain Carlson heard an alarming message from his air refueling technician in the back of the plane. Carlson said, "As we were reaching traffic pattern altitude, the boom operator from the back told me, 'Hey, I think something happened down there guys, there's smoke. There's smoke down there.'"

Before the crash, an airman in the control tower saw the plane was unrecoverable. "He's going down, get the crash phone!" The crash phone—a hotline that simultaneously notifies the command post, police, fire, and medical first responders of an emergent situation—was dead. Several agonizing seconds passed before the emergency generator kicked on and restored power, allowing the tower to make notifications. Several first responders were already en route. They had seen, heard, and felt the plane go down. The tower suspended runway operations, allowing emergency vehicles to cross the runway unimpeded by landing aircraft.

Jodie McGeehan stood in shock. Her two oldest sons ran toward the flight line, guided by the dark column of smoke.

The busload of security policemen from C Flight were nearly part of the accident. One of them recalls looking up as the plane flew overhead, its wings vertical; the pilot seemed to make eye contact with him. Security policemen were the first on the scene. They scrambled down the stairs of the bus. Some ran instinctively toward the fire and smoke. The intense heat pushed them back. The cops spread out, encircling the fiery crash site, protecting the scene, and keeping others at a safe distance.

Across the flight line, inside the fire station, Assistant Fire Chief Mirasole and head nurse, Major Cochran, were discussing the hospital shooting. The lights went out, followed by the rumbling sound of an explosion. Chief Mirasole knew Bud Holland was in the air practicing the maneuvers he had discussed in the planning meeting the previous week. As Chief Mirasole moved to respond, he told Cochran, "Plane down ... you stay with me."

Chief Mirasole moved outside to his truck, followed by Cochran. The chief looked across the flight line. He said, "All I could see was, it looked like the WSA was on fire. I had Engine 7 already at gate 17, which is located adjacent to the crash site, opening the gate. They were at taxiway delta waiting to cross the runway, and they were eyewitnesses to the incident. We responded over there. I was the third truck in. Response time was about one minute. We went in, and I remember going down the road with all the parts and the pieces, and the fire was quite large and quite hot."

When they arrived on scene, Cochran noted, "It was obvious that there was not much use for my services right away, because the plane was down and there weren't any bystanders that seemed injured at the time."

Pat McGeehan outran his brother and slipped through a gate leading to the flight line. From under the wing of a parked KC-135, he looked into the distance and watched as firemen pumped water into the black void that enveloped the pieces of his father's burning plane.

The intensely hot fire threatened to destroy an electrical substation outside the WSA. Engine 3 arrived on scene and attacked the flames as Engine 7 found a hydrant for resupply. Chief Mirasole said, "We attacked the fire ... to save the substation, started knocking down the fire at the fuselage—the only area of the aircraft we could identify. I went around to the backside to see how far the fire went into the WSA area. I ascertained that it didn't go into the WSA. I directed Crash 1 to go around on the WSA side of the accident and start knocking down the fire from the substation to the fuselage. At that point ... I pulled out, coordinating with the cops, told them I wanted a five-hundred-foot cordon."

After talking with the security police, Chief Mirasole drove down the road to set up a command post on the perimeter. He was approached by several airmen from the Survival School who had watched the plane go down. "They advised me just as I was going to set up my command post that they did see somebody eject from the aircraft and they were planning on going to the accident site. We redirected them to do a search on the west side of the road."

Initially, the toxic black smoke rose straight into the sky; as the wreckage burned, the black cloud turned dark gray and began to drift. The wind carried caustic fumes and particulate to the first responders on the perimeter. The cordon was increased to one thousand feet after several airmen were overcome by fumes and began vomiting.

As teams searched for the ejected aviator, the firefighters continued knocking down the flames. Firefighters with hand lines moved into the crash site as fire rescue crews searched for casualties. They found four bodies among the burnt wreckage. The object the witnesses had seen fly from the plane was Lieutenant Colonel McGeehan's ejection hatch. He had initiated the ejection sequence but the ejection had been interrupted by the impact. All four crew members, Robert Wolff, Kenneth Huston, Mark McGeehan, and Bud Holland, were killed.

Several security police leaders responded to the scene. Among them were the chief of security police, the first sergeant, C Flight shift commander 1st Lt Scott Kolar and security flight chiefs MSgt Pete Le Grand and MSgt Madison Palmer. Le Grand and Palmer were busy helping secure the perimeter of the crash site. As the situation began to stabilize, Le Grand turned to the task of relieving the day shift flight from their duty guarding the WSA. When he went to round up his flight, Le Grand discovered they had been relieved of duty. Someone had decided the cops had been traumatized by what they had witnessed. They had been disarmed and driven to the Deel Community Recreation Center, where they sat sequestered in a room.

Le Grand thought the young airmen would be better off returning to duty and working through the trauma of the incident together. Le Grand said he tracked them down. "They were all deer in the headlights, but I could tell they were relieved to see me." He stepped into the room and asked, "Ready to go to work?" They all smiled and followed him to the posting bus, returned to the armory for their weapons, and headed out to the WSA. Le Grand spent the rest of the evening visiting his airmen on their posts, allowing them to talk about what they had seen. The airman who saw the pilot fly overhead looking down at him was convinced the pilot was looking to him for help. He was relieved when his flight chief suggested the pilot was attempting to orient himself with the ground as he attempted to recover the aircraft.

Several witnesses had videotaped the practice flight. Security police were directed to locate and confiscate the videotapes for use in the accident investigation. One tape evaded confiscation and aired on local and national news, showing the B-52 circling the tower at low altitude, banking its wings until vertical, and falling into an explosive ball of fire.

The day after the crash, Fairchild Public Affairs put out a press release confirming that all four aboard the B-52 were killed in a crash while conducting a "local training mission" near Fairchild's control tower. Public Affairs asked for the media to assist them in notifying the public that Aerospace Day was canceled. The civilian press knew the crew had been practicing for the air show, and two days later they found Secretary of the Air Force Sheila Widnall at McChord Air Force Base in western Washington where they pressed her for answers. Widnall defended the Air Force policy on air shows. "The things we do in air shows are what we normally do in training missions."

Secretary Widnall may have assumed the Air Force had been following its regulations that prohibited aerobatic flight in its heavy aircraft. The video that played repeatedly on televisions across the nation showed otherwise. Newspaper and television reports suggested the plane was performing dangerous maneuvers before it crashed. Almost immediately, Congress began asking questions about the crash and wondered if the Air Force had forgotten its 1987 promise not to use its heavy aircraft to conduct aerobatic maneuvers. Four days after the crash, Widnall wrote to members of Congress telling them what the press was saying about the maneuvers was speculation. Widnall changed her stance three weeks later, telling Congress that Czar 52's maneuvers appeared to exceed the normal operating procedures but stopped short of blaming the maneuvers for the crash.

With few exceptions, everyone at Fairchild believed the crash was pilot error, and they knew who was flying the plane. Capt Alexander Brown said he spoke with Sgt Jan Daily, a civil engineering clerk with the Washington Air National Guard. Brown said Daily told him she saw the plane's wings rock back and forth about five times immediately before the crash. He said, "She saw the wings rock, remarked to herself that looked odd, walked into the building, and felt a pressure wave." Brown said, "That wing rock was, in my experience flying with Bud, characteristic of his taking control of the aircraft. That when you handed off aircraft control, particularly in the traffic pattern, he would oscillate the yoke about five times."

Jodie McGeehan didn't blame Bud Holland for the death of her husband. "I put all the blame on his superiors—they encouraged him and rewarded him for years." She feared nothing would change if Fairchild's leadership wasn't held accountable. At a memorial service, Jodie McGeehan detailed her concerns to Kenneth Pearce, a former B-52 pilot and close friend of her husband. Pearce wrote a letter to senior Air Force officials, who passed his letter on to their investigation board. In the letter, Pearce related that Lieutenant Colonel McGeehan unsuccessfully attempted to have Holland grounded after hearing complaints from his aircrews. Pearce also questioned the judgment of Holland, the maneuvers he flew in previous air shows, and the failure of Fairchild's leadership to stop his irresponsible flying.

An Air Force investigation board was formed to "obtain and preserve all available evidence for claims, litigation, disciplinary and administrative actions." The investigation was headed by Col Michael McConnell, the commander of the 93rd Operations Group, Castle AFB, California. Assisting him was a team of military specialists in the medical, aircraft maintenance, and legal fields. Other than the legal advisors, there were no law enforcement officers assisting in the investigation. Forty-nine interviews were conducted of current and former Fairchild commanders, aircrew, doctors, maintenance crews, firefighters, and cops. The investigation ruled out mechanical failure, weather factors, and medical conditions as a cause of the crash.

The board then focused on the airmanship and historical flying behavior of the crew. Testimony revealed all four crewmembers were skilled aviators, but only Bud Holland had a history of overly aggressive flying. The board found several instances of Holland flying in violation of USAF, ACC, and FAA regulations over a three-year period.

The investigation determined all of the crew died as a result of "multiple extreme injuries." However, Holland showed specific injuries suggesting his hands were on the controls at the time of impact. The report read, "The board determined that pilot error was a cause. The pilot violated regulatory provisions, flight manual guidance, and guidance from the wing commander, placing the aircraft outside established flight parameters at an attitude and altitude where recovery was not possible." Colonel McConnell concluded, "Based upon clear and convincing evidence, my opinion is that the 24 June 1994 aircraft accident was the result of pilot error, crew error, and several breakdowns in supervision and leadership. The accident was preventable."

The cause of "pilot error" is clear. The board found that Lieutenant Colonel Holland, by exceeding bank angles, speed, and altitude restrictions for maneuvering the aircraft during a circling approach, flew the aircraft into a stalled condition, departed controlled flight, and impacted the ground. The board's determination of "crew error" as a factor in the crash seems less clear. According to the report, "The accident crew, perhaps not recognizing a dangerous situation developing, allowed the pilot to enter into a stalled condition." The breakdown of supervision and leadership was evident. The report read:

> The pilot had a history of excessively aggressive flying and poor airmanship. The frequently changed wing leadership did not recognize this pattern of behavior. The 92nd Wing commander [Colonel Brooks] and his staff lacked an adequate understanding of regulations concerning air shows and maneuvering angles permitted in the traffic pattern. The 92nd Operations Group commander (OG/CC) [Colonel Pellerin] recommended, and the wing commander approved, air show maneuvers not complying with the Pilot's Flight Manual and USAF, ACC, and FAA regulations. The 92nd OG/CC flew the air show profile with the mishap pilot previously, did not recognize it was contrary to regulations and air discipline, and did not direct a profile change to bring it into compliance. The maneuver resulting in the accident was a direct extension of that exceedingly aggressive profile.

The investigation board acknowledged that Brooks rejected portions of Holland's profile because of its aggressiveness. But they noted he "did not direct the operations group to accomplish a total review of air show criteria after rejecting their profile. The wing commander ordered a flight profile that was less aggressive but was still not in compliance with ACC regulations and the Pilot's Flight Manual." The investigative report continued, "Lt Col Holland, despite the orders given him by the wing commander, flew a very reckless profile and ignored those orders, without being curtailed by onboard supervisors including the squadron commander, an instructor navigator, and the vice wing commander."

Captain Fleming supported the investigative board's conclusion that the crash was preventable. Fleming said, "From my position, this was not unknown, this was known, it could have been stopped, and it was elected to not be stopped, and maybe they were thinking just one more flight, he's gonna retire, and nothing will happen. The whole crew force is standing up and jumping up and down saying no, no, no. Too many events, too many times that he drew attention to himself. People, and I'm saying the senior leadership knew, is what I'm saying. And, I would not accept as a crew dog, an explanation or something from them saying that 'we didn't know.' The entire crew force would laugh if that was what was told to us."

Fleming suggested that Holland was protected by his rank and position. He said, "[T]he hypocrisy is amazing—if someone on the crew force had done one of the things that Lieutenant Colonel Holland routinely did, they would probably never fly again. And the hypocrisy for him to be in a position of the chief of standardization, which is why some people didn't say anything, is unconscionable."

Capt Peter Donnelly offered his insight: "I believe that Colonel Holland was doing what he was encouraged to do, rewarded for doing. ... The media has rewarded him with praise in the local paper. I know that the wing staff has rewarded him with praise and assignments to special missions. He flies the air show every year and everybody ... could see the way he flew at those air shows, and he was not reprimanded, he was rewarded. ... If he had been corralled in, he would have flown the way he was told to. I believe that, but if he wasn't, he was going to fly the way he wanted to and the way he was encouraged to. ... He was what the Air Force made him."

A few months after the investigation concluded, Colonel Pellerin was charged with three counts of dereliction of duty stemming from his recommendation to approve Holland's dangerous flight profile and for not taking action to end the pilot's unsafe flying. In 1995, Pellerin reached an agreement with a military court, pleading guilty to two of the three counts. Before sentencing, he said, "I accept full responsibility for not having prevented this. ... It was my duty to do so." He avoided jail time and dismissal from the Air Force; he was fined $7,500 for his involvement in the incident that cost four lives and a 73-million-dollar airplane. Pellerin suggested he would be paying a higher price. "This will haunt me for the rest of my life."

Elizabeth Huston, the wife of radar navigator Lieutenant Colonel Huston, who died aboard Czar 52, felt Pellerin was a scapegoat. She wondered why Holland's previous commanders hadn't stopped him earlier. Elizabeth Huston said Holland had performed the same maneuvers in the 1993 air show, and the wing commander at that time, Brigadier General Richards, patted him on the back saying, "Way to go, Bud."

According to *The Spokesman-Review*, John Nance, a consultant for aviation safety, agreed that Pellerin was a scapegoat. Nance, who is also a commercial airline pilot as well as a pilot in the Air Force Reserve, said the Pellerin case fits a pattern of protecting high-ranking officers. "The Air Force forms a protective shield over the chain of command. … The brotherhood demands the leadership be protected. It blames an individual to avoid blaming the system."

The interviews conducted by the aircraft accident investigation board of Holland's former commanders were not interrogatory. When questioned about their knowledge of Holland's unsafe flying, many of them could not recall or claimed to have no knowledge of specific incidents.

In the end, Col William Pellerin was the only living person held responsible for the crash. Col William Brooks, the wing commander at the time of the crash, was granted immunity in exchange for his testimony at Pellerin's court-martial. Brooks, who had been approved for promotion to the rank of brigadier general, was denied the promotion and retired a year after the crash to become a club golf pro. Brig Gen James Richards went on to work in the Pentagon for the Assistant Secretary of the Air Force. Lt Col Stephen Harper became an inspector general team chief at Air Combat Command Headquarters. Col David Capotosti was made the chief of safety for the 12th Air Force.

After the investigative board determined the crash was preventable, Gen John Loh, commander of Air Combat Command, personally reminded all of his wing commanders of the regulations concerning air shows. His warning apparently didn't reach Elmendorf Air Force Base, Alaska. In 2010, a C-17A cargo plane powered by four jet engines, and similar in size to the B-52, was practicing maneuvers for an air show. The plane took off, climbed rapidly, and immediately banked hard to the left. The plane leveled off, flying low over the airfield before executing an aggressive right turn over the base. The pilot ignored a stall warning alarm and continued the hard turn until it was too late. The crash was eerily similar to that of Czar 52, including the investigative determination that pilot error caused the death of four crewmembers after the right wing dropped to ninety degrees and the nose fell through the air. The plane plunged wing-first into the ground and disappeared in a ball of smoke and flame.

Czar 52 during unplanned go-around of control tower, 24 June 1994.
Aircraft Accident Investigation photo

Czar 52 departure from controlled flight. Copilot ejection hatch seen near the tail of the aircraft, 24 June 1994. Aircraft Accident Investigation photo

Czar 52 upon impact, 24 June 1994.
Aircraft Accident Investigation photo

Czar 52 crash site photo taken from WSA vantage point, 24 June 1994.
Aircraft Accident Investigation photo

Crash site showing relationship to Weapon Storage Area (above) and Survival School Campus (below), 24 June 1994. Aircraft Accident Investigation photo

Col Robert Wolff. Press photo

Lt Col Arthur "Bud" Holland. Press photo

Lt Col Kenneth Huston. Press photo

Lt Col Mark McGeehan. Press photo

Sheriff's Investigation

Representatives from the various law enforcement agencies who responded to Fairchild's hospital met to determine who would take charge of the investigation. Since the gunman was deceased and would not be prosecuted, the FBI would not assume jurisdiction but would be available to assist. Everyone agreed that the sheriff's office should be the primary investigative agency, since it had the manpower and experience to handle the scene. Air Force OSI agents also offered to assist and initiated their own investigation focusing on Air Force interests.

The Spokane County Sheriff's Office dispatched four teams of detectives to area hospitals to interview the wounded and collect their clothing and any ballistic evidence that might be recovered during surgery. Another team of detectives followed a lead to Arnold's Motel, where they confirmed the gunman had rented a room. Several detectives walked through the hospital crime scene, noting blood stains, shell casings, and bullet holes in cars, walls, windows, and floors. Identification officers followed behind taking notes, measurements, and photographs before collecting evidence. The Washington State Patrol had the latest in crime scene diagramming equipment—a laser-equipped surveying device—that helped them map the multi-acre crime scene, showing where every piece of evidence was located.

Only a few hours after the shooting, sheriff's detectives at the scene learned someone claiming to be Lois Mellberg was trying to contact them from Michigan. They wondered how Mellberg's family could know he was involved, since his name had not yet been released to the media. The detectives chose not to return Lois's phone call until local law enforcement could officially notify the next of kin. The process took much longer than they expected. By the time Mellberg's parents were told that he had been killed at Fairchild after going on a shooting spree, the news media had already named him as the killer.

Lois had learned about her son's involvement earlier that afternoon after receiving a phone call from Marlene Anderson, the manager of Arnold's Motel. Marlene said Lois initially sounded confused. "She went hysterical, screaming, 'Tell me he wasn't one of them!'" When Anderson told Lois that her son was the suspected killer, Marlene said Lois responded, "If you only knew the horrible things that [Fairchild] did to that boy."

In the days that followed, Lois Mellberg telephoned the agencies investigating the shooting, requesting information. Sheriff's detective James Hansen returned her calls and answered her questions. Initially, Lois provided the detective with information potentially useful to the investigation. But before long, her demeanor changed. She told Detective Hansen that she would not cooperate with the Air Force, believing they would cover up certain details of the case. She had refused to provide OSI access to her son's computer or his personal notes and records that had been shipped from Cannon AFB, arriving at the family home the day after the shooting. Lois acknowledged her son's actions at Fairchild were inexcusable, but she went on to enumerate how the Air Force had mistreated him. She told the detective that her son had tried to get several notations in his medical file corrected, and she believed the Air Force used its mental health system to imprison her son as a punishment for using his chain of command to try to change things. Lois also accused the late Dr. Brigham of directly interfering in her son's transfer to Mountain Home. Detective Hansen noted in his report, "It is apparent in the conversations with Mrs. Mellberg that she does blame the Air Force for what did happen ultimately to her son."

Lois Mellberg stopped contacting Detective Hansen after he informed her he was only interested in information that pertained to his investigation—the investigation of the multiple deaths and assaults committed by her son as well as the officer-involved shooting of her son.

At the onset of the investigation, there had been several reports of a second gunman, and at least two victims thought there had been two shooters inside the hospital. This was attributed to the chaos generated by the rapidly occurring violence. After further interviews, all of the witnesses agreed that there had only been one perpetrator. The Spokane County Sheriff's Office conducted an extensive investigation. An examination of ballistic evidence showed that Mellbeg's 75-round magazine still held 19 rounds when he was killed. Investigators determined that all of the malevolent bodily injury at the hospital was caused by bullets fired from the MAK-90 rifle carried by Dean Mellberg.

Politics and Media

Before the area was secure, television news crews were broadcasting live reports from the perimeter of Fairchild's hospital. Crews from Spokane, Seattle, and others from as far away as Oregon and New York, camped outside the crime scene to cover the developing story. Dave Fehling of CBS News reported from the perimeter, "Whatever it was troubling Dean Mellberg, it apparently led him to commit one of the most vicious mass shootings ever in the Northwest." Other reporters listed the number of dead and wounded and, as if they were keeping score, dubbed the incident the "worst mass shooting in Spokane history." Newscasters repeatedly broadcast the name of the perpetrator; some dubbed him the "Fairchild Assassin." His photograph was displayed prominently on television screens and in newspapers. The coverage and national attention paid to the Fairchild incident inspired at least one violent criminal. Just days after the Fairchild shooting, a convicted felon in Spokane threatened to kill his mental health care workers, indicating he would "do it Fairchild style." When police were alerted to the threat, they arrested the man and despite his criminal record, found him in possession of more than thirty firearms and a large quantity of ammunition.

In the early news coverage, one Spokane reporter referred to the incident as a "random act of lethal violence." Other Spokane reporters interviewed motel staff and others who had brief encounters with Mellberg in the weeks before the shooting and said, "Everyone that we spoke with today said that Mellberg never gave them a sign that he was capable of hurting so many people." Cheryl Chodun, with Detroit's WXYZ Channel 7 Action News, conducted interviews in Mellberg's hometown of Lansing and reported, "As friends remember Dean Mellberg today, they are shaking their heads in disbelief. Although it appears he was somewhat of a loner and was even picked on by others, the deadly rampage in Spokane yesterday was something no one could have predicted."

A CNN reporter traveled to Spokane and aired a story that showed a photograph of Mellberg, saying, "Dean Mellberg smiled in his pictures. The last few people to talk with him said he was polite—clean-cut one day, a killer the next; we'll never know why." Lansing's Channel 6 reporter Alex Montano said, "News of the tragedy shocked those who had known Mellberg as a quiet and shy student at Waverly High School. … An average student who never got into any trouble, participating in only one extra-curricular activity—choir." The same Channel 6 news crew interviewed seventeen-year-old Jaime Thorne after spotting her in a high school year-book choir photo sitting next to Mellberg. Jaime said, before the interview she informed the news crew she didn't really know Dean and didn't even know his last name. She said they told her it didn't matter. Jaime was unfa-miliar with the severity of Mellberg's crime and was embarrassed when she saw footage of her interview where she said, "He was very quiet. He seemed very polite and nice in class, and he always did what he was told, and he was just nice. He didn't do anything wrong to anybody. He was just quiet." Montano ended the story showing footage of Mellberg's Lansing home, saying, "And as a sheriff deputy guards the Mellberg household from media and other onlookers today, the family inside can only wonder what hap-pened to the choirboy who for a moment yesterday became a madman."

Investigative journalists with *The Spokesman-Review*, Jim Camden, Jess Walter, Jeanette White and others dug deep into the story. *The Spokesman-Review* ran exposés that raised pointed questions regarding the events that led to the Fairchild shooting. Spokane's KXLY 4 News aired a brief state-ment from Coeur d'Alene, Idaho, psychologist Craig Stempf. Stempf said the government does very little for those in the armed forces who need mental health care. "The military seems unwilling to undergo long-term treatment with serious psychological problems, and they would almost rather send the person into civilian life and discharge them."

Spokane's KREM 2 news began their 20 June 1994, 11 o'clock broad-cast by showing scenes from the hospital as anchor Nadine Woodward announced, "A lone gunman opens fire at Fairchild's base hospital." The screen switched to a close-up shot of a black semiautomatic rifle as anchor Charles Rowe proclaimed, "This is the type of gun that caused all the car-nage." For several days, Spokane's KHQ 6 news anchors delivered stories about the tragedy with a graphic of Mellberg's MAK-90 and 75-round drum magazine on the screen beside them. KHQ 6 reporter Bill Gross interviewed "Firearm Trainers" and showed footage of watermelons being shot by a semi-automatic AK-47 rifle.

National and local news stories cited the tragedy as the latest example of the need to impose stricter gun control laws. The day after the tragedy,

Washington State Senator Patty Murray reiterated her demand for a ban on "assault weapons." Murray spoke in the US Senate. "How many more people have to die before we realize how destructive and totally unnecessary these weapons are and ban them from this country?" Murray was referring to a bill recently approved by Congress that would ban future sales of nineteen specific semi-automatic rifles.

In a brief clip, Washington State Senator Slade Gordon countered Murray's comments, saying the tragedy in Spokane has done nothing to change his opposition to the bill. He pointed out, "The ban wouldn't have applied to the weapons which exist at the present time and in fact this perhaps shows the lack of utility of these laws." Some parents and spouses of the victims of the shooting at Fairchild supported the additional gun control laws.

Many of the survivors didn't see firearms as the cause of Fairchild's tragedy. Patrick Deaton, who was shot while seated in Fairchild's pharmacy lobby, told *The Spokesman-Review*, "Weapons don't kill people." He said, "What we need to do is change the hearts of people."

Orson Lee gave interviews to several media outlets from his hospital bed where he was recovering from shrapnel wounds caused by the gunman's bullet. Lee told Spokane's KHQ 6 News, "I would have liked to see somebody get him a lot sooner, and I think if I'd had a .45 I'd have tried to get him sooner."

Mark Hess, who was shot while exiting the pharmacy lobby, would later give an interview to Illinois Sauk Valley Media where he said, "If I had a gun, I could have stopped him. Nobody was in the way."

Deena Kelley, who was shot in the back while attempting to hide in the pharmacy lobby said, "Mellberg was determined. I have absolutely no doubt that he would have found a way to obtain a weapon regardless of any gun control measures. ... We live in a world where some people are bent on destruction. Tragically there are times when a deranged individual with a gun can only be stopped by someone of strong mind that has a gun and knows how to use it. It is my opinion that the shooter could have been stopped before anyone was killed if more military personnel had been wearing side arms on base."

Memorial

Three days after the shooting, I finished my only mandatory mental health counseling appointment and drove down Highway 2 headed to Airway Heights. I pulled into the Buckhorn Inn for a beer. The television at the end of the bar was tuned to the local news coverage of a memorial service taking place at the base chapel. Unaware of the memorial until that moment, I was caught off guard and wept openly as chaplains, family and friends eulogized the lives we lost. The bartender asked me if I had been there. I managed to tell her, "I was the one who stopped him." She and a few other patrons kept my beer glass full for the next few hours as I quietly drowned my grief until my buddies tracked me down and gave me a ride home.

The memorial took place on Thursday morning, 23 June 1994. Five hundred mourners gathered at the base chapel to remember the four lives lost at the hospital. They would be informed that Michelle Sigman, still hospitalized and in serious condition, had lost her unborn daughter, Taylor McKenzie, bringing the number of innocent lives lost to five.

Loudspeakers broadcast the service to the mourners who overflowed the bleachers set up outside the chapel. Spokane's KXLY News 4 cameras were placed a respectful distance across the street and captured the forty-minute service, which they broadcast live, uninterrupted by commercial or commentary.

Phil Williams, a longtime friend of Rande and Anita Lindner, described Anita as a "loving, devoted mother and a supportive and understanding wife, a caring daughter, a believer in our youth, and a person who many people could and did rely on." He spoke of their friendship and her volunteer work with Campfire and Civil Air Patrol. "Anita did what she did, not for recognition or for fame, but because she knew that people were counting on her, and that was what friends were supposed to do."

Phil recalled asking Anita how she managed to be so organized with so many activities and responsibilities as a parent.

"Anita told me something I believe was the motto she lived her life by. She said, 'If you believe that something is worth doing, give it your all or do nothing at all, because a job half-done does no one any good.' Anita always gave her all to whatever she did, her family, her community, her church, her friends. She believed in these things and she gave them her all. Good people like Anita and the other innocent people that we lost in this tragedy are hard to find. But they have made our lives richer for knowing them … I am proud to call Anita my friend and I will miss her."

Chaplain David Knight read "a statement concerning Christin McCarron."

"There will be many who seek to vilify Dean Mellberg. Dean Mellberg was not a monster, but a monstrous thing has been done. Eight-year-old Christin is gone, and yet now her story must be told and remembered. … Christin Francis McCarron … entered into eternal life on June 20 1994. She was born on February 13 1986, in Spokane, Washington. Christin was a person of great heart who cared dearly for everyone she knew. Favorite pasttimes included bicycling with her brother and family through Manito Park and camping with her family. Christin was an avid reader. She loved school, especially researching history, and rock collecting. Christin was a member of Balboa Elementary Montessori class. Christin was active in fundraising with her class to support Cross Walk (a temporary children's shelter that was Christin's favorite charity), rain forest preservation, and other charities. She attended church at Our Lady of Lourdes in Spokane. Christin will be forever in the hearts of those who loved her. She is survived by her parents, Echo and Greg McCarron of Spokane, and one brother, Ryan. … Greg and Echo wish the Fairchild Air Force community to know that they bear no anger and no bitterness for what has happened. They wish you to know that they love all of the people of Spokane and Fairchild Air Force Base. Blessed be the children for theirs is the kingdom of heaven."

Billy Brigham eulogized his brother.

"Tom graduated from high school at the age of sixteen, attended Purdue University on an athletic scholarship, and graduated at age nineteen. He went on to graduate school at Auburn University. At the age of twenty-one, Tom married Susan Harold-Brigham, and later that year received his master's degree. From there he went to medical school, where he graduated with high

honors. He did his residency in psychiatry and was commissioned as a major in the US Air Force at the age of twenty-nine."

"I just read quickly through a list of visible things that Tom accomplished in a short period of time. This list would give the impression that Tom was a man in a hurry. But his credentials and diplomas do not tell us enough about the man who we knew. A man who was a devoted husband, who did and shared so many things with his wife. One who was an active and engaged father to his two children. … Tom will be missed as a brother, a son, a husband, a father, and friend."

Survival School psychologist James Mitchell, Alan London's clinical supervisor, spoke about his colleague.

"Those of us in mental health in the military serve two masters. We must balance our concern and compassion and care for the patient with the awesome responsibility of ensuring that those people who have access to the terrible weapons of war are suitable for that. Alan was better at that than anyone that I have ever met. He and I spent many hours reviewing his caseload and talking about his concerns in terms of meeting the needs of his patients and meeting his responsibility to the military."

"I know the depth of his caring for his wife. I know the depth of his patriotism for his country. And I know the depth of his concern for his patients. He had the ability to restore hope and inspire passion in people to move forward into wellness. And if we can take one thing from this and pass it on to others around us, it's that ability to restore hope and inspire a commitment to move forward into wellness. We are all poorer for his passing. I shall miss him as a friend and a colleague."

The day after the memorial service, social worker Krista Pierson returned to the mental health center for the first time since the shooting. She saw where bullets had impacted the cinderblock walls, and she saw the blood stains on the carpet. She said, "It was all so surreal." She had just returned from Dr. London's funeral service and was helping Kathy London clean out her husband's office.

The two women heard a loud rumble and saw billowing black smoke coming from the flight line. As they carried a box to a car outside, they began crying when they heard the sound of sirens. Pierson said, "We didn't know what had happened, but we knew it was bad."

Four days later, on the morning of 28 June 1994, a second memorial service would take place at the base chapel, the sad result of yet another tragedy, one that had been foreseen and warned about.

Anita Lindner. Photo courtesy of Lindner family

Dr. Alan London. Photo courtesy of London family

Dr. Thomas Brigham. Photo courtesy of Brigham family

Christin and Ryan McCarron.
Reprinted by permission of McCarron family

Lawsuit

After they were released from the hospital, the survivors continued to heal. They looked forward to reversing their colostomies, regaining the use of their limbs and healing mentally. Some would never again walk without pain, a limp, or the constant threat of falling. Most experienced the symptoms of mental trauma commonly found in veterans of war. And for many the trauma still affects them today.

After the shooting, Orson Lee became more aware of his surroundings and found himself looking over his shoulder, something he hadn't done since his days in combat. But Lee said his wife was even more affected than he was. "If you were in a car and watched your spouse get gunned down, you'd have trouble too. ... I spent eleven months in Korea and fourteen months in Vietnam. When you're in a combat situation, nothing moves within two hundred to three hundred yards that you don't see. I've experienced that kind of thing. My wife hasn't."

Survivors experienced nightmares and insomnia. They developed an aversion to hospitals and crowded public spaces. They suffered depression and anxiety. They jumped at loud noises and were abnormally wary of strangers. A year after the shooting, Marlene Moe said, "You never sit with your back to the door. ... I always make sure where the exits are. I'm suspicious of everyone around me."

Not long after the shooting, SSgt Joe Noone realized he was experiencing symptoms of trauma. He said, "I've been in a couple of situations in which I've worried, unrealistically, that someone was going to pull a gun. It's going to take a while."

Thirteen-year-old Sam Spencer had nightmares that prompted him to sleep with a hatchet under his pillow and his hunting knife within reach of his bed. About a year after the shooting, his leg had healed somewhat but was still painful to walk on. Sam said, "That's the way it's going to be," and refused to let it stop him from pursuing his interests. He played basketball for his junior high and grudgingly took to the bench when the pain in his leg became too much. He was able to take a gun safety class in his 4H club and managed to go deer hunting.

Not long after the shooting, Fairchild's hospital staff and mental health personnel had to go back to work in the same building where their colleagues had lost their lives. The walls had been painted and the carpet replaced, but some of the bullet damage remained.

Social worker Krista Pierson said it was difficult seeing patients so soon afterwards. "I was dealing with my own grief … and I had to detach myself to help them. I saw myself as the walking wounded caring for the walking wounded." Even today, she is unsure if her emotional wounds will ever heal completely. But she has managed to move on with her life.

Some people felt more confident after surviving the incident, but many more felt survivor's guilt—guilt from not being able to save lives or for simply surviving a tragedy while others did not. Kevin Seeley still feels a twinge of guilt for unknowingly helping the gunman. Seeley held the bathroom door open for Mellberg as he struggled to get inside with his oversized gym bag prior to the shooting.

Margaret Lum returned to work at a Spokane flower shop only days after escaping the hospital's shot clinic. She said, "I was making an arrangement, and my boss was blowing up balloons, not thinking anything of it till one of them popped. … I screamed and literally jumped on the counter in tears." Later that afternoon, a woman walked in and ordered flowers for a funeral. Margaret got goosebumps when she learned the woman was Susan Brigham. "I was stunned. I felt so guilty for being alive. She was so sweet when I told her that I was there and that I was so sorry for her loss. We hugged and cried and hugged. She told me not to feel guilty, that her husband would be so happy to know that people survived." Margaret promised Mrs. Brigham that she would attend the memorial service and live the best life that she could.

Today, Margaret can talk about her experience at the hospital without crying, and she has learned to control her startle response. "I go shooting with my husband and have learned to breathe at the sound of different gun shots. I pray that others have found their peace with this incident."

Over the years, many of the survivors have found at least some relief through the passage of time and counseling. As Marlene Moe said, you could "what if" and "why" the situation forever. "But you have to learn to live with it the rest of your life."

In the two years that followed the shooting, survivors and their families filed twenty-nine claims against the Air Force, totaling 160 million dollars. The claims were denied, prompting a team of lawyers representing the survivors to file nineteen lawsuits against the federal government, alleging forty-one acts of negligence. The legal process would take years.

The US government fought to avoid paying restitution, but Fairchild Air Force Base stepped up. Several of Fairchild's airmen volunteered and were given a budget to assist the survivors.

One of the volunteers was SMSgt Curt Luce. He frequently visited Rande Lindner and encouraged him to seek counseling as he attempted to cope with the loss of his wife Anita. Rande said, "He's made a big difference, knowing that there's at least someone on the base who does care." Senior Master Sergeant Luce also helped the Moes by giving Dennis someone to talk to and driving him to medical appointments. Luce and other volunteers helped Eva Walch maintain her independence. They installed a wheelchair ramp at her front door and a sprinkler system in her yard to keep her meticulous lawn and flowerbeds flourishing. Eva said, "It's really hard for me to ask for anything. Curt makes it kind of easy. … If there wasn't a Curt, I think we'd be knocking down the doors of Fairchild."

Not everyone who was victimized by the tragedy filed a lawsuit. Many were prohibited from doing so, ever since a Supreme Court ruling in 1950 determined the US government is not liable for injuries to members of the armed forces that result from the negligence of other armed forces members.

The ruling became known as the Feres doctrine; and in 1998, when the lawsuit finally reached Spokane's US District Court, Justice Department attorneys cited the Feres doctrine when they moved to have the lawsuit thrown out. The judge agreed that the government was negligent, but also ruled that the Feres doctrine applied to the case. He dismissed all but two of the lawsuit's claims of negligence.

In March 2000, the Ninth Circuit Court of Appeals upheld the survivors' right to sue the government for the negligent processing of Mellberg's enlistment and their failure to properly diagnose and treat his mental disorders, as well as discharging him without provisions for medical treatment. A new trial date was set for September 2001.

The survivors weren't looking to win the lottery. Eva Walch said, "I don't think we should get millions, but a judgment could make life a lot easier." Many of the survivors were struggling financially. The Air Force had promised to pay for their medical expenses, but at least one survivor said they had been slow to pay and had refused to pay some counseling costs. The slow pace of the judicial system was frustrating. Rande Lindner, who lost his wife in the tragedy, felt the government was dragging its feet in hopes some of the victims would go away. Many of them were in their seventies, and one had already died waiting for the trial.

Two weeks before the trial date, Justice Department lawyers shocked the survivors' attorneys by requesting mediation. They agreed to settle the case as long as all of the survivors agreed to the terms. Eva Walch resisted and wanted to see the case go to trial. She said, "We were ready to go through the ordeal for the truth to come out." But with the Justice Department promising to appeal any undesirable ruling, extending the already seven-year-long process, all of the survivors eventually agreed to settle.

The government agreed to pay $17 million to the twenty-nine plaintiffs. The award would not be split evenly. The amount each survivor received was determined by the extent of their injuries.

It may have added insult to injury if the survivors had known that the gunman's mother was the sole beneficiary of his Service Group Life Insurance policy. The policy remained in effect for six months after his separation, making her eligible to promptly collect $100,000.

Accountability and Change

Susan Brigham was enraged. When she arrived at the crime scene, she was denied the opportunity to see her husband while he was "still warm and lifelike." When she was finally allowed in his office there were so many military men in the room she couldn't properly say goodbye.

She sought counseling from a member of the crisis team dispatched to Fairchild after the shooting. But the psychologist she confided in added insult to injury. Susan said, "I will never forget Dr. Shue's response as I told him of my tremendous guilt. He informed me that my type of thinking was as grandiose and delusional as Mellberg's."

Then Susan received a box of her husband's personal effects that he had kept in his office. A photograph of Dr. Brigham and his children taken while hiking in the Canadian Rockies was still splattered with blood. Susan had given her husband the framed picture for Father's Day the day before he was killed. Later, Susan and her son were spinning a globe that her husband had kept in his office when she realized the dark brown streak running across the Pacific Ocean was, again, her husband's blood.

Even if she wanted to, Susan was prevented from suing the Air Force over her husband's death due to the Feres doctrine. But what she wanted more than money was accountability. She also knew that her husband, who had fought to improve the military's mental health system, wouldn't have wanted a lawsuit. She said, "Tom hated litigation. What he wanted was change." Instead, Susan Brigham channeled her anger into a resolution to find out how the military mental health system allowed her husband and his colleague to be killed by a dangerous patient. She researched Mellberg's background and the events that led up to the tragedy and spent the next three years lobbying Congress and the Air Force for answers, accountability, and change.

Susan arranged to meet with senior Air Force mental health policy makers. Prior to the meeting she sent a letter to Washington D.C., warning them that she knew more about the situation than they might have thought. She told them that her husband shared with her the joy he experienced in his job but also the frustrations he experienced as he did his best to deliver expert psychiatric care in the face of military incompetence and ineptitude. Susan also wrote that Dr. Brigham couldn't believe it when he heard that Mellberg had been diagnosed with autism. She said he knew Mellberg was manipulating the staff at Wilford Hall. She said her husband was incredulous when Mellberg was returned to active duty. Susan said Dr. Brigham had never seen anyone who looked and acted so normal, and yet was imbued with a very apparent underlying evil. She asked the officials to explain why the Air Force thought Mellberg's right to stay in the service outweighed so many innocent people's right to life. Susan ended her letter telling the Air Force officials that her husband died because he was a principled man. She accused them of defending a failed system instead of standing up for the individuals who upheld the military code of honor and ethics. She asked them why—"Where are your principles?"

In February of 1995, Susan flew to Washington on a "widow's pension." She met with the Psychiatry Consultant to the Air Force Surgeon General, Colonel Jay Weiss, and vented her rage as she lobbied for change. Susan also met with Lieutenant General Marcus Anderson, the Air Force Inspector General. The general pointed out that Dr. Brigham and Dr. London only mentioned once in their reports that Mellberg was dangerous and that the term dangerous is vague. Susan countered, "How many times do you ever see that in anybody's records?"

The general admitted that mistakes were made in Mellberg's case. But he likened the shooting to an unpredictable plane crash. Susan said, "Well, general, when you put Dean Mellberg out on the street without any treatment, it was like putting a plane in the air without any fuel." She asked, "When my son turns twelve and asks why his Daddy died, what should I tell him?"

The general said he hoped she would tell him his father died for his country.

"No, general, he didn't. He died because of his country."

Due in part to Susan Brigham's quest and pressure from Congress, Secretary of the Air Force Sheila Widnall ordered the assembly of a special management review team to look into the Mellberg case. The review team consisted of Air Force medical, legal, and mental health experts. Their goal was to "assess and reach conclusions about whether medical and administrative decisions were reasonable" and to "provide recommendations for improvement of administrative processes and directives to prevent a recurrence of a similar event."

The team interviewed key personnel at all of Mellberg's previous duty stations to determine if regulations and procedures had been followed. Two months after the shooting, the team released a report listing four findings.

- The personnel reviewing Mellberg's enlistment documents failed to follow up on his disclosure of previous treatment for a mental condition that might have disqualified him from enlistment.
- On three separate occasions, squadron leadership elected to retain Mellberg on active duty despite strong recommendations from mental health professionals to discharge him.
- While at Wilford Hall Medical Center, a change in diagnoses, miscommunications, and misinterpretation of medical board documentation resulted in Mellberg's reassignment instead of discharge.
- Mellberg was able to affect his treatment by purging unfavorable documentation from his medical records.

The report suggested Lois Mellberg's disruptive behavior, complaints, and interference with her son's medical treatment at Wilford Hall Medical Center were contributing factors in her son's being retained in the Air Force. The review team's recommendations to prevent a reoccurrence of the tragedy amounted to clarifying administrative discharge regulations, modifying medical board paperwork, and reviewing medical record control procedures. They ultimately concluded the Air Force could not have anticipated nor prevented the tragedy.

Initially, the report was not made public. When Susan finally received a copy, after repeated requests, she was not satisfied with the findings. She said, "It's like they didn't learn a thing. ... The magnitude of the errors was so great and they're just changing minutiae."

Susan was incensed that military mental health professionals could still be overruled by commanders who had no mental health training. She was also concerned that the report didn't address the fact that military mental health practitioners serve two masters, treating patients while at the same time reporting to the patient's commander about their fitness for duty. The dual role places doctors in the sometimes dangerous position of being the patient's adversary rather than their advocate.

When Congress pressed the military to consider making changes to the system, perhaps adopting the civilian mental health model, Secretary Widnall responded by saying that military mental health doctors would "continue the necessary and very important dual role."

Susan sent a letter to General Ronald Fogleman, chief of staff of the Air Force, and referenced the special management review's report which she said revealed a series of violations of regulations, medical malpractice, poor judgment and the negligent discharge of a mentally ill airman. She expressed her disappointment that the Air Force had not sought accountability. Susan also sought permission to disseminate the special management review's report to Air Force wing commanders and psychiatrists, hoping to share the lessons to be learned from the system failure.

In October 1997, the Department of Defense made changes to its mental health instructions. The new instructions included a requirement to develop treatment plans for "imminently dangerous" service members before they are discharged. They also defined imminent and potential dangerousness and established requirements to take precautions against threatened injury.

When Susan Brigham learned of the changes she said, "There was a moment of elation, followed by days of crying. … It doesn't bring back five dead and heal twenty-two wounded."

Trauma to Recovery

It was about 1725 when I finished clearing the hospital cafeteria. I turned the volume up on my radio as I stepped back into the hallway. The law enforcement desk radioed asking for my status and location. I responded, "Secure, inside the hospital." Within minutes, security policeman, MSgt Scott Dearduff and OSI Special Agent Jim Carroll approached, telling me I was needed at the on-scene command post. I argued that there was still work to be done but eventually conceded. We walked through the hallway of the oddly quiet hospital, noticing shell casings on the floor and narrow rips in the blood-stained carpet where bullets had skipped off the concrete subfloor. When I arrived at SA Carroll's vehicle outside the ER, I reached to wipe the sweat from my brow. It was then that I realized I was still wearing my bicycle helmet. I unbuckled the helmet saying, "I didn't know I still had this thing on."

A nearby SP laughed. "Damn, Brown, you're fucked up. You must be in shock." I denied it. I had been surrounded by signs of trauma and violence but had emotionally shut down in order to focus on the job. At the time, I felt fine. Numb but fine.

SA Carroll drove down the ER driveway, turning left onto Graham Road, headed for the perimeter. In the distance, I saw the woman lying behind the blue minivan. Time slowed as the sight of her lifeless body passed from the windshield to the driver's side window. I turned in my seat and watched through the rear window as she slowly faded in the distance. When I faced forward again, I saw the gunman lying unattended in the grass, his body now covered with a white sheet, solidifying the fact that he was dead. I can't describe how it felt to realize I had killed a man. It wasn't sympathy or remorse. I felt mildly exhilarated from prevailing in a gunfight, but any sense of victory was trumped by the knowledge that innocent people had been injured and killed. Even the sorrow and guilt I felt for the casualties was muted. I was emotionally flatlined.

At the command post, I met with Detective Hansen of the Spokane County Sheriff's Office. He informed me that they would formally interview me at a later date, but for now he just needed to ask a few questions. After giving him a brief synopsis of my observations and the actions I took, I pointed toward the sidewalk in front of the annex where I had fired my pistol and said, "My brass should be in the grass near that telephone pole." A security police NCO approached and said he was there to take me back to the squadron. I had almost made it to the front seat of his vehicle when another NCO approached and told me he needed my gun. Reluctantly, I surrendered my entire duty belt including my holstered handgun, handcuffs, radio, and flashlight. Being disarmed at the scene of my gunfight left me feeling vulnerable; being relieved of duty prior to the end of my shift felt punitive.

Before we drove off, someone retrieved a spare duty belt from the trunk of their car and handed it to me saying it would help me to "not stand out as having been disarmed." I fastened the conspicuously light belt around my waist and we drove onto base toward the squadron building. I began to speak to the sergeant about the shooting and my concern for the woman behind the van. He cut me off telling me he didn't want to know, and added, "You will be debriefed properly at the law enforcement desk." I half expected him to read me my Miranda rights. He tried to make small talk as I stared silently out the window, feeling as empty as the holster on my hip.

The law enforcement desk was bustling as they continued to make notifications and coordinate the activity at the hospital. I sat alone in an interview room just outside the law enforcement desk. I couldn't stop thinking there must be something more productive I could be doing. I wondered what was going on back at the hospital and wanted to be back on the scene. I didn't want to be sitting in a room, especially one designated for interviewing criminals. I went back up to the desk and asked if I could use a phone to let my family know I was all right. Without explanation, someone told me it would be best if I did not talk to anyone for a few days.

I spent the rest of my shift in the interview room, periodically stepping out to the hall as various commanders came by to shake my hand and congratulate me. After I thanked them we stood in the hall staring at each other in awkward silence. At 2200 members of my flight began trickling back to the squadron. The building was unusually quiet, void of the usual war stories that typically follow a night of police work. Everyone was exhausted, but I wasn't ready to leave. I kept asking if there was anything I could do to help at the scene.

My supervisor and flight chief didn't want me to stay in my dorm room that evening. They claimed they didn't want me to be bothered by other airmen wanting to hear about the shooting. I think they just didn't want me to be alone. Tech Sergeant Robinson said I could stay in the guest room of her home. Before heading to her house, I went to my dorm room to change clothes. I hurriedly stripped off my uniform shirt and body armor. I slipped out of my black leather shoes and kicked them into the corner. I noticed the bottom and sides of the soles glistened with splashes of dried blood. On my way out the door, I changed the outgoing message on my answering machine, hoping to get word to my family.

"Hi, this is Andy. If you heard the news, don't worry. I'm okay."

I retrieved my personal handgun and arrived at Robinson's singlewide trailer in an Airway Heights mobile home park just in time to watch the 11 o'clock local news. I sat on a couch in her dark living room hoping to learn more about what happened at the hospital. Reporters broadcast live from the perimeter. "A man who was discharged from the Air Force for psychological reasons comes back to Fairchild Air Force Base and kills the psychologist, the man who recommended he be discharged." I heard the gunman's name for the first time. "Twenty-year-old Dean Mellberg, from Lansing, Michigan … went on a shooting rampage" before he "was eventually shot and killed by a military policeman." By the end of the broadcast, I learned that four people had been killed and over twenty others had been wounded, including children. I was quietly overwhelmed, feeling only a subdued sadness and a faint sense of failed duty.

I wasn't tired, but I lay down in Robinson's guest bedroom with my Taurus resting on the bed beside me. I closed my eyes and was back at the base. The radio call replayed in my head and I saw myself responding down Graham Road as the cars rolled slowly past me. I saw the crowd fleeing toward me and heard the gunfire. I saw the gunman and heard myself shouting and returning fire. I saw the gunman's feet kick as he flew into the air and landed on his back. I saw the woman lying lifeless behind the minivan. I saw the red pool on the white tile of the cafeteria floor.

Throughout the night, I experienced a wide-eyed tingling alertness as if I had grasped a live wire. I jumped at every creak inside the unfamiliar home. Every voice outside, every car door closing and footstep on the gravel brought me down the dimly lit hallway peeking through curtains, with pistol in hand. My nights of restful sleep were over.

Two days after the shooting I met with detectives Grabenstein and Hansen from the sheriff's office and Special Agent Jim Carroll from OSI in a billeting room, for my formal interview. It was the first time I spoke in detail about what I saw and did at the hospital. As I recalled the images, I was choked with emotion and had to occasionally stop the interview to go outside and sob. The interview was cathartic. I left feeling refreshed but the relief was short-lived.

Military crisis teams flew in from Fort Lewis and Travis Air Force Base the day after the shooting. Psychiatrists, psychologists, and social workers met with various groups and individuals in an attempt to help them cope with the tragedy. I attended one mandatory counseling session with twenty-five other cops. We sat around a conference table and took turns speaking about our role in the response and how we felt about it. Most of the cops gave brief reports, short on details and generally ending with a statement such as "I'm dealing with it." Only one person in the group was in touch with his emotions or willing to share them in a room full of cops. He had been on the emergency services team helping search the annex. He described how he vomited after seeing the body of one of the doctors.

When it was my turn, I briefly described responding to the scene and encountering the gunman. I ended by saying, "I returned fire and stopped him." I couldn't articulate what I was feeling at the time and wasn't asked to elaborate.

Pending completion of the sheriff's investigation I was relieved of patrolman duty and worked an unarmed position watching over the prisoners in our confinement section. I worked alone and missed the camaraderie I had with my flight. Most of the other cops in the squadron seemed apprehensive to approach me, let alone talk to me. One day, before my shift, I walked into the guard mount room to say hello to my flight. A group of airmen were in the corner talking and laughing. When they saw me they went silent. I prodded them until one of them sheepishly admitted what they were laughing about.

"There's a newspaper at the front gate with a photo of Mellberg on the front page and someone drew a bullet hole on his head."

I said, "Did they put a hole in his shoulder too?"

"No."

"Oh yeah? Well I did."

I used humor as a coping mechanism, hoping it would let others know I was comfortable talking about the incident. Not long after the shooting, an issue of *Airman Magazine* came out with an article about the incident and a photo of me on the back cover. My co-workers asked me to autograph copies for them. I didn't know why they wanted my autograph but I didn't refuse. Borrowing from an Air Force recruiting slogan, I signed the magazines and wrote, "Aim high. I did."

Photograph of SrA Brown that appeared on the back of *Airman Magazine* 1994

I felt a need to talk, but when the incident came up in conversation it was only briefly discussed before someone changed the subject. I got the impression people were uncomfortable hearing me talk about the incident. I eventually stopped talking about it, but I couldn't stop thinking about it.

Friday, 24 June 1994, was my first day off after the shooting. I felt a sense of relief as I drove out the gate, headed to Mountain Home, Idaho, for the comfortable companionship of my friends Erik and Tracy Turner. As I drove down Highway 2, something in the distance drew my attention. I looked through my driver's side window toward the base and saw a tall wide column of ominous black smoke. Further down the road I stopped at a small-town diner and saw on the television that a plane had gone down at Fairchild. I knew a plane crash would require a security police response, but I needed to get away.

When I got back from my weekend with the Turners, I immediately put in a request for leave, hoping to return to Mountain Home or spend some time with my family in Port Orchard. My leave request was denied so that I would be available to attend an award ceremony.

Award Ceremony, 30 June 1994. From Left to Right: SSgt Deborah Foster, Sgt Steven Walker, Sgt Michael Lecker, SSgt Joseph Noone, 2nd Lt Timothy Street, Sgt Kevin Schindler, TSgt Gloria Robinson, MSgt John Shenk and 1st Lt Scott Kolar, SrA Andy Brown. Courtesy of FAFB Historian

On 30 June 1994, ten days after the shooting, I stood on a platform at the edge of Fairchild's parade ground with four security policemen and five other personnel who had been at the hospital. Gen John Loh, commander of Air Combat Command, traveled from Langley Air Force Base, Virginia, to speak and present the awards. The ceremony was put together so fast the citation accompanying my medal hadn't been printed yet. It seemed to me that the Air Force rushed to focus on the heroics of the day in an attempt to divert attention away from the tragedy.

As local television news cameras filmed the event, Loh gave a speech to bleachers full of military and civilians. "From tragic events come some very heroic acts." I was presented with the Airman's Medal, a decoration awarded for heroic actions at the voluntary risk of life not involving actual combat. General Loh said, "We do not give the Airman's Medal for ordinary events. We do not give the Airman's Medal for extraordinary events. We give the Airman's Medal only for heroic acts of courage."

The other awardees received Commendation Medals for their acts of heroism. 1st Lt Scott Kolar, MSgt John Shenk, TSgt Gloria Robinson, and Sgt Kevin Schindler were recognized for searching and securing the scene. 2nd Lt Timothy Street, SSgt Deborah Foster, SSgt Joseph Noone, Sgt Michael Lecker and Sgt Steven Walker received Commendation medals for evacuating the hospital, distracting the gunman, and treating the wounded.

Countless others—both security policemen and hospital personnel—deserved medals. When hospital leadership attempted to submit select personnel for awards, they were stymied by higher command. As a compromise, four months after the incident, everyone assigned to the 92nd Medical Group, whether they were at the hospital during the incident or not, received an Achievement Medal with an identically worded citation recognizing them for their "quick and selfless actions" and their "high degree of courage and professionalism by aiding and protecting co-workers and victims even as the attack was in progress."

The day after the award ceremony *The Spokesman-Review* ran an article by staff writer J. Todd Foster with a photo of me saluting General Loh. The headline read, "Airman gets top honor for stopping gunman." The article revealed my name, but Foster's opening line read, "A nearsighted, baby-faced bicycle cop received the Air Force's highest peacetime honor."

I turned down several requests for television and print media interviews, not because I was concerned about how they would portray me, but because I never liked being in the spotlight. I also naively hoped that if I refused interviews, the story would fade away and allow the families to start putting the trauma behind them. I received several awards from community groups, the Red Cross, law enforcement associations, and the Air Force. I reluctantly accepted the praise. It was difficult accepting awards that stemmed from an event that ended five innocent lives and altered numerous others.

Part of me was proud of my actions but I also second-guessed myself. I regretted the fact that I had given the gunman verbal warnings before returning fire. I also questioned my response time. During the initial response, my mind's perception of time was altered and it seemed like an eternity passed before I got on scene and stopped the killing. I ran the scenario through my mind, wondering if I could have somehow gotten there quicker and saved more lives.

For several months, the incident was heavily covered by *The Spokesman-Review*. The newspaper was my sole source of information regarding the victims and the status of the investigation. I hadn't known any of the people who were wounded or killed, but the more I learned about them the more I grieved. I read that Christin McCarron had been "a giggling eight-year-old" whose mother described as "a very, very sweet person" who "always thought of others' feelings." Christin's death hit me the hardest.

When I read that Christin had been in the cafeteria when she was shot, I realized it was her blood on the shoes that lay in the corner of my room. I hadn't worn them since the night of the incident, but I couldn't bring myself to throw them away. Several days later, I could no longer live with the painful reminder. I came home from work and retrieved a shoebox from my wall locker. My chest tightened as I gently picked up the shoes. A lump swelled in my throat as I placed them in the box and carried them to the parking lot. Tears squeezed from my eyes as I shut out the vision of a scared little girl and my inability to save her. I laid the shoes to rest in the dormitory dumpster, feeling an irreverent guilt, like I was throwing away the memory of the little girl. But I will always remember Christin Francis McCarron, a precious eight-year-old girl.

Three months after the shooting, I was cleared to return to duty. I was glad to be back on the road and working patrol with my fellow SPs again. Some of my peers felt comfortable talking to me about the shooting, although it was not as helpful as I had hoped. When one young SP asked me, "How does it feel to have murdered someone?" I abruptly explained to him the difference between murder and justifiable homicide. I didn't feel guilty taking the life of a killer. But after being asked repeatedly if I felt guilty about killing someone, I began to wonder if something was wrong with me. I asked my command if I could speak with a counselor. Wanting to talk to someone familiar with officer-involved shootings, I sought out Dr. Deanette Palmer who counseled officers of the Spokane Police Department. After speaking with Dr. Palmer, I was relieved to learn I was dealing normally with the trauma. It felt good to talk and I continued seeing her for a couple of weeks until I discovered I had been relieved of duty for receiving psychological counseling.

I didn't care if people knew I was seeing a psychologist, but I was too proud to suffer the stigma of being a disarmed cop. Law enforcement is a trust-dependent profession. Cops are entrusted with firearms. They are entrusted to secure the safety of the community. Other cops entrust them with their lives. If their command doesn't trust them to carry a gun, it sends a message that maybe their co-workers shouldn't trust them either. Being relieved of duty for mental health counseling made me feel like an outsider, no longer a part of the team.

I told Dr. Palmer I didn't need further counseling and asked her to write a letter to my squadron telling them I was fit for duty. She was angry to hear that I had been relieved of duty and notified my squadron that there was no reason to disqualify me from weapons handling duty. I went back to working patrol. I stuffed any emotions that surfaced and stopped trying to process how the incident was affecting me.

Like many of those who were involved in the incident, I was offered orders out of Fairchild and was told I could choose my next assignment. I delayed accepting the offer, as I didn't want to leave Spokane and the friends I had made. When strangers started recognizing me and referring to me as the guy who shot Mellberg, a fresh start at a new base began to sound like a good idea. I asked for an assignment to Australia, but there were no openings for a senior airman. At the suggestion of several people, I requested and received an assignment to Hawaii, where I would spend the next three years.

In January 1995, I checked in with the 15th Security Police Squadron at Hickam AFB, on the island of Oahu. My desire for anonymity was quashed when I was introduced to my new co-workers as "the guy from Fairchild that shot that dude."

I worked as a patrolman and lived in the cop dorm. When we got to-gether for a few beers, the shooting usually came up in the form of jokes like "Don't piss Brown off or he'll shoot you." I laughed it off, but wondered if I would ever be able to put the shooting behind me. I couldn't stop thinking about it: everything I saw, heard, and smelled triggered an unwelcome memory of the dead, the wounded, or the gunman. Along with the thoughts came an ever-present anxiety. I hoped the memories and anxiety would fade with time, but they only seemed to get worse. I couldn't sleep, and I became increasingly irritable and intolerant of others. My only escape came from seclusion and alcohol. I remained sober on the job. But off-duty, I holed up in my dorm room and only socialized if alcohol was involved.

Hickam was my second overseas tour, and although Hawaii had been a US state since 1959, it seemed like a foreign country to me. Unlike my tour on Crete, I was unable to embrace the culture or appreciate the beauty of the islands. The Hawaii I saw was no post card. I only saw the crowds, crime, drug addiction, poverty, and racism.

In an attempt to find happiness, I fulfilled a longtime dream and bought a 1997 Harley-Davidson Springer. Riding improved my mood temporarily, but before long I was frustrated by the fact that I was limited to riding in circles around the small island.

I did my best to hide my anxiety and irritability from my superiors and co-workers and was still confident and capable of performing as a patrolman. That confidence faded one night when I was at the main gate helping the gate guards process a drunk driver. It was a call that had become second nature to me, but as I demonstrated the field sobriety tests to the subject, my hands trembled and my voice quaked. It was as embarrassing as it was alarming.

I applied for and received a position as a security police criminal investigator, hoping that a break from the road would help me relax. I graduated Military Police Investigator (MPI) School at Fort McClellan, in Alabama, at the top of my class. At MPI School, we learned forensics, crime scene processing, and interview and interrogation techniques. I put those skills to good use at Hickam, where we worked cases involving drugs, theft, assault, forgery, and fraud. Identifying suspects and obtaining confessions was exciting work. We worked long hours, but it was rewarding—our investigations section maintained a 95 percent solve rate.

It had been nearly a year since the shooting but the passage of time had done little to lessen my symptoms. The anxiety, irritability and intrusive thoughts persisted. I was also depressed and withdrawn, spending much of my off-duty time alone in my room. I desperately searched the newly emerging Internet trying to find out what was wrong with me. I read about post-traumatic stress disorder (PTSD) for the first time.

I would later learn the condition known today as PTSD is not a new phenomenon. It is referenced in the writings of the ancient Greeks and is evident in the post-war traditions of Native Americans. It has been present in all of America's wars—known by different names. In the US Civil War, it was referred to as soldier's heart; in the First World War, it was shell shock; in the Second World War, it was called battle fatigue. Veterans of the Vietnam War were the first to be diagnosed with post-traumatic stress disorder. It is not limited to veterans. Although it is commonly associated with combat, it can result from experiencing any event that threatens death or serious bodily injury.

PTSD can change the way you view the world. Symptoms can include nightmares, flashbacks and intrusive thoughts or memories of the traumatic event. One factor of PTSD involves traumatic memories that are filed away in the subconscious. Everyone has conscious memories of minor traumas they have experienced. When you touch a hot stove or are bitten by a dog, your mind takes note and reminds you to be cautious around hot stoves and aggressive dogs. If the trauma is life threatening, even the smallest detail related to the event can be stored in your subconscious and create psychological distress without apparent cause. A normally innocuous sight, sound or smell, if associated with a trauma, can trigger the mind to enter survival mode and release stress hormones. Being in a crowd; hearing a balloon pop, a car backfire, or a baby cry; being in a hospital or smelling fresh cut grass on a summer day can trigger a fight or flight stress response. The increased level of stress hormones causes anxiety, irritability, insomnia, hypervigilance, exaggerated startle response and more.

On 2 May 1995, I self-referred for an appointment with Hickam's mental health clinic. According to my medical records, the appointment was to help address my "post-traumatic stress disorder-like symptoms." I was perplexed when the psychologist's first order was to have me complete psychometric tests, one of which consisted of more than 550 true or false questions such as:

"My soul sometimes leaves my body."

"Evil spirits possess me at times."

"When I am with people I am bothered by hearing very queer things."

"I see things or animals or people around me that others do not see."

Although I found the questions irrelevant and insulting, I completed the tests, believing it was the first step toward resolving my symptoms.

A week later when I met with the psychologist again, I realized I was wrong. After interpreting my test results she determined nothing was wrong with me. She noted in my medical records: "No indication of any significant mental/emotional problems or need for treatment. Patient appears to have adjusted well following involvement in line of duty event." I might have pursued counseling elsewhere but chose not to when I learned I had once again been relieved of duty for seeking mental health care. Per my request, the psychologist informed my squadron that there was "no indication of any reason to remove patient from sensitive duties." I went back to work. My ability to feel joy, empathy and gratefulness decreased and my anxiety and irritability continued to rise.

In addition to the intrusive thoughts, I often consciously thought about the shooting. I ran the scenario through my head trying to see if I could have stopped the gunman sooner. I was obsessed with finding out how long it took me to get to the scene.

I made several Freedom of Information Act requests to the Air Force for documents relating to the shooting. I received stacks of redacted reports and statements but was repeatedly denied a copy of the recorded telephone and radio traffic that would reveal my response time.

My assignment to Hickam ended in January 1998, and I received orders to Kirtland Air Force Base in Albuquerque, New Mexico, where I was assigned to the 377th Security Forces Squadron. For a short time, I worked as a patrolman until an investigator position opened up. The crime rate at Kirtland was similar to Hickam but we had fewer investigators to share the workload. The stack of case files that accumulated on my desk seemed to grow taller every time I took a phone call.

I jumped and cringed whenever the phone rang. If something didn't go as planned or work as I expected, I became furious. My antiquated computer and multi-line office phone were frequent targets of my rage. Oddly enough, throwing the computer keyboard across the room or banging the handset of the phone into the keypad didn't improve their performance. When I started losing my temper in the interview room, yelling at subjects when they lied to me, I knew I had reached a critical point. I holed up in my office, unplugged the phone, and quit working cases. I couldn't articulate what was wrong with me. I tried to explain it to my supervisor and co-workers by telling them, "My nerves are shot."

I had come to realize that the job I loved had become just another source of stress. It was apparent that I could either be a cop, or receive mental health counseling, but not both. So I accepted the fact that I would be relieved of duty and made an appointment with Kirtland's mental health services. I met with an Air Force psychologist who quickly recognized I was exhibiting symptoms of post-traumatic stress disorder. Over the next several months, he worked diligently yet unsuccessfully to mitigate my symptoms with psychotherapy and a series of various medications.

I had hoped to serve at least twenty years in the Air Force before I retired. But with no hope of regaining my mental well-being, I made the frightening and difficult decision to accept a medical separation in hopes of finding peace in the civilian world. After serving ten years, I left the Air Force with a diagnosis of chronic post-traumatic stress disorder.

I spent a week riding my Harley from New Mexico to Washington State. I traveled the older highways, meandering through beautiful country, stopping whenever I chose, sleeping on desolate rest-area picnic tables and in small-town motels. I ended up back in Spokane to visit Erik Turner, who had also recently separated from the Air Force. When I met Erik's niece, Rhonda, I decided to make Spokane my new home.

Rhonda and I eventually moved into a small house in a densely packed North Spokane neighborhood. With the exception of family gatherings, I didn't socialize, and even then I relied on alcohol to calm my anxious nerves. I avoided crowds and public places. When we did go out, I compulsively sat in the last row of movie theaters and kept my back to the wall in restaurants, always aware of exits and entrances. At home, I kept the doors locked, the window shades closed, and loaded guns at the ready. I traded in the Taurus for a variety of reliable handguns and never left the house unarmed.

Rhonda and I got married in 2002; a few months later, when I learned she was pregnant I bought a GunVault, a small quick-access handgun lockbox that I kept bedside. Our son was born in 2003, and our daughter followed three years later. When they were old enough to be curious about guns, I taught them the rules of safe and responsible firearm handling. Even so, if my firearms weren't on me, they were locked up.

I was a proud and attentive father, but I was still on edge. I slept about four hours a night, and the sleep I did get wasn't restful. I awoke at the slightest noise. I was easily startled, easily frustrated, and quick tempered. I frequently yelled and threw things. Although I was never physically abusive, my outbursts were frightening and concerning. I wasn't the father or the husband I wanted to be.

We soon discovered our next door neighbor was a user and dealer of crystal methamphetamine. My hyper alertness was easily justified: the dregs of society came and went from his house at all hours of the night. To little avail, I confronted the neighbor about his house being a constant source of fighting, barking dogs, and cars racing up and down the street. One day as I walked from my house to my truck parked on the street, a pit bull broke through the neighbor's gate and charged toward me aggressively. The snarling dog stopped short just as I turned and pointed a pistol at its head. The neighbor called the dog off and they both retreated into his home. Things seemed to quiet down afterward. I worked with a Spokane police officer and provided him with my notes of illicit activity and vehicle license plates. After they raided the house, it was sold to new owners and peace returned to the neighborhood.

I went through several jobs as an industrial laborer. The transition to the civilian workforce was difficult and I clashed with my co-workers and supervisors. I quit some jobs and was fired or laid off from others. Although I always seemed to find work, I worried about my ability to support my family in the long term. I missed law enforcement, but wasn't ready for the stress that came with the job. My wife was supportive and encouraged me to continue pursuing mental health care.

I grew increasingly negative and cynical, a mindset fed by television and radio newscasts reporting a constant stream of crime and tragedy. I listened to radio talk shows that preached doom, gloom, and a political us-versus-them mentality. I began to assume the worst of everyone I encountered, believing they were selfish, stupid or out to get me. When I saw an aggressive driver or was followed too closely in traffic, I quietly raged as if it were a personal affront. When I saw a bumper sticker espousing politics that were the opposite of my beliefs, I was filled with hateful disdain. I dwelled on the past and worried about the future, concerned only for the safety and survival of my family and myself. I paid little attention to the present moment and the positive things in my life. On the outside, I appeared normal. But if you looked closely, you might see my unconsciously clenched jaw and hands balled into fists or tremoring with the electric current of anxiety.

I continued mental health counseling with civilian therapists as well as the Spokane Veterans Affairs Medical Center. I attended PTSD group therapy and private counseling sessions. The talk therapy wasn't helping, and I stopped taking the various medications I was prescribed when the side effects became worse than the symptoms they were supposed to relieve. Nothing calmed my anxiety better than beer, except maybe whiskey. Like many people with PTSD, I wasn't a danger to myself or others, but I didn't like the person I had become. My reliance on alcohol and my growing negative outlook on life threatened to ruin my marriage. I continued looking for answers, hoping to hang onto the only positive thing I had in life, my family.

Some people said I should just get over it, but it wasn't as easy as flipping a switch. Over the years, I read countless books on trauma, PTSD and finding peace as I searched for the secret—the quick and easy cure. I would eventually discover my path to recovery from PTSD consisted of a series of deliberate steps.

In 2006 I found a job in a Border Patrol communications center, working the radio, monitoring alarms, and running record checks. I hadn't worked a law enforcement-related job in six years, and it felt good to assist the agents in the field.

We sold our house and bought a mobile home on a rural piece of property on the outskirts of Spokane. While we waited to take possession of our new home, my family and I stayed with my in-laws, who lived on a corner lot in a North Spokane neighborhood. I was moving some of our household goods into my father-in-law's shop when I noticed several sheriff's deputies slowly patrolling the area. As one of them rolled by, I asked who they were looking for. The deputy gave me the description of a young white male but didn't mention why they were searching for him.

I went back to my work, and about ten minutes later, a man matching the description emerged from behind the shop. The only way he could access that area was to have jumped a chain link fence in the back yard. He approached me asking for a ride, and I agreed without hesitation. I walked back toward the driveway, trying to draw him out to where he might be spotted by a passing deputy. He started to follow me, but his instincts told him to run. My instincts told me to give chase. I didn't know why the deputies were looking for him, I didn't know if he was armed, and I didn't know his intentions.

I pursued him, shouting, "Stop!" and "Get on the ground now!" He ran to the back yard. He could either jump the fence into the street or burst through the back door of the house where my wife, kids and mother-in-law were.

He was ignoring my commands until he glanced over his shoulder. When he saw the stainless steel revolver I had slipped from my pocket, he melted facedown into the grass. I continued shouting instructions, ordering him to cross his ankles and put his arms out to his sides. He complied, all the while telling me I was crazy and insisting all he wanted was a ride.

A deputy pulled up outside the fence. He emerged from his car, laughing at the sight of his prey laid out on the grass with a "civilian" holding him at gunpoint and Gunnar, my in-law's German wirehaired pointer, barking in his ear. I slowly pocketed my pistol and took a step backward, showing the deputy my empty hands. The subject got up and made a move toward the fence. I yelled for him to stay on the ground, but he refused and kept insisting I was crazy as he climbed over the fence and graciously entered into the deputy's custody.

Later, several deputies rallied outside the house, and took down my information. They let me know they were grateful for my assistance, especially the deputy who had been tracking the subject on foot for several miles. The man was a known felon who had fled after he was caught burglarizing a woman's home. I couldn't stop myself from giving chase. I also couldn't stop trembling from the rush of adrenaline I felt afterward. I looked forward to living in the country, where I hoped I wouldn't have to deal with the criminal element.

I was able to relax a little after moving to the country, and I occasionally slept better. I continued various forms of mental health treatment with little effect. I still relied on alcohol to calm my anxiety, and I still had a negative outlook. Or, as Rhonda would say, I was in my hole.

In 2008, after nearly fourteen years of Freedom of Information Act requests, denials, and appeals, I received a package in the mail containing the digital audio recordings of the law enforcement radio transmissions from the day of the incident. That night while Rhonda was at work, after I put the kids to bed, I stood in my living room and played the CD. The static hissed through the stereo speakers and was suddenly interrupted by the radio call, "Fairchild Police to all posts and patrols, we have an alarm at the ER." I noted the time and imagined myself responding three-tenths of a mile on a bicycle. I imagined my encounter with the gunman. My skin tightened and grew cold, and the hair on my arms and neck stiffened when my twenty-four-year-old voice interrupted my thoughts: "Fairchild-Six, shots fired I took him down he's down this is Police Six he's down!" I looked at the clock. From the time of the initial dispatch to my radio call, less than two minutes had passed. I realized that I couldn't have gotten to the hospital any faster. At that moment, I finally began to forgive myself.

I began talking publicly about the shooting and my experience with post-shooting trauma. I found talking to be therapeutic. I found the process of writing and repeatedly confronting the details of the incident greatly diminished their effect on me.

I removed as much negativity from my life as possible and took a break from the fear-generating news and mass media. I made a conscious effort to focus on the positive. After a while, I was able to see and appreciate the good things around me.

After reading about the usefulness of Buddhist practices in healing from trauma, I began to practice acceptance and mindfulness. I worked toward accepting where I was and what I had in life. I made an effort to experience the present moment, not dwelling on the past or worrying about the future. I endeavored to be more empathetic and forgiving of other people. When I came to realize that everyone is struggling with something, I became more forgiving toward myself and others.

I stopped self-medicating with alcohol and found I could control my anxiety with meditation and focusing on my breath. When I was overwhelmed with stress, my breathing was shallow and rapid. By slowing down and focusing on my respirations, I was able to clear my mind and calm my anxiety. (I later learned that this technique is also known as combat breathing.)

I had tried acupuncture, acupressure, herbal supplements and medication. Some of those things helped, but the effect was temporary, a Band-Aid on an untreated wound. I finally found relief through some relatively new programs at the Spokane Veterans Administration—prolonged exposure therapy and cognitive processing therapy. Instead of the usual talk therapy or masking symptoms with medication, these programs helped me process the shooting and uncover the root of my symptoms. I realized I had a lot of subconscious negative thoughts and those thoughts contributed to my negative feelings and symptoms. When I learned to recognize and challenge those thoughts I began to crawl out of the dark hole I had fallen into. The programs also helped further diminish the guilt I had been carrying around.

I am back to carrying a gun and a badge for the Department of Homeland Security. I am in a much better place and have a greater appreciation for life. I am grateful for my loving wife, my beautiful family, a roof over my head, and a job I enjoy.

One year after the twin tragedies, Fairchild created a memorial park and erected a large black concrete monument in the middle of a manicured lawn near walking trails and a playground. Two plaques on the monument list the names of the people killed at the hospital, and the four aviators who died aboard Czar 52. A larger plaque above the names holds a poem:

> Let peace be our companion on a walk beside the trees.
> Our spirits like our banner yet are lifted on the breeze
> So pause with us awhile and know that you are not alone.
> Our hearts will e'er be with you though immortalized in stone.

Ever since my return to Spokane, I have visited the memorial on the anniversary of the hospital tragedy. In 2014, I was asked to speak at a ceremony marking the twentieth anniversary. I didn't think it was my place to speak in memoriam of those killed. But when I learned they wanted the event to focus on the resiliency of the survivors, I agreed to speak. It took me fifteen years to find peace, but I am a survivor. On 20 June 2014, I stood at a lectern in Fairchild's Memorial Park and spoke to those in attendance:

> Twenty years ago today, a beautiful summer afternoon turned to tragedy. A man with a rifle moved through the hallways and parking lots of Fairchild's hospital leaving a trail of chaos and devastation in his path.

I spoke of the lives lost, those who were wounded and my response to the shooting. My speech continued:

> My actions have been called heroic, but there were many heroes among the patrons and staff at the hospital that day. If not for their actions, the bloodshed and loss of life would have been greater.

I described some of the selfless actions that occurred inside the hospital. I also spoke of the response to the B-52 crash four days later and the trauma experienced by those who were there. My speech continued:

I have been in contact with many of the people who were there that day—doctors, nurses, med techs, fire fighters, cops, and survivors. Few, if any, escaped without mental trauma; and in varying degrees they still struggle with it today. I won't speak for them, but I will tell you about my experience.

After summarizing my struggle with the effects of trauma and my eventual recovery, I ended the speech saying:

I may never be the person I was before the shooting, but in some ways I am stronger for it, and I have found peace. I haven't lost the habits I developed as a patrolman—I am still vigilant for evil and ready to stand in its way when it threatens innocents. There was a time when all I could see was darkness, but today I practice a balanced awareness; I see the beauty of the world while I am watching for danger. Today—I can once again appreciate the simple wonder of a cloudless summer day.

I will never forget the survivors and heroes of June 1994. And although I never met them, I will never forget Christin McCarron, Anita Lindner, Thomas Brigham, Alan London, and Taylor Sigman. Because I didn't know them I was hesitant to speak at this memorial ceremony. I was worried that I wouldn't pay them a fitting tribute. But whether you knew the fallen or not, we can all honor them today, with a greater appreciation of life.

Afterword

Mass public murder is not a new phenomenon and has likely been happening since the dawn of civilization. One of the earliest known accounts was observed in Malaysia in the year 1516, by Portuguese writer and world traveler Duarte Barbosa. It was again observed in Malaysia by British Explorer, Captain James Cook in 1770. Both Cook and Barbosa recorded instances of lone tribe members, armed with swords, indiscriminately attacking fellow villagers without apparent cause. The unprovoked attacks would continue until the intervention of other armed tribesmen. The Malay referred to the phenomenon as *mengamok*—to make a furious and desperate charge. Today the term is known simply as running amok. In a translated version of *The Book of Duarte Barbosa*, he wrote,

> They take a dagger in their hands and go out into the streets and kill as many persons as they meet, both men, women and children, in such wise that they are like mad dogs, killing until they are killed. These are called *amuco*. And as soon as they see them begin this work, they cry out saying *amuco, amuco*, in order that people may take care of themselves and they kill them with dagger and spear thrusts.

Running amok was at one time believed to be a cultural condition occurring only in primitive tribes. In 1849, amok was recognized as a psychiatric condition having two forms: *Beramok*, in which the perpetrator suffered from a depressive mood disorder and experienced a personal loss; and *amok*, in which the perpetrator suffered from a depressive, psychotic, or personality disorder and attacked out of revenge for a perceived insult or injustice. In 1994, Amok was listed in the fourth edition of the *Diagnostic and Statistical Manual of Mental Disorders* (DSM-IV). Regardless of its origin or definition, throughout history, brave men and women have been responding to the call of "*Amuco*".

After studying 160 active-shooter incidents, the FBI released a report in 2014 that showed the majority of the incidents lasted from two to five minutes and were over before police could intervene. Forty percent of the incidents were ended by either citizen intervention or the attacker committing suicide. The study identified twenty-one incidents where unarmed citizens successfully intervened, and seven incidents where armed citizens or off-duty law enforcement successfully ended the threat. The FBI concluded in their report, "Even when law enforcement was present or able to respond within minutes, civilians often had to make life and death decisions, and therefore, should be engaged in training and discussions on decisions they may face."

The current protocol taught by law enforcement agencies tells citizens they have the best chance of surviving an incident of mass public murder if they run, hide or fight.

> RUN: Whenever you are out in public, get into the habit of noting the location of escape paths and exits. At the first sign of trouble, leave the area and put as much distance as possible between you and the threat as quickly and safely as you can.

> HIDE: If the threat is imminent and you cannot escape, find a place to hide, preferably one that will protect you from gunfire. If you seek shelter in a room, lock the door and block it with furniture or other obstructions. Once you have hidden, look around your environment for items to use as improvised weapons and continue to look for an opportunity to escape.

> FIGHT: If you are appropriately armed or otherwise capable, bringing the fight to the attacker is the quickest way to end the threat and save lives. Additionally, if you are unable to escape and have hidden and the threat is approaching and imminent, bring the fight to the attacker. If you are not appropriately armed, use improvised weapons and commit to the attack with sudden and violent aggression until the threat is neutralized.

Even if you are properly armed and present during the onset of a mass public murder, you may not be in a position to effectively employ your defensive weapon without exposing yourself or your loved ones to danger. You may need to close the distance to engage the attacker or you may decide that your best option is to retreat to safety. In any case, be aware that the police, and possibly other armed citizens, will be responding to the scene. Do everything you can to avoid looking like the perpetrator. Make sure your weapon is not visible when police arrive and immediately obey their commands.

A 2013 survey conducted by PoliceOne.com showed that nearly ninety percent of law enforcement officers believe that casualties would be decreased if armed citizens were present at the onset of an active-shooter incident. Ninety-one percent of police officers surveyed support citizens lawfully carrying concealed firearms.

Whether an incident of mass public murder is an act of terror or the result of mental illness, the killing will continue until the perpetrator chooses to stop or until they are stopped by first responders. Police officers acknowledge they are statistically unlikely to arrive in time and they understand that like the Malaysian villagers in the sixteenth century, citizens who find themselves at the scene of twenty-first century violence will be the first responders. The vast majority of law enforcement officers support the citizens' right to defend themselves and others with the modern day equivalent of the dagger and spear.

If you are one of the millions of citizens who has made the commitment to bear arms in defense of self and loved ones, I applaud you. I also implore you to seek professional training. Your training should be ongoing and consist of more than basic marksmanship. Learn how to safely handle and efficiently deploy your defensive weapon in a variety of situations and practice until it becomes instinctive. Become knowledgeable in the judicious use of deadly force and what actions to take after the threat has ended. Massad Ayoob, a police officer, defensive firearm instructor, and use of force expert, has written several books that will help guide you in that effort. A good one to begin with is *Deadly Force: Understanding Your Right to Self Defense*. Reading a book is not a substitute for hands-on training. To truly learn firearm skills, I recommend Mr. Ayoob's firearm training classes, classes offered by the Firearms Academy of Seattle or a similar professional level of training. I also recommend that people seek training in the treatment of traumatic injury and bleeding control and that they carry a first-aid trauma kit.

Incidents of mass public murder do not occur frequently enough to warrant fear. But criminal violence does happen often enough that you should consider how you would respond. If you are trained in the use of firearms, carry them whenever and wherever possible. Even if you choose not to carry a defensive weapon, you should have a plan in place should you ever find yourself threatened by violence.

The best way to protect yourself from becoming a victim of any crime is to avoid looking like an easy target. Criminals prefer victims who appear unaware. Whenever you are out in public take a break from your mobile media device, keep your head up and be aware of your surroundings. Being vigilant is not necessarily a byproduct of paranoia. When you are watchful, you are more likely to realize when you are in danger, but you also afford yourself the opportunity to see the beauty of the world around you that would otherwise go unnoticed.

Being watchful has the added benefit of providing your mind with the subtle clues it needs to fuel your intuition. You may not consciously interpret the signs of danger but your subconscious mind will intuitively warn you. Your intuition can manifest as a gut feeling, fear or humor. On 20 June 1994, numerous people inexplicably canceled their medical appointments prior to the shooting at Fairchild's hospital. Countless people who interacted with Dean Mellberg expressed a genuine fear of him. Several of Mellberg's co-workers joked that he would kill them. Several hospital staff members joked that the noises they heard on the afternoon of 20 June 1994, were gunshots. In his book, *The Gift of Fear*, Gavin de Becker reveals how you can tap into your intuition and learn to trust it to keep you safe. Mr. de Becker rejects the myth that violent acts are unpredictable and uses real life examples in his book to reveal the sometimes subtle precursors of violent crime.

Another book that may help you identify the warning signs that someone has the potential for violence or homicidal behavior was written by Dr. Gregory K. Moffatt. Dr. Moffatt is a clinician who specializes in the prevention of homicidal and violent behavior. In his book, *Blind-Sided: Homicide Where It Is Least Expected*, Dr. Moffatt attempts to debunk the myth that mass public murder happens without warning. He cites case studies of homicides at schools and workplaces and lists twenty-two hierarchical traits that can be used to assess a person's propensity for violence. Dr. Moffatt's list of traits is included in the Reference Material section of this book.

Lt Dan Marcou, a thirty-three-year police veteran and trainer, has been working to educate the public on how to identify potential perpetrators of mass public murder before they act. Lieutenant Marcou developed a list of five phases that most mass public murderers go through as they progress toward their crime. Marcou says if a citizen recognizes the signs that someone is in any of the first four phases and notifies law enforcement, they may prevent a tragedy. Morcou's five phases are also listed in the Reference Material section of this book.

What more could have been done to prevent the mass murder at Fairchild AFB and many of the similar incidents that have occurred since then? Fixing America's failing mental health care system would be a good place to start.

American mental health care began a steady decline beginning in the mid-1950's with a movement known as deinstitutionalization. Over a span of several decades, the majority of America's state psychiatric hospitals were systematically emptied and closed. The number of inpatient beds and psychiatric services available to the mentally ill has been decreasing ever since, but the need for those services has remained unchanged. The community mental health centers, which promised to fill the void left by deinstitutionalization, were underfunded and unable to meet the demand for mental health care.

America's mental health crisis was compounded by the civil rights movement of the 1960s and 70s. Lawyers, with no experience in mental health, filed class-action lawsuits that led to changes in the laws regarding the treatment of the mentally ill. The new laws prevent the involuntary treatment of even the severely mentally ill unless they meet a narrow set of criteria defining dangerousness. Unless a petitioner can prove a person is an imminent threat to themselves or others, they cannot be mandated to receive treatment. Research has shown that half of all individuals with severe psychiatric disorders are not competent to assess their own need for treatment—they are too sick to care for themselves and too sick to realize they need help. Consequently, many people with severe mental illness end up homeless, incarcerated or victimized.

According to Psychiatrist E. Fuller Torrey, founder of the Treatment Advocacy Center, people with untreated severe psychiatric illness make up one third of America's homeless population and approximately sixteen percent of the jail and prison inmate population. Additionally, approximately thirteen thousand people with severe mental illness commit suicide each year.

Individuals with severe psychiatric illness also commit at least half of the mass public murders in America. It is important to note that not everyone with mental illness will become violent and not all mass public murderers are mentally ill. However, *The New York Times* conducted a study of "rampage homicides" that occurred between 1949 and 1999 and published an article on 9 April 2000, where *The Times* concluded, of the 100 incidents studied, "At least half of the killers showed signs of serious mental health problems" and "48 killers had some kind of formal diagnosis, often schizophrenia." Similar studies have reached the same conclusion.

Removing the obstacles that prevent treatment would not only protect the mentally ill from becoming victims of their illness, it would also prevent certain incidents of violence, including mass public murder. One possible solution would be the implementation of Assisted Outpatient Treatment. More information as well as other possible solutions to America's mental health crisis can be found in Dr. Torrey's book: *The Insanity Offense: How America's Failure to Treat the Seriously Mentally Ill Endangers Its Citizens.*

I was reluctant to publish a book about the Fairchild shooting, out of concern that others would be inspired to emulate the killer. If after reading this book you find the killer worthy of emulation, I urge you to reconsider. Even if the media publicizes your name and photograph, your notoriety will be short-lived. Someone will likely write a book revealing your true nature and your intimate secrets that didn't make headlines. They will know that you didn't have the courage to persevere in a sometimes difficult world. They will know how you took your frustration out on innocent men, women, and children. If you want to demonstrate true courage, reach out for help and accept the counsel of a mental health professional. Persevere until you find a noble purpose and the strength to make a peaceful and positive impact on your community.

I have no animosity toward the Air Force and cherish the time I spent in the service. I did not write this book out of malice. I did it in an effort to improve the system and prevent future tragedies. I also hope my story will help remove the stigma associated with PTSD and other mental illness and encourage others to seek help. Ultimately, this story needed to be told. The men and women at Fairchild are inspirational. Their story is proof that behind the scenes of every tragedy, is a story of humanity, bravery and compassion. Their story is evidence of something we all need reminding of now and then. The number of good people in this world will always outnumber the bad.

Reference Material

Lieutenant Marcou's five phases of a mass public murderer

1. Fantasy Phase: During this phase, the would-be perpetrator fantasizes about the news coverage he'll receive. He pictures breaking the body count record of previous active killers, and going out in a blaze of glory. He may draw pictures of the event, make Web postings and discuss these desires with friends and foes alike.

2. Planning Phase: During the planning phase, the potential killer lays out the who, what, when, where and how of the crime. He may put plans in writing and will often discuss these plans with others. The potential killer will determine the weapons needed and how they will be obtained. He will decide how to travel to the target location and how to dress to conceal his weapons without arousing suspicion.

3. Preparation Phase: After forming the plan, the subject may obtain weapons, ammunition and/or explosives. He may conduct a practice run or walkthrough of the operation, preparing himself for the assault. Potential killers have been known to call friends and tell them not to go to school or work on a certain day, in order to keep them out of danger.

4. Approach Phase: By the approach stage, the suspect has made his plans and has committed himself to carry out the act. At this point, he is moving toward the intended target and will most likely be carrying the tools that he will use to commit the crime.

5. Implementation Phase: Once the attack begins the perpetrator will continue killing until he decides to stop or is stopped by force. The sooner someone—anyone—effectively intervenes through an act of courage, the fewer casualties will result.

From Dr. Gregory K. Moffatt's book: *Blind-Sided: Homicide Where It Is Least Expected*

Traits of a Potentially Violent Person

- History of aggressive behavior
- Subjective fear of person by others
- Threatening behaviors/statements of intent to do harm
- Specific victim
- Social isolation
- Antisocial behavior
- Absence of support system
- Lack of or weak social skills
- Clear feeling of being wronged by target
- Severe situational stress
- Job instability
- Substance abuse
- Poor self-image
- Suicide attempts/ideation
- Fantasies of violence
- Presence of aggressive models
- Divorce/marital instability
- Loss of job
- Poverty
- Available weapon
- Male gender
- Age 23–45

FROM: 92 MEDGP/SGHA (247-2731)   Date: 14 June 1993

SUBJ: Mental Health Evaluation on Amn Dean A. Mellberg.
      SSN: 369-72-5062

TO: 92 MS/CC

1. This medical statement concerns the above-named individual, who was
evaluated at the Mental Health Clinic, Fairchild AFB, WA, on 3, 4, and 7 June
1993. He completed psychological testing in conjunction with this evaluation
on 7 June 1993. This evaluation contains sensitive medical information, and
needs to be treated with customary confidentiality. Release it only to those
with an official need to know. He was evaluated at your request due to his
demonstrating aggressive and destructive attitudes towards himself and others.

2. My diagnosis, in DSM-IIIR terms, following evaluation is:

     Axis I (Clinical Syndromes): 300.02 Generalized anxiety disorder

     Axis II (personality disorder or significant features): V71.09, No Diagnosis, Strong
          Obsessive—Compulsive features

     Axis III: (physical disorders): None Affecting

     Axis IV: (psychosocial stressors): 1, None

     Axis V: (global assessment of functioning) Current GAF: 55, Moderate Symptoms
          GAF Past Year: 55, Moderate Symptoms

3. Airman Mellberg, both upon initial presentation and later during
psychometric testing demonstrated a significant level of anxiety. He appeared
tense, and addressed both officer and enlisted personnel as "Sir" innumerable
times, and was even observed saluting officers who passed by on the opposite
side of the street when he was taking breaks from his testing. Further, he
took well over 12 hours to complete a test battery that typically takes about
three hours to complete, and the data provided from that testing proven to be
invalid, primarily because of his efforts to skew testing in a favorable
direction. He adamantly denies any expression of any destructive thoughts or
conflicts with his peers, but when pressed will admit to a minimal amount of
the behaviors which brought him to the attention of his commander and this
clinic.

Dr. London's memo to maintenance squadron commander, page 1

4. COMMENTS AND RECOMMENDATIONS:
    a. There is no evidence of mental defect, emotional illness, or psychiatric disorder of such nature as to warrant disposition through military medical channels under the provisions of AFR 35-4.
    b. This individual is mentally responsible for his behavior and possesses sufficient mental capacity to understand and cooperate intelligently as a respondent in any administrative proceeding which might involve him, if necessary.
    c. At the present time there is evidence of a definite mental health abnormality and/or personal history of mental disease or emotional illness of sufficient severity to permanently disqualify him her from the Sensitive Duties Program (SDP) as described in AFR 35-99/35-36.
    d. This individual was previously evaluated on 24 July 1992 at the Behavioral Analysis Service, Lackland AFB, during Basic Military Training. At that time, it was strongly recommended that AB Mellberg be administratively separated. The issues and behaviors that created problems for him then have not subsided, and are likely to continue to create friction between him and the military environment. This individual is clearly unsuited to further military service due to the behavior he has demonstrated which is compatible with the diagnoses given above. Prompt administrative separation from the U.S. Air Force is strongly recommended under the provisions of AFR 39-10, Paragraph 5-11(i).
    e. While not currently suicidal or out of touch with reality, there is a potential that he could rapidly decompensate under the stresses of facing an administrative separation. While hospitalization is not warranted at this time, I recommend that he be monitored closely until a decision has been made and that decision has been fully implemented.

4. If you have any further questions, please contact me at the Mental Health Clinic (2731).

Alan W London

Alan W London, Capt, USAF, BSC
Chief, Psychology Services

Dr. London's memo to maintenance squadron commander, page 2

FROM: Mental Health Center   8 Sep 93
       92 Medical Group/SGHA
       713 Hospital Loop, Suite #127
       Fairchild AFB, WA 99011-8701

SUBJ: Mental Health Evaluation on Amn Dean A. Mellberg
       SSN: 369-72-5062

  TO: 92 MS/CC

1. This medical statement concerns Amn Mellberg, who was reevaluated on 12 Aug. 93 and 1 Sep. 93. This evaluation contains sensitive medical information, and needs to be treated with customary confidentiality. Release it only to those with an official necessity to know. Amn Mellberg was evaluated at your request today in response to his somewhat frantic efforts to file a legal charge against his former roommate at Fairchild AFB.

2. Our diagnosis, in DSM-III-R terms, following reevaluation is:

    Axis I (Clinical Syndrome); Rule out Brief Reactive Psychosis
                                 History of generalized anxiety disorder,
                                 300.02

    Axis II (Personality Disorder or significant features); V71.09,
                                 Probable Paranoid Personality Disorder

    Axis III (Physical Disorders); None affecting

    Axis IV (Psychosocial Stressors); 3, Moderate

    Axis V (Global assessment of functioning); Current GAF; 50, Moderate
                                 Symptoms GAF Past Year; 60,
                                 Moderate Symptoms

3. Airman Mellberg has been extremely guarded with the information he has provided us throughout his visits at the Fairchild AFB Mental Health Clinic. This has been exemplified not only with his testing which was completely invalid due to his extreme guardedness, but also with his interviewing responses. On 12 Aug. 93, he denied any of the specific symptoms of generalized anxiety that were enumerated for him although he appeared to demonstrate some of them during the interview. Instead of answering many of the question appropriately, he frequently answered them with questions to the interviewer. He uttered many platitudes such as "There are no problems, just challenges." He adamantly denied any intention of harming either himself or other persons, even when careful probing was performed. He also denied any psychotic symptoms such as hallucinations or delusions. He returned to the

TB

Dr. Brigham's memo to maintenance squadron commander, page 1

Mental Health Clinic on 1 Sep. 93 by command. During this interview he was slightly less guarded and more open, his affect was less intense. He acted surprised to hear that his former roommate had accused him of implying threats to harm him. This was the only subject that caused Amn Mellberg to raise his voice. Careful probing was again performed to elicit a possibility of suicidal or homicidal thoughts, but Amn Mellberg refused to endorse such ideas. Amn Mellberg was called to the Mental Health Clinic on 3 September 1993 to participate in a conflict resolution session with A1C Rayner, First Sergeant Jones, Dr. London and myself. Despite A1C Rayner's apparent true expression of regret for the discomfort he had caused Amn Mellberg with his allegation, Amn Mellberg was unfazed. He called the allegation against him a "crime against humanity." He felt just compensation for it would be 1 million dollars, because he believed his life was ruined as a result of it. At one point in the interview he appeared as if he would attack A1C Rayner as he rose out of his chair yelling loudly and moving toward A1C Rayner. Several times in the interview Amn Mellberg's thought processing was noted to be rather loose. At other times he spoke as if he were quoting the King James version of the Bible in a rather inappropriate context.

4. Amn Mellberg was called to the Mental Health Clinic once again on 7 September 1993 to determine whether the conflict resolution session had any impact upon him over the long weekend. He indicated that he still felt that the allegation against him was a "crime against humanity" and that he would pursue every legal option possible to make A1C Rayner pay for this deed. He did not imply that he would physically harm A1C Rayner. He would not admit to any special powers or abilities. Amn Mellberg was assessed at this interview by a county mental health professional for detainability. He was judged not detainable, but was very much encouraged to be voluntarily admitted to the hospital. He agreed to do this; however, upon settling in to the Main West Psychiatric Unit at Sacred Heart Medical Center, he expressed his strong desire to leave the hospital. Considerable efforts were then made by another county mental health professional to convince him to remain at the hospital. When he was picked up by the ambulance from Fairchild AFB to be taken to the AEROVAC plane, he delayed the ambulance party considerably while he attempted to call every resource available that he thought might prevent his being hospitalized. These resources included various types of attorneys, various commanders at Fairchild AFB, and reportedly even his congressman.

5. As can be seen from the above history, Amn Mellberg is clearly unsuited for duty in the United States Air Force. If he is thought to have a Brief Reactive Psychosis at Willford Hall Psychiatric Unit, he will probably be set up for a medical evaluation board. If he is not thought to have an Axis I disorder other than Generalized Anxiety, he may be returned to his duty section at Fairchild AFB for administrative separation. This would presumably be done on the basis of his probable Paranoid Personality Disorder.

6. We will attempt to keep you abreast of the developments regarding Amn Mellberg. Please do not hesitate to call (247-2731) if you have any questions.

THOMAS E. BRIGHAM, Maj, USAF, MC
Chief, Mental Health Services

Dr. Brigham's memo to maintenance squadron commander, page 2

EXCEPTION TO SF 502
APPROVED BY NARS 7/76

MEDICAL RECORD	NARRATIVE SUMMARY (CLINICAL RESUME)	
DATE OF ADMISSION 3 Sep 93	DATE OF DISCHARGE	NUMBER OF DAYS HOSPITALIZED

(Sign and date at end of narrative)

PATIENT'S IDENTIFICATION DATA AND REASON FOR EVALUATION: 19 year old male, ADAF, E-2 referred for Commander Directed Evaluation on 3 June 93 following a vague threat to harm his roommate.

HISTORY OF PRESENT ILLNESS: Airman Mellberg has been extremely guarded with the information he has provided us throughout his visits at the Fairchild AFB Mental Health Clinic. This has been exemplified not only with his testing which was completely invalid due to his extreme guardedness, but also with his interviewing responses. On 12 Aug 93, he denied any of the specific symptoms of generalized anxiety that were enumerated for him although he appeared to demonstrate some of them during the interview. Instead of answering many of the questions appropriately, he frequently answered them with questions to the interviewer. He uttered many platitudes such as "There are no problems, just challenges." He adamantly denied any intention of harming either himself or other persons, even when careful probing was performed. He also denied any psychotic symptoms such as hallucinations or delusions. He returned to the Mental Health Clinic on 1 Sep 93 by command. During this interview he was slightly less guarded and more open, his affect was less intense. He acted surprised and angry to hear that his former roommate had accused him of implying threats to harm him. This was the only subject that caused Amn Mellberg to raise his voice. Careful probing was again performed to illicit a possibility of suicidal or homicidal thoughts, but Amn Mellberg refused to endorse such ideas. He made no aggressive moves towards to the interviewer.

Amn Mellberg was seen again on 3 Sep 93 in conjunction with Amn Rayner, the individual who had made the allegation against him. In addition, Dr London, Amn Cook (the Mental Health technician), and SMSgt Jones (the first sergeant of both Amn Rayner and Mellberg) were present for a conflict resolution appointment. During this appointment both Amn Rayner and Amn Mellberg were given the opportunity to express their thoughts and feelings about the situation. Amn Rayner was able to apologize for the hurt feelings that he had produced in Amn Mellberg. Amn Mellberg was not able to express any concern for the fear that he had caused in Amn Rayner. Amn Mellberg indicated that he believed that a "crime against humanity" had been performed when Amn Rayner made the allegation. He believed that just compensation for this crime would be approximately 1 million dollars, since he believed that his career had been ruined by this allegation. He absolutely refused to accept the notion that his career had been ruined by his <u>response</u> to the allegation rather than the allegation itself (despite the repeated reassurances of SMSgt Jones).

(Use additional sheets of this form (Standard Form 502) if more space is required)

SIGNATURE OF PHYSICIAN	DATE	IDENTIFICATION NO.	ORGANIZATION

PATIENT'S IDENTIFICATION (For typed or written entries give: Name · last, first, middle; rank; grade; hospital or medical facility)	REGISTER NO	WARD NO

MELLBERG, DEAN
369-72-5062   Page 1 of 3
FAIRCHILD AFB, WA 99011-8701
DATE DICTATED: 7 SEP 93   DATE TYPED: 7 SEP 93

NARRATIVE SUMMARY (CLINICAL RESUME)
Standard Form 502
General Services Administration and
Interagency Committee on Medical Records
TYPIST'S INT: CAS
MARCH 1979 502-115-01

Narrative Summary regarding Mellberg prepared by Dr. Brigham and sent to Wilford Hall Medical Center, page 1

MEDICAL RECORD	NARRATIVE SUMMARY (CLINICAL RESUME)	
DATE OF ADMISSION 3 Sep 93	DATE OF DISCHARGE	NUMBER OF DAYS HOSPITALIZED

(Sign and date at end of narrative)

At one point in the interview Amn Mellberg became quite loose in his thought processing. Many times he assumed the affect and speech of an Elizabethan pastor pronouncing statements from the King James Bible. Amn Mellberg's total focus upon this allegation and his belief that it had ruined his life was extremely concerning to the clinicians present. At one point, Amn Mellberg yelled in a very low voice at Amn Rayner and moved forward in his chair as if to attack Amn Rayner. He did not, however, attack him.

In light of this evaluation, Dr Mitchell, the staff psychologist at the Survival School as well as Dr Raisini, the Chief of psychiatric services at Wilford Hall were contacted regarding this case. They both thought it would be appropriate to air-evacuate Amn Mellberg to an Air Force psychiatric inpatient unit where he could be evaluated more thoroughly and safely.

PAST PSYCHIATRIC HISTORY: Given generalized anxiety disorder diagnosis during bootcamp at Lackland. Suggestion made to separate him at that time. No counseling or medications.

SOCIAL HISTORY: No friends. Highschool quite "sad". No substance or alcohol abuse. No tobacco. Says he gets along well with parents and older brother, but no phone number could be discovered for the parents.

FAMILY HISTORY: No psychiatric illness known.

HOSPITAL COURSE: After approximately one hour at the civilian hospital, the patient decided he wanted to leave (despite having been ordered to remain there by this physician). He was convinced to remain by the county Mental Health Professional after extensive consultation with Drs London and Brigham. While at the hospital, overnight, he attempted to call the base commander and his congressman, as well as chaplains and attorneys at JAG.

LABS: None

MENTAL STATUS EXAMINATION: The patient is alert and fully orientated. Affect is flat with the exception of occasional angry grimaces. Mood is angry to anxious. Thought processing is circumstantial at times, tangential at others and frankly loose at certain points in the conversation. Thought content includes the overvalued idea (if not delusion) that Amn Rayner intended to cause the patient irreparable harm by making the allegation to his sergeants several months ago.

(Use additional sheets of this form (Standard Form 502) if more space is required)

SIGNATURE OF PHYSICIAN	DATE	IDENTIFICATION NO.	ORGANIZATION

PATIENT'S IDENTIFICATION (For typed or written entries give: Name - last, first, middle; rank; grade; hospital or medical facility)	REGISTER NO	WARD NO

MELLBERG, DEAN A.
369-72-5062   Page 2 of 3
FAIRCHILD AFB, WA 99011-8701
DATE DICTATED: 7 SEP 93   DATE TYPED 7 SEP 93   TYPIST'S INIT CAS

NARRATIVE SUMMARY (CLINICAL RESUME)
Standard Form 502
General Services Administration and
Interagency Committee on Medical Records
MARCH 1979 502-115-01

Narrative Summary regarding Mellberg prepared by Dr. Brigham and sent to
Wilford Hall Medical Center, page 2

EXCEPTION TO SF 502
APPROVED BY NARS 7/76

MEDICAL RECORD	NARRATIVE SUMMARY (CLINICAL RESUME)	
DATE OF ADMISSION 3 Sep 93	DATE OF DISCHARGE	NUMBER OF DAYS HOSPITALIZED

(Sign and date at end of narrative)

The patient also appears to be grandiose although he will not admit to any special associations with the supernatural world. The patient has made vague threats to harm others, but will not admit to actual plans to harm others when confronted. He had expressed no thoughts of harming himself in the course of his treatment. Appearance; clean, pressed BDU's, extremely short cropped hair, extremely rigid stature. Psychomotor activity is mildly retarded. The patient moves in a somewhat automoton-type fashion. Speech, as noted before, varies from extremely soft to yelling and at times assumes the role of a preacher.

PHYSICAL EXAM: Pertinent for severe acne, otherwise normal.

DIAGNOSIS: IAW DSM III-R:

Axis I (Clinical Syndrome); Rule out Brief Reactive Psychosis 298.80
        History of generalized anxiety disorder, 300.02.

Axis II (Personality Disorder or significant features); V71.09,
        Probable Paranoid P.D.

Axis III (Physical Disorders); None affecting

Axis IV (Psychosocial Stressors); 3, Moderate

Axis V (Global assessment of functioning) Current GAF; 50, Moderate
        Symptoms GAF Past Year; 60, Moderate Symptoms

RECOMMENDATION: We are referring Amn Mellberg for an extensive psychiatric evaluation to rule out brief reactive psychosis and treat it as well as possible if it exists. We consider this patient dangerous. Amn Rayner is aware of the risk posed to him by Amn Mellberg. Amn Mellberg will be air-evacuated with the attendance of a mental health technician. He may be administered 100mg IM Thorazine q6 hours prn severe agitation. He will be maintained in soft restraints or leathers if necessary. These precautions are necessary because he is totally involuntary - he has no insight into his problem.

THOMAS E. BRIGHAM, Maj, USAF, MC
Chief, Mental Health Services

(Use additional sheets of this form (Standard Form 502) if more space is required)

SIGNATURE OF PHYSICIAN	DATE	IDENTIFICATION NO.	ORGANIZATION	
PATIENT'S IDENTIFICATION (For typed or written entries give: Name - last, first, middle, rank; grade; hospital or medical facility)			REGISTER NO	WARD NO

MELLBERG, DEAN A.
369-72-5062   Page 3 of 3
FAIRCHILD AFB, WA 99011-8701
DATE DICTATED: 3 SEP 93   DATE TYPED 3 SEP 93

NARRATIVE SUMMARY (CLINICAL RESUME)
Standard Form 502
General Services Administration and
Interagency Committee on Medical Records
TYPIST'S INT: CAS
MARCH 1979 502-115-01

Narrative Summary regarding Mellberg prepared by Dr. Brigham and sent to
Wilford Hall Medical Center, page 3

DEPARTMENT OF THE AIR FORCE
WASHINGTON DC 20330-1000

OFFICE OF THE SECRETARY

The Honorable Dave Camp
United States Representative   FEB 1 4 1994
135 Ashman
Midland, Michigan 48640

Dear Mr. Camp:

This is in reply to your inquiry in behalf of Airman First
Class Dean A. Mellberg regarding his current situation.

Airman Mellberg's commander verified that he was accused by
his roommate of indecent acts and behavior. The commander also
confirmed that no disciplinary action was taken against Airman
Mellberg because the accusations could not be substantiated. As a
result of interviews with several different doctors, Airman
Mellberg was air evacuated to the Psychiatric Inpatient Unit at
Wilford Hall Medical Center where he is currently undergoing treatment. On November 1, 1993, a physical evaluation board considered
Airman Mellberg's case in an informal hearing and recommended that
he be found physically unfit for further military service and discharged, with entitlement to disability severance pay and a 20
percent disability rating. He did not concur with the recommended
findings and requested a formal hearing of his case. The formal
physical evaluation board was scheduled for December 8, 1993, but
never convened. The case was recalled by Wilford Hall Medical
Center on December 27, 1993.

On January 4, 1994, Airman Mellberg's records met another
medical board which recommended he be returned to duty for
appropriate administrative disposition. Airman Mellberg was
briefed on January 5, 1994, and concurred with the recommended
findings. He will be returned to duty upon his release from
Wilford Hall Medical Center.

We appreciate your interest in Airman Mellberg and trust this
information is helpful.

Sincerely,

THOMAS W. SHUBERT, Lt Col, USAF
Congressional Inquiry Division
Office of Legislative Liaison

Air Force memo responding to Congressman Camp's inquiry

_DAVE CAMP
4TH DISTRICT, MICHIGAN

MEMBER:
COMMITTEE ON
WAYS AND MEANS

SUBCOMMITTEE ON
SELECT REVENUE MEASURES

SUBCOMMITTEE ON
HUMAN RESOURCES

Congress of the United States
House of Representatives
Washington, DC 20515-2204

137 CANNON BUILDING
WASHINGTON, D.C. 20515-2204
(202) 225-3561
FAX (202) 225-9679

DISTRICT OFFICES:

135 ASHMAN
MIDLAND, MI 48640
(517) 631-2562
FAX (517) 631-6271

3508 WEST HOUGHTON LAKE DRIVE
SUITE 1
HOUGHTON LAKE, MI 48629
(517) 366-4922

308 WEST MAIN ST.
OWOSSO, MI 48867
(517) 723-6759
TOLL FREE 1-800-342-2455

February 22, 1994

Mrs. Lois Mellberg

Dear Lois:

Thank you for contacting me requesting assistance from the United
States Air Force (USAF). I appreciate hearing from you.
Enclosed is correspondence received from the USAF on February 21,
1994, in response to the Congressional inquiry placed on your
son, Dean's behalf.

As I am sure you are aware, the USAF states Dean will be returned
to duty in the very near future. I am sure this was good news
for both you and Dean, and I am pleased to have been of
assistance. If Dean encounters any further difficulty at his new
duty station, please contact me and I will inquire further with
the USAF.

Once again, thank you for informing me of your concerns. If I
can offer additional assistance, please do not hesitate to call.

Sincerely,

DAVE CAMP
Member of Congress

DLC/tmg
enclosure

Congressman Camp letter to Lois Mellberg

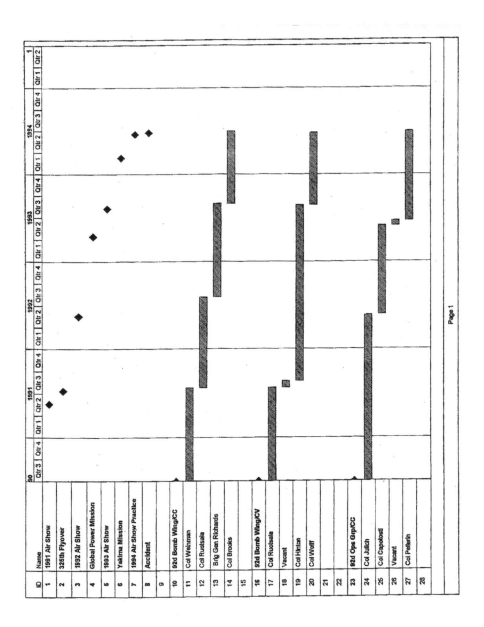

92 Bomb Wing Leadership Continuity, page 1.
Aircraft Accident Investigation Report

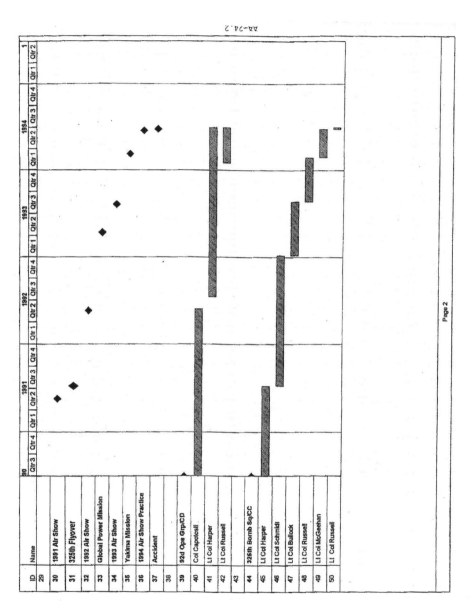

92 Bomb Wing Leadership Continuity, page 2.
Aircraft Accident Investigation Report

Bibliography

Shooting

Bonnie Harris, and Jess Walter, "Ousted Airman Killed His Psychologist First." *The Spokesman-Review* [Spokane] 21 June 1994: A1+. Print

Lynch, Jim, and Bill Morlin. "They Knew It Was Real When Gunman Was Shot." *The Spokesman-Review* [Spokane] 21 June 1994: A7. Print.

Harris, Bonnie. "'Hell of a Shot' Downed Gunman." *The Spokesman-Review* [Spokane] 23 June 1994: A10. Print.

Hansen, Dan. "Computer Glitch May Have Saved His Life." *The Spokesman-Review* [Spokane] 23 June 1994: A10. Print.

Olivera, D. F. "Mellberg Teaches Lessons to Military." *The Spokesman-Review* [Spokane] 29 June 1994: B8. Print.

Foster, J. Todd. "Airman Gets Top Honor for Stopping Gunman." *The Spokesman-Review* [Spokane] 1 July 1994: A1+. Print

Boggs, Alison. "Convicted Felon Arrested at Home Filled With Guns." *The Spokesman-Review* [Spokane] 01 July 1994: B3. Print.

White, Jeanette. "Alton Spencer Doing Just Fine after *Not* Being Shot." *The Spokesman-Review* [Spokane] 20 Aug. 1994: A1. Print.

Jeanette, White. "Pitching In When the Calls Came, Spokane's Hospitals Were Ready for the Disaster." *The Spokesman-Review* [Spokane] 28 Aug. 1994: F6. Print.

Walter, Jess. "Airman Never Fit in to the Military." *The Spokesman-Review* [Spokane] 02 Oct. 1994: A1+. Print.

Mortenson, Erik. "Learning to Live Again." *Eugene Register* 6 Nov. 1994: A1+. Print.

Sitaramiah, Gita. "Acts Of Heroism Honored Lifesaver Awards From The Local Red Cross Chapter Were Given To 32 People Who Rushed To The Aid Of Others." n.d.: n. pag. *The Spokesman-Review*. 02 Mar. 1995. Web.

Sitaramiah, Gita. "Fast-talking Hero." *The Spokesman-Review* [Spokane] 18 Apr. 1995: B3. Print.

Camden, Jim. "Lawmakers Seek Mellberg Investigation." *The Spokesman-Review* [Spokane] 18 May 1995: A1+. Print.

Camden, Jim. "Fighting Anger, Seeking Answers." *The Spokesman-Review* [Spokane] 21 May 1995: A1+. Print.

Camden, Jim. "Bipartisan Group Seeks Probe." *The Spokesman-Review* [Spokane] 21 May 1995: A10. Print.

Camden, Jim, and Jeanette White. "Fairchild: One Year Later, The Pain Persists." *The Spokesman-Review* [Spokane] 18 June 1995: n. pag. Web.

Camden, Jim. "Fairchild: One Year Later Air Force 'Didn't Learn A Thing,' Widow Says." *The Spokesman-Review* [Spokane] 18 June 1995: n. pag. Web.

Camden, Jim. "Carnage Fuels Gun Debate." *The Spokesman-Review* [Spokane] 19 Jun. 1995: A1+. Print.

White, Jeanette, and Camden, Jim. "Their Lives Linked By Tragedy." *The Spokesman-Review* [Spokane] 19 Jun. 1995: A4. Print.

Camden, Jim. "Military Rethinks Discharge." *The Spokesman-Review* [Spokane] 17 Nov. 1997: A1+. Print.

Lawsuit

Morlin, Bill. "Woman's Shooting-spree Suit Alleges 41 Acts of Negligence." *The Spokesman-Review* [Spokane] 05 Dec. 1995: B3. Print.

SIGMAN v. UNITED STATES. United States Court of Appeals, Ninth Circuit. 29 Mar. 2000. *FindLaw*. Web.

Camden, Jim. "Victims Settle in Fairchild Shootings." *The Spokesman-Review* [Spokane] 13 Aug. 2001: A1+. Print.

Plane Crash/Fairchild AFB

Bogan, Christopher. "City Stalls as Ash Falls." *The Spokesman-Review* [Spokane] 19 May 1980, volcano watch/special report ed.: 10. Web.

Carollo, Russell. "Fairchild Delights 'whole Family'." *The Spokesman-Review* [Spokane] 18 May 1987: A5. Print.

Carollo, Russell. "SAC Waived Limits on Aerobatics." *The Spokesman-Review* [Spokane] 02 June 1987: A1. Print.

Carollo, Russell, and Jim Camden. "Air Force Details Events Leading to Fairchild Crash That Killed 7." *The Spokesman-Review* [Spokane] 13 June 1987: A1+. Print.

Camden, Jim. "Grounded-SAC Ends Show Plans for 'best of the Best'." *The Spokesman-Review* [Spokane] 13 June 1987: A8. Print.

Carollo, Russell, and Jim Camden. "Tanker Flew Too Close to B-52 Path." *The Spokesman-Review* [Spokane] 13 June 1987: A1+. Print.

Carollo, Russell, and Jim Camden. "Air Show Routine Violated Safety Rules." *The Spokesman-Review* [Spokane] 16 Apr. 1988: A1+. Print.

Carollo, Russell. "Fairchild Crash Leads to Tough Air Show Rules." *The Spokesman-Review* [Spokane] 25 May 1988: A1+. Print.

Camden, Jim. "Aerospace Day Features Gulf War Pilots, Planes." *The Spokesman-Review* [Spokane] 17 May 1991: B1-B2. Print.

Camden, Jim. "Tail Gunners Fly out of Fairchild, into History." *The Spokesman-Review* [Spokane] 01 Oct. 1991: A1+. Print.

Sowa, Tom. "Air Show Impresses Young, Not-so-young." *The Spokesman-Review* [Spokane] 18 May 1992: A6. Print.

Camden, Jim. "A Farewell Flight of History." *The Spokesman-Review* [Spokane] 26 May 1994: B3. Print.

Seattle Times Staff. "Air Force Secretary Says B-52 Crash Shouldn't Halt Shows." *Seattle Times* 27 June 1994: n. pag. Web.

Camden, Jim. "Experts Study Wreckage of B-52 Foley, Dicks Ask Air Force to Review Its Policy on Air Shows." *The Spokesman-Review* [Spokane] 28 June 1994: A7. Print.

Camden, Jim. "A Special Flight." *The Spokesman-Review* [Spokane] 29 June 1994: A1+. Print.

Camden, Jim. "Air Force Changes Statement on Crash." *The Spokesman-Review* [Spokane] 02 Sept. 1994: B3. Print.

Camden, Jim. "Air Force Says It Won't Happen Again." *The Spokesman-Review* [Spokane] 30 Sept. 1994: A1. Print.

Camden, Jim. "B-52 Crash May Result in Court-martial." *The Spokesman-Review* [Spokane] 16 Nov. 1994: A1+. Print.

Camden, Jim. "Ex-Fairchild Commander May Get Immunity in Crash." *The Spokesman-Review* [Spokane] 19 Nov. 1994: A1+. Print.

Camden, Jim. "Fairchild Flight Chief Faces Court-Martial March 14 Col. Pellerin Faces Three Counts Of Dereliction Of Duty." *The Spokesman-Review* [Spokane] 13 Jan. 1995: n. pag. Web.

Camden, Jim. "Crash Was near Warheads." *The Spokesman-Review* [Spokane] 27 Apr. 1995: B2. Print.

Camden, Jim. "Air Force Reprimands, Fines Colonel: Officer Who Was In Charge Of Flight Operations Says B-52 Crash Will Haunt Him For Rest Of His Life." *The Spokesman-Review* [Spokane] 23 May 1995: n. pag. Web.

Kong, Major. "Flying the B-52." Web log post. *Daily Kos*. N.p., 09 Dec. 2012. Web.

Reports

US General Accounting Office. "Strategic Air Command: KC-135A Crash and the Need for SAC Air Show Regulations". Report to Congress, July 1988. http://www.gao.gov/assets/150/146691.pdf

Spokane County Sheriff Department, Report: Case No: 94-052251

TIG Report. Special Management Review: *The Mellberg Case, Fairchild AFB WA*, PN 94-702. The Inspector General of the Air Force, 19 Aug. 1994.

United States Air Force Aircraft Accident Investigation Board Report. B-52H, S/N 61-0026. HQ 12th Air Force, 05 Sep. 1994.

United States Air Force Aircraft Accident Investigation Board Report. C-17A, T/N 00-0173. 3RD Wing Joint Base Elmendorf-Richardson, Alaska, 27 Sep. 2010.

PoliceOne.com. *Gun Policy & Law Enforcement Survey.* Http://police-praetorian.netdna-ssl.com/p1_gunsurveysummary_2013.pdf. Web.

Acknowledgments

I want to thank the following people for helping me become the person I am today and for their help in making this book possible.

For their personal guidance:
    Judy "Ma" Barker (my Mom)
    Aunt Gloria Hink

For their patience, love and support:
    Rhonda
    Ben
    Eleanor

For their friendship:
    Erik and Tracy Turner
    Lenny, Morgan, Mike and Mark

For their professional guidance:
    Charles Remsberg
    Massad Ayoob
    Marty Hayes
    Combat Arms Training and Maintenance

For their help in telling the stories and producing this book:
    The men and women of the 92nd Medical Group and Fairchild
        Air Force Base
    Jim Camden
    Jess Walter
    Jeanette White
    Susan Brigham
    Pat McGeehan
    Russ Davis of Gray Dog Press

Dennis Held
John Simlett
Dick Margulis
Gary Provost
Rhonda Brown
Massad Ayoob
Mike Brewer
Robin Samuels
Herman Gunter III

For assisting me on my journey toward recovery:
Dawn Gray
Rhonda Brown
Robert Jackson
Thich Nhat Hanh

My friends and mentors from the:
366th Security Police Squadron
7276th Security Police Squadron
92nd Security Police Squadron
15th Security Police Squadron
377th Security Police Squadron

Index

92nd Air Refueling Squadron, 15
92nd Air Refueling Wing, 117
92nd Bomb Wing, 15, 33, 49, 50, 51, 115, 117, 121, 156, 163
92nd Logistics Group, 79
92nd Maintenance Squadron, 57
92nd Medical Group, 33, 63, 160, 257, 305
92nd Operations Group, 47, 50, 51, 52, 79, 123, 154, 267
92nd Security Police Squadron, 83, 144
92nd Services Squadron, 184
325th Bomb Squadron, 15, 49, 50, 51, 52, 117, 122, 153, 154
9010 annex building, 1, 196, 208, 210, 235

A
aerobatics, 16, 18, 85
Air Combat Command (ACC), 79, 257, 269, 305
Airman's Medal, 305
air shows:
    Alaska 2010, 269-270
    Canada 1993, 154
    Fairchild 1991, 45-47
    Fairchild 1992, 51-53
    Fairchild 1993, 79-82, 84-85
Airway Heights, Washington, 82, 83, 212, 285, 301
Albuquerque, New Mexico, 125, 149, 310
Amarillo, Texas, 125, 148
amok, 319
Anderson, Brian, 259
Anderson, Marcus, 296
Anderson, Edgar "Andy", 76
Anderson, Marlene, 169, 279
Anderson, Karl, 76, 177
Approach Phase, 169-172, 175-176, 325
army surplus, 5, 167
Arnold, Margaret, 26-27
Arnold's Motel, 167, 168, 169, 279

ATC Form 341 (Air Training Command), 24-25
award ceremony, 304-306
Ayoob, Massad, Foreword, 321

B

B-52 Stratofortress, 17, 18, 45, 46, 49-52, 79-81, 115-116, 119, 121-122, 154-156, 159, 161-163, 257-262, 265-266
   See also BUFF.
   B-52 Pilot's Flight Manual (Dash 11), 45, 49, 52, 159, 266, 267
   crashes:
      Arizona, 121
      Czar 52, 260-269
   description of, 16, 47, 48
   mentioned, 3, 85, 184, 269, 316
   photo of, 15, 19, 270, 271, 272
Baker, Delwyn, 192, 193, 194, 195, 229-230, 231, 233, 252
Baldwin, Timothy, 188-189, 195
Ballog, Dennis, 162
Barbosa, Duarte, 319
Barshney, Ann, 191, 231, 232, 236, 248
Barton, Victor, 229-230
Base Exchange (BX), 17, 140
Basic Military Training School (BMTS, basic training):
   Andy Brown, 33-34
   Dean Mellberg, 12-13, 22-27, 69, 106, 136
   mentioned, 8, 21, 29, 31, 55, 65, 68
Bates, Dale, 232, 233
BDU-48 (training bomb), 120
Behavior Analysis Services (BAS), 25, 26, 27, 65
Benson, Jim, 119, 122
Beretta, handgun, 34, 83, 84, 144, 209, 210, 212
   See also M9.
   mentioned, 2, 214
bicycle:
   Andy Brown, 1-2, 5, 143-145, 196, 209, 305, 314
   Dean Mellberg, 58, 71, 94, 130, 132, 141, 147, 166
bike patrol, 1, 143, 144, 196
Blind-Sided, 322, 326
Blue Angels, 16
Brigham, Billy, 286-285
Brigham, Thomas, 3, 64, 69, 72-78, 103, 175-177, 280, 289, 295-296
   aid given to, 235-236, 237, 248
   eulogy, 286-287

Brigham, Thomas (continued)
    memo to Mellberg's commander, 74-75, 329-330
    mentioned, 71, 180, 246, 317
    narrative summary, 78, 331-333
    photo of, 289
Brigham, Susan, 3, 75-76, 103, 237, 286, 292, 295-298
Brooks, William, 82, 156, 159-162, 257-258, 267, 269
    photo of, 222
Brown, Alexander, 46, 52, 81, 156, 265
Brown, Andy:
    15th Security Police Squadron, 307
    92nd Security Police Squadron, 83, 144
    366th Security Police Squadron, 35, 38
    377th Security Police Squadron, 310
    3711th Training Squadron, 33
    7276th Security Police Squadron, 41
    bike patrol, 1, 143, 144, 196
    firearms use:
        Fairchild, 2, 83-84, 210-211
        Spokane, 312-314
    expert marksman, 34, 42
    Fort Dix, 35
    Hickam Air Force Base, 307-310
    Iraklion Air Station, 41-42
    Kirtland Air Force Base, 310-311
    Law Enforcement Tech School, 33-35
    mental health:
        Fairchild Air Force Base, 306-307
        Hickam Air Force Base, 308-310
        Kirtland Air Force Base, 310-311
        Spokane, Washington, 311-315
    mental rehearsal, 42, 84
    Military Police Investigator (MPI) School, 308
    Mountain Home Air Force Base, 35, 37-40
    photo of, 35, 145, 303, 304
    Port Orchard, Washington, 5-8, 35, 40, 42, 143, 304
    Riyadh, Saudi Arabia, 143
    Security Police Creed, 37
    South Kitsap High School, 6-7
Brown, Pauline, 194, 230, 245
building 9010 (Annex), 1-2, 63, 166, 168, 175-179, 193, 195, 196, 208-210, 214-
    217, 232-236, 246
    photo of, 173, 197, 198, 199, 201, 206, 220, 223

BUFF, 47, 49, 156, 257, 260, 262
Bullock, David, 53, 79, 80
Buzogany, Joseph, 90, 92, 94

C

Camp, Dave, 99, 114, 139-140
    letter to Air Force, 99
    letter from Air Force, 113-114, 334
    letter to Lois Mellberg, 114, 335
Campbell, John III, 100-102, 108, 152
Cannon Air Force Base, 3, 113, 125, 136, 142, 147
Capotosti, David, 50-53, 79, 269
Carlson, Stephen, 258, 262
Carroll, Jim, 218, 299, 301
Carroll, Mike, 166, 167
Cathey, Steven, 95
Chain, John Jr., 16-18
Chapman, Christopher, 20
Clovis, New Mexico, 125, 126, 141, 142, 147-149
Cochran, Teresa, 160, 263
Collins, Delbert, 240, 241, 242
Combat Arms Training and Maintenance (CATM), 42, 168
Cook, James, 319
Cook, Jeff, 3, 74, 77-78
Coppi, Stephen, 81, 122
Cornett, Michael, 20
Countess, Clem, 50, 80-81, 82, 115-116, 261
Cox, Neal, 182, 240
Crime Stop, 187, 207, 208, 213

D

Daily, Jan, 265
Danley, Melissa, 191, 196, 231-232, 233, 250
David Grant Medical Center, 78
Davis-Perritano, Melinda, 132, 138
Dawson, Stephen, 61, 64-66, 70-71, 72, 93
Day, Buddy, 189
Day, Richard, 79
Deaconess Hospital, 251, 252
Deadly Force, 321
Dearduff, Scott, 299
    photo of, 222
Deaton, Patrick, 174, 181, 232, 233, 283

de Becker, Gavin, 322
Deehan, Paul, 161
Déjà Vu Gentlemen's Club, 168-169
Delrosario, Joneil, 179
DeSantis, Jim, 245
Diagnostic and Statistical Manual of Mental Disorders (DSM), 319
Donnelly, Peter, 154, 268
Dugue, Brett, 46, 115
Dunmore, Cedric, 89, 95, 96, 98

E
Earl, David, 163, 235
E-Dub, 48, 52, 116, 122
Elliott, Daniel, 196, 236, 237
Elmendorf Air Force Base, 165-166, 269
Erks, Rodney, 20
Estes, George, 168, 178, 236, 237
expert marksman, 34, 42, 68, 141

F
Fagras, Gordon, 182
Fairchild Air Force Base, 1-3, 6, 15-18, 45-47, 49-53, 55-85, 113, 115-123, 143-
     145, 153-164, 168, 170-248, 257-270, 286, 293, 301
     dental clinic, 63, 67, 233, 234
     hospital, 1-3, 63-64, 67, 145, 166, 170-219, 229-248, 255, 279-280, 281
          photo of, 171, 172, 173, 197-206, 220-221, 223, 229
     mentioned, 31, 42, 92, 103, 105, 109, 112, 132, 133, 136, 166, 251, 253, 255,
          279, 280, 281, 282, 283
Fantasy Phase, 107-108, 113, 325
Felix, David, 121
Feres doctrine, 293, 295
Firearms Academy of Seattle, 321
firearms, 5, 27, 34, 68, 75, 281, 283, 311
     concealed carry, 321, 322
     restrictions, 83, 167, 240
Five Phases of a Mass Public Murderer, 322-323, 325
Fleming, Shawn, 50, 79, 82, 115, 116, 117, 155, 156, 268
Fogleman, Ronald, 298
Foley, Tom, 258
Ford, Brandon, 246
Ford, Heather, 238
Fort Dix, 35
Foster, Almon, 176, 184

Foster, Deborah, 189, 305
    photo of, 304

G
Gadbois, William, 189, 230, 231
Garcia, Antonio Jr., 161
Garrett, Deborah, 132, 133
Gerken, Ruth, 175, 180, 187, 237, 238
Goodman, Caroline, 178
Gordon, Slade, 283
Grabenstein, Rick, 301
Grant, Robert, 163, 257
Gray, Brittany, 175, 176, 240
gun control, 240, 282-283, 166-167
Gunther, Lynn, 162
GunVault, 311
Guth, William, 136, 140

H
Hamilton, Paul, 17, 18, 20
Hansen, James, 280, 299, 301
Harper, Stephen, 53, 79, 81, 82, 156, 269
Heritage Park, 49
Hess, Mark, 175, 176, 180, 246, 247, 248, 283
Hickam Air Force Base, 307, 308, 309, 310
Hinton, Larry, 53
Hoard, Tyrone, 179
Holland, Arthur "Bud", 154-156
    1991 Air Show, 45-47
    1992 Air Show, 51-53
    1993 Air Show, 79-82
    air show planning, 159-163
    Black Rock Desert, 115-117
    change-of-command flyover, 49-51
    Czar 52, 257-270
    dangerous, 3-4, 18, 51, 81, 123, 153, 154, 155, 163, 259, 265, 267, 268
    fear of, 3-4, 51-52, 80-81, 115-117, 119, 121-123, 153, 155-156, 160-163
    Mead High School, 53
    photo of, 276
    Yakima, Washington, 119-123
Holland, Sarah, 155
Hollis, Steve, 122
Hunsinger, Dennis, 159

Huston, Elizabeth, 269
Huston, Kenneth, 161, 258, 264, 269
    photo of, 277
Hutchinson, Chief (First Sergeant), 59, 60, 61, 62, 63

I

Implementation Phase, 176-196, 325
Ingalsbe, Richard, 161
Inspector General, 269, 296
    complaints, 71, 99, 135-136
    reports, 105, 108
intuition, 3, 68, 90, 126, 128-129, 166, 177, 178, 322
investigation:
    crash of Czar 52, 266-268
    mass murder, 279-280
Iraklion Air Station, 41, 42, 43
Isaak, Doyle, 163, 176, 177
Ivy, William, 121

J

Jackson, Ronald, 26
Jessee, Tami, 238
Johnson, Frank, 20
Johnson, Gary, 72
Johnson, Joe, 194, 230, 245
Johnson, Morgan, 143
Jones, Eric, 52, 53, 119-123, 155
Jones, First Sergeant, 70, 74
Joplin, Orbin "Hap", 174, 181
Julich, Arnold, 47, 50

K

Karns, Omer, 174, 181, 244
KC-135, 16, 17, 18, 19, 45, 156, 159, 160, 258, 263
    photo of, 15
Keene, Elizabeth, 88, 90, 92, 94, 95, 100
Kelley, Becky, 175, 181
Kelley, Deena, 175, 181, 188, 252, 283
Kemph, Phil, 21-25, 27
Kendall, Payton, 2, 55
Kershner, Preston, 193
Kervina, Eric, 126
Kirtland Air Force Base, 126, 310

Knight, David, 77, 286
Kolar, Scott, 215-217, 264, 305
    photo of, 304
L
Lackland Air Force Base, 21, 24-25, 33, 99, 150
    See also Wilford Hall Medical Center.
    See also Basic Military Training School.
    mentioned, 8, 13, 64, 78, 105, 107, 129
    photo of, 36
Langer, Kirk, 165-166
Langley Air Force Base, 305
Lansing, Michigan, 9, 12, 281, 282, 301
Lanzano, Gia-Evita, 97-99, 102
LaPoint, Sarah, 96
Lasich, Daniel, 243
lawsuit, 291-294
Leal, Roberto, 125, 132, 138-142, 148
Lecker, Michael, 184, 185, 186, 239, 305
    photo of, 304
Lee, Marlene, 179
Lee, Orson, 179, 180, 216, 234, 283, 291
Le Grand, Pete, 264
Liberty Motel, 166, 167
Lien, Sheri, 186
Lindner, Anita, 195, 229, 230, 317
    eulogy, 285-286
    photo of, 288
Lindner, Rande, 285, 293
Lish, Dave, 187
Loh, John, 269, 305
London, Alan, 61, 63-65, 69, 73-76, 109, 175-176, 317
    aid given, 235, 236, 237, 240
    eulogy, 287
    memo to Mellberg's commander, 64-65, 327-328
    orders to Alaska, 166
    photo of, 289
London, Kathy, 64, 287
Lowry Air Force Base, 27, 29
Lubbock, Texas, 125, 149, 150
Luce, Curt, 293
Lum, Margaret, 184, 185, 292

M

M9 handgun, 34, 42, 83, 144
    qualification course, 34
M16 rifle, 6, 35, 38, 144, 217
    Mellberg, 27, 68, 128, 141
MacGyver, 107, 108
Magen, Jed, 105-107
MAK-90 rifle, 166, 176
    drum magazine, 167, 168, 176, 192, 282
Marcou, Dan, 322-323, 325
Martin, Ben, 219
Martinez, Richard Jr., 194
mass public murder, 319-325
    Dana Point, California, 68
    Dearborn, Michigan, 68
    dry run, Cannon AFB, 129
    Fairchild Air Force Base, 171-196, 207-219
        aborted attempt/dry run, 168
        crime scene photos, 171, 197-206, 220, 221, 223
    Five Phases of, 322-323, 325
    intervention, 321-323, 325
    Malaysia, 319
    prevention, 322-324
    Royal Oak, 68
    survival protocol, 320
McBride, Master Sergeant, 233-234
McCarron, Christin, 174, 183, 186, 244, 245, 246, 306, 317
    eulogy, 286
    photo of, 290
McCarron, Greg, 286
McCarron, Echo, 246, 286
McCarron, Ryan, 174, 182, 183, 238, 240, 246, 286
    photo of, 290
McConnell, Michael, 266
McCormick, Doug, 246
McCray, Douglas, 186
McCullough, Michael, 163-164
McGeehan, Brendan, 153
McGeehan, Collin, 153
McGeehan, Jodie, 153, 155, 162, 261, 262, 266
McGeehan, Mark, 117, 119, 123, 153-155, 156, 161, 162, 258, 259, 264
    photo of, 278
McGeehan, Pat, 153, 263

McGowan, Patrick, 128
media:
    Airman Magazine, 302, 303
    Camden, Jim, 17, 282
    CBS, 281
    Chodun, Cheryl, 281
    CNN, 255, 281
    Fehling, Dave, 281
    Foster, J. Todd, 305
    Gross, Bill, 282
    KHQ, 282, 283
    KREM, 282
    KXLY, 249, 250, 282, 285
    Montano, Alex, 282
    Police magazine, *39*
    PoliceOne.com, 321
    Rowe, Charles, 282
    Sauk Valley Media, 283
    The Spokesman-Review, 3, 17, 51, 255, 269, 282, 283, 305, 306
    Walter, Jess, 282
    White, Jeanette, 255, 282
    Woodward, Nadine, 282
    WXYZ, 281
Mellberg, Dean:
    alarm clock, 57, 70-72, 93, 100
    Arnold's Motel, 167, 168, 169, 279
    barbershop, 66, 75
    basic training, 21-27
    bullied, 9-12
    Cannon Air Force Base, 3, 113, 125-142, 147-149
    choir, 10, 282
    Clovis, 125, 126, 141, 142, 147-149
    conflict resolution meeting, 73-75
    "crime against humanity", 74, 106
    dangerous, 3, 30, 61, 78, 128, 151, 295, 296
    diagnoses/symptoms:
        antisocial personality, 90, 101
        anxiety disorder, 25, 64, 69, 73, 93, 106
        Asperger syndrome, 106
        attending to internal stimuli, 90, 92, 101
        autism, 100, 101-103, 106, 107, 108, 133-134, 296
        brief reactive psychosis, 73, 78
        obsessive–compulsive, 25, 64, 69, 97

Mellberg, Dean: (continued)

    diagnoses/symptoms: (continued)

        organic mental disorder, 88, 92

        paranoid/paranoid personality disorder, 73, 88, 92, 101, 106, 133-134, 152

        passive aggressive, 70

        personality disorder, 92, 140

        psychotic/psychosis, 73-74, 78, 92, 97, 98

        schizophrenia/schizoid, 88, 92, 97, 100, 101, 103

    discharge recommendations:

        basic training (BAS), 25-26

        Cannon Air Force Base, 133-134

        Fairchild Air Force Base, 65-66, 72

        Wilford Hall Medical Center, 88, 92, 94, 96, 97, 102, 108, 114

    Elmendorf Air Force Base, 165-166

    enlistment document discrepancies, 12, 293, 297

    Fairchild 1993, 55-78

    Faith "girlfriend", 107-108, 113, 129-130, 151, 169

    fear of, 2-3, 68, 72, 77, 78, 89, 91, 103, 129, 132, 134, 138, 148, 169

    Fitzsimmons Army Medical Center, 31

    hygiene, 11, 30, 166

    journal entries, 57, 58, 60, 61, 64, 66, 69, 70-71

    Lackland Air Force Base, 13, 21, 76, 78, 99, 105, 107, 111, 129, 150

    Lansing, Michigan, 9-13

    letters to:

        Air Force Inspector General, 135-136

        Congressman, 99-100, 135, 139-140

        Faith, 129-130

        home, 111

        MEB, 92-93

        separation authority, 136-138

    Liberty Motel, 166, 167

    loan, 58, 63, 93, 100

    MAK-90 rifle, 166, 176

        drum magazine, 167, 168, 176, 192, 282

    media coverage, 281, 282, 301

    Medical Evaluation Board (MEB), 88, 91, 92, 93, 94, 103, 105, 107, 108, 112

    mental health referrals:

        basic training, 25-26

        Cannon Air Force Base, 132

        Fairchild Air Force Base, 61, 78, 72

        Lowry Air Force Base, 30-31

    Minnesota Multiphasic Personality Inventory (MMPI), 64, 133

    neuropsychological evaluation, 101-102

Mellberg, Dean: (continued)
    perceived injustices, 100, 113, 136, 137-138, 139-140, 152
        basic training, 24, 27
        Fairchild AFB, 60, 69, 70-72, 74, 75
        Wilford Hall, 92-93
    personal loss, 140-141, 151
    perverse behavior, 11, 30, 58, 59-60, 90-91, 95, 127
    Physical Evaluation Board (PEB), 91, 94, 95, 96, 97, 101, 102, 103
    sexual assault, 94
    sharp objects, 92
    Spokane 1994, 166-196
    Sportsman's Surplus, 68, 168
    Waverly High School, 9, 126, 282
    Wilford Hall Medical Center, 78, 88-103
Mellberg, Gary, 9, 56
Mellberg, Lois, 9, 10, 56, 66, 108, 114, 132
    letter from congressman, 335
    post shooting, 279, 280
    Wilford Hall, 96, 97, 98, 99, 102, 105, 297
Melton, Terri, 190
Memorial Park, 316
Mirasole, Robert, 160, 263
Mitchell, James, 64, 73-75, 287
Moe, Dennis, 174, 175, 180, 182, 183, 188, 237, 238, 253
Moe, Kelly, 174, 182-183, 238, 253
Moe, Marlene, 174, 175, 182, 183, 187, 188, 237, 238, 239, 253, 291, 292
Moe, Melissa, 174, 183, 186, 187, 253
Moffatt, Gregory, 322, 326
Morrison, Stacy, 208
Mountain Home Air Force Base, 35, 37-39, 112-113, 280, 304
Mt. Saint Helens, 6
Murray, Lorraine, 192, 194, 231
Murray, Patty, 283

N
Nance, John, 269
Noone, Joseph, 189-190, 192, 243-244, 291, 305
    photo of, 304

O
Offutt gate, 1, 63, 145, 196, 247
Olenoski, Joe, 184, 185, 186
Olenoski, Stacy, 184, 185, 186

Orth, Danette, 225, 226, 227
Orth, Scott, 225, 226, 227
OSI (Air Force Office of Special Investigations), 213, 218, 248, 279, 280, 299, 301
Otto, Gail, 7
Overton, Kent, 208, 211, 213

P

Palmer, Deanette, 307
Palmer, Madison, 264
Peak, Lance, 237, 244
Pearce, Kenneth, 266
Pearson, Cecily, 168
Pellerin, William, 79, 81, 82, 123, 153-156, 161-163, 267-269
Pentecost, Brandy, 174, 183, 187, 238, 240
Persian Gulf War, 45, 47
Petrin, Milton, 241, 242, 243
Physical Evaluation Board (PEB), 91, 94-97, 101-103
Pierson, Krista, 69, 287, 292
Pinault, Michael, 176
Pitts, Connie, 251
Planning Phase, 166-168, 325
plane crashes:
        Arizona desert 1984, 121
        Elmendorf Air Force Base 2010, 269
        Fairchild Air Force Base 1987, 17-20
                photo of, 19
        Fairchild Air Force Base 1994, 260-269
                photo of, 270-274
        Ramstein Air Base 1988, 160
Port Orchard, Washington, 5, 6, 7, 8, 35, 40, 42, 143, 304
Precision Measurement Electronics Laboratory (PMEL), 12, 112, 132
        Cannon AFB, 125, 126, 127, 128
        Fairchild AFB, 31, 55, 57, 68, 72, 77, 109, 113
        Lowry AFB, 29
Preparation Phase, 166-168, 325
Prescott, Sam, 3, 128, 129, 148
Post-Traumatic Stress Disorder (PTSD), 291, 308-310, 312-314, 324
        coping with, 315

R

Rayner, Erik, 57-62, 70-75
Rayner, Stacy, 58, 59, 60, 71
Raynes, Airman First Class, 177, 235

Recruit Housing and Training Facility (RH&T), 21
    photo of, 28
Remsberg, Charles, 42
Richards, James, 81, 82, 269
Riggan, Derek, 52
Riyadh, Saudi Arabia, 143, 145
Rizzo, Tony, 211-217, 219, 242
Roberts, Hazel "Joy", 175, 188, 252
Robinette, Randy, 101
Robinson, Gloria, 212-214, 301, 305
    photo of, 304
Rodriguez, Joe III, 25, 26, 27
Rogers, Laura, 177, 235
Romine, Deland, 192
Root, Dave, 190-192, 243-245, 247
    photo of, 250
Ruark, William, 130
Ruotsala, Michael, 46, 51

S
Sacred Heart Medical Center, 76, 77, 238, 252
Sanders, Don, 251
Santa Fe Railway, 125
Sauter, Mrs. (choir teacher), 10-11
Schindler, Kevin, 216, 217, 218, 305
    photo of, 304
Schmidt, Jerry, 49
Seeley, Kevin, 177, 235, 237, 246-247, 248, 292
Shea, Cathy, 176, 177
Shenk, John, 144, 214, 215, 216, 217, 305
    photo of, 304
Shoppette, 55, 84
Shubert, Thomas, 113
Shue, Philip (Dr.), 295
Sigman, James, 193
Sigman, Michelle, 175, 181, 188, 243, 245, 252, 285
Sigman, Taylor McKenzie, 285, 317
Simpson, Herb, 145
Singer, Dan, 144
Singleterry, James, 182, 238, 239-240
Slaughenhoupt, Jay, 46
Snow, Lisa, 133, 134, 137
South Kitsap High School, 6

Spencer, Alton, 255
Spencer, Sam, 183, 238, 252, 291
    photo of, 249
Spencer, Sharry, 255
Spokane Police, 248, 307, 312
Spokane, Washington, 6, 15, 16, 45, 55, 76, 77, 83, 119, 166, 247, 248, 251, 253, 283, 311, 313
    mentioned, 94, 174, 184, 207, 214, 281, 282, 285, 286, 292, 307, 312, 316
Spokane County Sheriff's Office, 212, 232, 248, 253, 279-280, 299, 301, 302, 313
Sportsman's Surplus, 68, 168
Sprague, Donald, 234
Stan/Eval, 46, 79, 116, 119, 123, 154
Stempf, Craig, 282
Stewart, LeDeane, 177
Strategic Air Command (SAC), 16, 18, 79
    heavies, 16, 18, 265
Street, Timothy, 230, 231, 244, 305
    photo of, 304
Sunwest Bank, 148
Survival School (SERE), 16, 64, 73, 184, 225, 233, 234, 260-261, 263, 287
    photo of, 274

T
Tappel, John, 175, 193, 243, 245-246
Taurus PT92 handgun, 83, 301, 311
The Book of Duarte Barbosa, 319
The Gift of Fear, 322
The Insanity Offense, 324
The Tactical Edge: Surviving High-Risk Patrol, 41
Thompson, Don, 51, 123, 154, 161
Thorne, Jaime, 282
Thunderbirds, 16
Thunderhawks, 16, 17, 18, 47
Torrey, E. Fuller, 323, 324
Training Instructor (TI), 21-27, 33, 106
Traits of a Potentially Violent Person, 322, 326
Travis Air Force Base, 78, 302
Turner, Erik, 40, 304, 311
Turner, Tracy, 40, 304
Tutini, Karina, 184, 185, 239

U

Urick, Doris, 178, 181
Urick, John, 178, 181

V

Veterans Affairs Medical Center, Spokane, Washington, 312, 315

W

Walch, Eva, 174, 175, 181, 188, 243, 253, 293, 294
Walker, David, 130, 131, 132, 135
Walker, Steven, 213, 230-231, 305
 photo of, 304
Ward 4D, 78, 88, 96, 103
 photo of, 87
Washabaugh, Walter "Mark", 99
Washington State Patrol, 7, 212, 248, 279
Waverly High School, 9-10, 126, 282
Weapon Storage Area (WSA), 79, 260-264
 photo of, 274
Weingartner, Nancy, 93, 94, 97, 98, 99, 102, 103
Weinman, Arnold, 50
Weiss, Jay, 296
Wellsandt, Mark, 233-234
Werder, Jennifer, 177, 235, 237
White, Leland, 50
Whitener, Sally, 126, 131, 132, 133, 134, 135, 138, 139, 140, 142
Widnall, Sheila, 258, 265, 296, 298
Wilford Hall Medical Center, 63-64, 76-78, 88-103, 105, 109, 113, 114, 125, 132,
 133, 136, 137, 138, 152, 167, 296, 297, 331, 332, 333
 photo of, 87
Williams, Phil, 285
Wilson, Nathaniel, 55, 56, 67, 68, 69
Wolff, Robert, 115, 156, 159, 257-258, 259, 261, 264
 photo of, 275

Y

Young, Mark, 130-131

Z

Zehr, David, 161
Zucchetto, Anthony, 174, 182, 183, 238, 240, 252
Zucchetto, Janessa, 174, 183, 186, 187, 245, 252